Introduction to Computer Networking

Introduction to Computer Networking

Edited by Gerald Davies

CLANRYE
INTERNATIONAL
www.clanryeinternational.com

Clanrye International,
750 Third Avenue, 9th Floor,
New York, NY 10017, USA

ISBN: 978-1-63240-706-1

Cataloging-in-Publication Data

Introduction to computer networking / edited by Gerald Davies.
    p. cm.
Includes bibliographical references and index.
ISBN 978-1-63240-706-1
1. Computer networks. 2. Network computers. I. Davies, Gerald.
TK5105.5 .I58 2018
004.6--dc23

For information on all Clanrye International publications
visit our website at www.clanryeinternational.com

Contents

Preface

Computer networks are a fundamental part of computer science. It enables computing devices with networks to share information with each other by using data links. The most common devices which use the computer network technology are servers, desktops, laptops, mobiles, etc. Computer networking is also important because it helps in allowing access to digital audio, world wide web, fax machines, digital video, printers, etc. to the network devices. This book studies, analyses and upholds the pillars of computer networking and its utmost significance in the modern times. For all those who are interested in this field, this textbook can prove to be an essential guide.

To facilitate a deeper understanding of the contents of this book a short introduction of every chapter is written below:

Chapter 1- Interconnected autonomous computers form computer networks, which are helpful in sharing information and resources with the use of cables or wireless media. The field is born as a result of a merger between computer and communication. This is an introductory chapter which will briefly introduce all the significant aspects of computer networks.

Chapter 2- Ideal cable types allow for large amounts of data to be transferred along longer distances. A coaxial cable has an inner tubular insulator layer and a tubular conducting shield. Broadband coaxial cables allow for a typical bandwith of 300 MHz. The major components of data communication systems are discussed in this section.

Chapter 3- Data link control devices allow for the transmission of data and the correction of data errors. The transmission from a source is carried through a data terminal equipment (DTE) to data circuit terminal equipment (DCE), which converts data into signals. Since communication channels may sometimes fail to deliver data, the use of error detection and correction helps in guaranteeing data delivery. This chapter has been carefully written to provide an easy understanding of the varied facets of data transmission and link control.

Chapter 4- Internetworking is a method of inter-connecting various computer networks together. The most famous example of internetworking is Internet, which is incorporated using Internet protocol suite as the hardware differs in the combined networks. Internet Protocol (IP) delivers information from the source host to destination host using the IP address. The chapter closely examines the key concepts of internetworking to provide an extensive understanding of the subject.

Chapter 5- Network security refers to the measures taken to ensure protection and prevention against activities such as misuse, unauthorized access, etc. A network may be private or public and the access to it is granted depending on its type. However, there is a possibility that a third-party may try to access private information. This intrusion is prevented with the use of cryptography, which is the study as well as the practice to create a secure communication. All the diverse principles of network security have been carefully analyzed in this chapter.

I would like to share the credit of this book with my editorial team who worked tirelessly on this book. I owe the completion of this book to the never-ending support of my family, who supported me throughout the project.

Editor

An Overview of Computer Networks

Interconnected autonomous computers form computer networks, which are helpful in sharing information and resources with the use of cables or wireless media. The field is born as a result of a merger between computer and communication. This is an introductory chapter which will briefly introduce all the significant aspects of computer networks.

Computer Networks

The concept of Network is not new. In simple terms it means an interconnected set of some objects. For decades we are familiar with the Radio, Television, railway, Highway, Bank and other types of networks. In recent years, the network that is making significant impact in our day-to-day life is the Computer network. By computer network we mean an interconnected set of autonomous computers. The term autonomous implies that the computers can function independent of others. However, these computers can exchange information with each other through the communication network system. Computer networks have emerged as a result of the convergence of two technologies of this century- Computer and Communication as shown in figure. The consequence of this revolutionary merger is the emergence of a integrated system that transmit all types of data and information. There is no fundamental difference between data communications and data processing and there are no fundamental differences among data, voice and video communications. A brief overview of the applications of computer networks is presented.

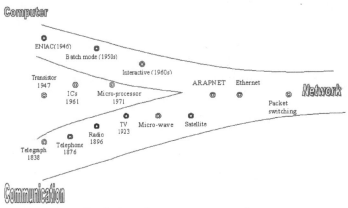

Evolution of computer networks

Historical Background

The history of electronic computers is not very old. It came into existence in the early 1950s and during the first two decades of its existence it remained as a centralized system housed in a single large room. In those days the computers were large in size and were operated by trained personnel. To the users it was a remote and mysterious object having no direct communication with the users. Jobs were submitted in the form of punched cards or paper tape and outputs were collected in the form of computer printouts. The submitted jobs were executed by the computer one after the other, which is referred to as batch mode of data processing. In this scenario, there was long delay between the submission of jobs and receipt of the results.

In the 1960s, computer systems were still centralize, but users provided with direct access through interactive terminals connected by point-to-point low-speed data links with the computer. In this situation, a large number of users, some of them located in remote locations could simultaneously access the centralized computer in time-division multiplexed mode. The users could now get immediate interactive feedback from the computer and correct errors immediately. Following the introduction of on-line terminals and time-sharing operating systems, remote terminals were used to use the central computer.

With the advancement of VLSI technology, and particularly, after the invention of microprocessors in the early 1970s, the computers became smaller in size and less expensive, but with significant increase in processing power. New breed of low-cost computers known as mini and personal computers were introduced. Instead of having a single central computer, an organization could now afford to own a number of computers located in different departments and sections.

Side-by-side, riding on the same VLSI technology the communication technology also advanced leading to the worldwide deployment of telephone network, developed primarily for voice communication. An organization having computers located geographically dispersed locations wanted to have data communications for diverse applications. Communication was required among the machines of the same kind for collaboration, for the use of common software or data or for sharing of some costly resources. This led to the development of computer networks by successful integration and cross-fertilization of communications and geographically dispersed computing facilities. One significant development was the APPANET (Advanced Research Projects Agency Network). Starting with four-node experimental network in 1969, it has subsequently grown into a network several thousand computers spanning half of the globe, from Hawaii to Sweden. Most of the present-day concepts such as packet switching evolved from the ARPANET project. The low bandwidth (3KHz on a voice grade line) telephone network was the only generally available communication system available for this type of network.

The bandwidth was clearly a problem, and in the late 1970s and early 80s another new communication technique known as Local Area Networks (LANs) evolved, which helped computers to communicate at high speed over a small geographical area. In the later years use of optical fiber and satellite communication allowed high-speed data communications over long distances.

A computer network or data network is a telecommunications network which allows nodes to share resources. In computer networks, networked computing devices exchange data with each other using a data link. The connections between nodes are established using either cable media or wireless media. The best-known computer network is the Internet.

Network computer devices that originate, route and terminate the data are called network nodes. Nodes can include hosts such as personal computers, phones, servers as well as networking hardware. Two such devices can be said to be networked together when one device is able to exchange information with the other device, whether or not they have a direct connection to each other.

Computer networks differ in the transmission medium used to carry their signals, communications protocols to organize network traffic, the network's size, topology and organizational intent.

Computer networks support an enormous number of applications and services such as access to the World Wide Web, digital video, digital audio, shared use of application and storage servers, printers, and fax machines, and use of email and instant messaging applications as well as many others. In most cases, application-specific communications protocols are layered (i.e. carried as payload) over other more general communications protocols. This formidable collection of information technology requires skilled network management to keep it all running reliably.

History

The chronology of significant computer-network developments includes:

- In the late 1950s, early networks of computers included the military radar system Semi-Automatic Ground Environment (SAGE).

- In 1959, Anatolii Ivanovich Kitov proposed to the Central Committee of the Communist Party of the Soviet Union a detailed plan for the re-organisation of the control of the Soviet armed forces and of the Soviet economy on the basis of a network of computing centres.

- In 1960, the commercial airline reservation system semi-automatic business research environment (SABRE) went online with two connected mainframes.

- In 1962, J.C.R. Licklider developed a working group he called the "Intergalactic

Computer Network", a precursor to the ARPANET, at the Advanced Research Projects Agency (ARPA).

- In 1964, researchers at Dartmouth College developed the Dartmouth Time Sharing System for distributed users of large computer systems. The same year, at Massachusetts Institute of Technology, a research group supported by General Electric and Bell Labs used a computer to route and manage telephone connections.

- Throughout the 1960s, Leonard Kleinrock, Paul Baran, and Donald Davies independently developed network systems that used packets to transfer information between computers over a network.

- In 1965, Thomas Marill and Lawrence G. Roberts created the first wide area network (WAN). This was an immediate precursor to the ARPANET, of which Roberts became program manager.

- Also in 1965, Western Electric introduced the first widely used telephone switch that implemented true computer control.

- In 1969, the University of California at Los Angeles, the Stanford Research Institute, the University of California at Santa Barbara, and the University of Utah became connected as the beginning of the ARPANET network using 50 kbit/s circuits.

- In 1972, commercial services using X.25 were deployed, and later used as an underlying infrastructure for expanding TCP/IP networks.

- In 1973, Robert Metcalfe wrote a formal memo at Xerox PARC describing Ethernet, a networking system that was based on the Aloha network, developed in the 1960s by Norman Abramson and colleagues at the University of Hawaii. In July 1976, Robert Metcalfe and David Boggs published their paper "Ethernet: Distributed Packet Switching for Local Computer Networks" and collaborated on several patents received in 1977 and 1978. In 1979, Robert Metcalfe pursued making Ethernet an open standard.

- In 1976, John Murphy of Datapoint Corporation created ARCNET, a token-passing network first used to share storage devices.

- In 1995, the transmission speed capacity for Ethernet increased from 10 Mbit/s to 100 Mbit/s. By 1998, Ethernet supported transmission speeds of a Gigabit. Subsequently, higher speeds of up to 100 Gbit/s were added (as of 2016). The ability of Ethernet to scale easily (such as quickly adapting to support new fiber optic cable speeds) is a contributing factor to its continued use.

Properties

Computer networking may be considered a branch of electrical engineering, telecommunications, computer science, information technology or computer engineering, since it relies upon the theoretical and practical application of the related disciplines.

A computer network facilitates interpersonal communications allowing users to communicate efficiently and easily via various means: email, instant messaging, chat rooms, telephone, video telephone calls, and video conferencing. Providing access to information on shared storage devices is an important feature of many networks. A network allows sharing of files, data, and other types of information giving authorized users the ability to access information stored on other computers on the network. A network allows sharing of network and computing resources. Users may access and use resources provided by devices on the network, such as printing a document on a shared network printer. Distributed computing uses computing resources across a network to accomplish tasks. A computer network may be used by computer crackers to deploy computer viruses or computer worms on devices connected to the network, or to prevent these devices from accessing the network via a denial of service attack.

Network Packet

Computer communication links that do not support packets, such as traditional point-to-point telecommunication links, simply transmit data as a bit stream. However, most information in computer networks is carried in *packets*. A network packet is a formatted unit of data (a list of bits or bytes, usually a few tens of bytes to a few kilobytes long) carried by a packet-switched network.

In packet networks, the data is formatted into packets that are sent through the network to their destination. Once the packets arrive they are reassembled into their original message. With packets, the bandwidth of the transmission medium can be better shared among users than if the network were circuit switched. When one user is not sending packets, the link can be filled with packets from other users, and so the cost can be shared, with relatively little interference, provided the link isn't overused.

Packets consist of two kinds of data: control information, and user data (payload). The control information provides data the network needs to deliver the user data, for example: source and destination network addresses, error detection codes, and sequencing information. Typically, control information is found in packet headers and trailers, with payload data in between.

Often the route a packet needs to take through a network is not immediately available. In that case the packet is queued and waits until a link is free.

Network Topology

The physical layout of a network is usually less important than the topology that connects network nodes. Most diagrams that describe a physical network are therefore topological, rather than geographic. The symbols on these diagrams usually denote network links and network nodes.

Network Links

The transmission media (often referred to in the literature as the *physical media*) used to link devices to form a computer network include electrical cable (Ethernet, HomeP-NA, power line communication, G.hn), optical fiber (fiber-optic communication), and radio waves (wireless networking). In the OSI model, these are defined at layers 1 and 2 — the physical layer and the data link layer.

A widely adopted *family* of transmission media used in local area network (LAN) technology is collectively known as Ethernet. The media and protocol standards that enable communication between networked devices over Ethernet are defined by IEEE 802.3. Ethernet transmits data over both copper and fiber cables. Wireless LAN standards (e.g. those defined by IEEE 802.11) use radio waves, or others use infrared signals as a transmission medium. Power line communication uses a building's power cabling to transmit data.

Wired Technologies

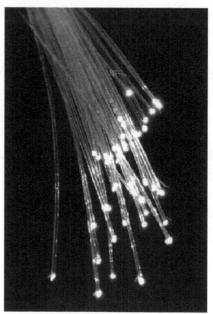

Fiber optic cables are used to transmit light from one computer/network node to another

The orders of the following wired technologies are, roughly, from slowest to fastest transmission speed.

- *Coaxial cable* is widely used for cable television systems, office buildings, and other work-sites for local area networks. The cables consist of copper or aluminum wire surrounded by an insulating layer (typically a flexible material with a high dielectric constant), which itself is surrounded by a conductive layer. The insulation helps minimize interference and distortion. Transmission speed ranges from 200 million bits per second to more than 500 million bits per second.

- ITU-T G.hn technology uses existing home wiring (coaxial cable, phone lines and power lines) to create a high-speed (up to 1 Gigabit/s) local area network

- *Twisted pair wire* is the most widely used medium for all telecommunication. Twisted-pair cabling consist of copper wires that are twisted into pairs. Ordinary telephone wires consist of two insulated copper wires twisted into pairs. Computer network cabling (wired Ethernet as defined by IEEE 802.3) consists of 4 pairs of copper cabling that can be utilized for both voice and data transmission. The use of two wires twisted together helps to reduce crosstalk and electromagnetic induction. The transmission speed ranges from 2 million bits per second to 10 billion bits per second. Twisted pair cabling comes in two forms: unshielded twisted pair (UTP) and shielded twisted-pair (STP). Each form comes in several category ratings, designed for use in various scenarios.

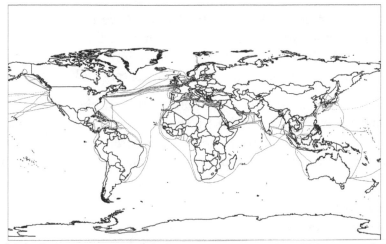

2007 map showing submarine optical fiber telecommunication cables around the world.

- An *optical fiber* is a glass fiber. It carries pulses of light that represent data. Some advantages of optical fibers over metal wires are very low transmission loss and immunity from electrical interference. Optical fibers can simultaneously carry multiple wavelengths of light, which greatly increases the rate that data can be sent, and helps enable data rates of up to trillions of bits per second. Optic fibers can be used for long runs of cable carrying very high data rates, and are used for undersea cables to interconnect continents.

Price is a main factor distinguishing wired- and wireless-technology options in a business. Wireless options command a price premium that can make purchasing wired computers, printers and other devices a financial benefit. Before making the decision to purchase hard-wired technology products, a review of the restrictions and limitations of the selections is necessary. Business and employee needs may override any cost considerations.

Wireless Technologies

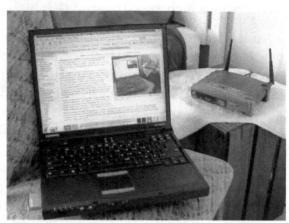

Computers are very often connected to networks using wireless links

- *Terrestrial microwave* – Terrestrial microwave communication uses Earth-based transmitters and receivers resembling satellite dishes. Terrestrial micro-waves are in the low gigahertz range, which limits all communications to line-of-sight. Relay stations are spaced approximately 48 km (30 mi) apart.

- *Communications satellites* – Satellites communicate via microwave radio waves, which are not deflected by the Earth's atmosphere. The satellites are stationed in space, typically in geosynchronous orbit 35,400 km (22,000 mi) above the equator. These Earth-orbiting systems are capable of receiving and relaying voice, data, and TV signals.

- *Cellular and PCS systems* use several radio communications technologies. The systems divide the region covered into multiple geographic areas. Each area has a low-power transmitter or radio relay antenna device to relay calls from one area to the next area.

- *Radio and spread spectrum technologies* – Wireless local area networks use a high-frequency radio technology similar to digital cellular and a low-frequency radio technology. Wireless LANs use spread spectrum technology to enable communication between multiple devices in a limited area. IEEE 802.11 defines a common flavor of open-standards wireless radio-wave technology known as Wifi.

- *Free-space optical communication* uses visible or invisible light for communications. In most cases, line-of-sight propagation is used, which limits the physical positioning of communicating devices.

Exotic Technologies

There have been various attempts at transporting data over exotic media:

- IP over Avian Carriers was a humorous April fool's Request for Comments, issued as RFC 1149. It was implemented in real life in 2001.

- Extending the Internet to interplanetary dimensions via radio waves, the Interplanetary Internet.

Both cases have a large round-trip delay time, which gives slow two-way communication, but doesn't prevent sending large amounts of information.

Network Nodes

Apart from any physical transmission medium there may be, networks comprise additional basic system building blocks, such as network interface controller (NICs), repeaters, hubs, bridges, switches, routers, modems, and firewalls.

Network Interfaces

An ATM network interface in the form of an accessory card. A lot of network interfaces are built-in.

A network interface controller (NIC) is computer hardware that provides a computer with the ability to access the transmission media, and has the ability to process low-level network information. For example, the NIC may have a connector for accepting a cable, or an aerial for wireless transmission and reception, and the associated circuitry.

The NIC responds to traffic addressed to a network address for either the NIC or the computer as a whole.

In Ethernet networks, each network interface controller has a unique Media Access Control (MAC) address—usually stored in the controller's permanent memory. To avoid address conflicts between network devices, the Institute of Electrical and Electronics Engineers (IEEE) maintains and administers MAC address uniqueness. The size of an Ethernet MAC address is six octets. The three most significant octets are reserved to identify NIC manufacturers. These manufacturers, using only their assigned prefixes, uniquely assign the three least-significant octets of every Ethernet interface they produce.

Repeaters and Hubs

A repeater is an electronic device that receives a network signal, cleans it of unnecessary noise and regenerates it. The signal is retransmitted at a higher power level, or to the other side of an obstruction, so that the signal can cover longer distances without degradation. In most twisted pair Ethernet configurations, repeaters are required for cable that runs longer than 100 meters. With fiber optics, repeaters can be tens or even hundreds of kilometers apart.

A repeater with multiple ports is known as a hub. Repeaters work on the physical layer of the OSI model. Repeaters require a small amount of time to regenerate the signal. This can cause a propagation delay that affects network performance. As a result, many network architectures limit the number of repeaters that can be used in a row, e.g., the Ethernet 5-4-3 rule.

Hubs have been mostly obsoleted by modern switches; but repeaters are used for long distance links, notably undersea cabling.

Bridges

A network bridge connects and filters traffic between two network segments at the data link layer (layer 2) of the OSI model to form a single network. This breaks the network's collision domain but maintains a unified broadcast domain. Network segmentation breaks down a large, congested network into an aggregation of smaller, more efficient networks.

Bridges come in three basic types:

- Local bridges: Directly connect LANs

- Remote bridges: Can be used to create a wide area network (WAN) link between LANs. Remote bridges, where the connecting link is slower than the end networks, largely have been replaced with routers.

- Wireless bridges: Can be used to join LANs or connect remote devices to LANs.

Switches

A network switch is a device that forwards and filters OSI layer 2 datagrams (frames) between ports based on the destination MAC address in each frame. A switch is distinct from a hub in that it only forwards the frames to the physical ports involved in the communication rather than all ports connected. It can be thought of as a multi-port bridge. It learns to associate physical ports to MAC addresses by examining the source addresses of received frames. If an unknown destination is targeted, the switch broadcasts to all ports but the source. Switches normally have numerous ports, facilitating a star topology for devices, and cascading additional switches.

Multi-layer switches are capable of routing based on layer 3 addressing or additional logical levels. The term *switch* is often used loosely to include devices such as routers and bridges, as well as devices that may distribute traffic based on load or based on application content (e.g., a Web URL identifier).

Routers

A typical home or small office router showing the ADSL telephone line and
Ethernet network cable connections

A router is an internetworking device that forwards packets between networks by processing the routing information included in the packet or datagram (Internet protocol information from layer 3). The routing information is often processed in conjunction with the routing table (or forwarding table). A router uses its routing table to determine where to forward packets. A destination in a routing table can include a "null" interface, also known as the "black hole" interface because data can go into it, however, no further processing is done for said data, i.e. the packets are dropped.

Modems

Modems (MOdulator-DEModulator) are used to connect network nodes via wire not originally designed for digital network traffic, or for wireless. To do this one or more carrier signals are modulated by the digital signal to produce an analog signal that can be tailored to give the required properties for transmission. Modems are commonly used for telephone lines, using a Digital Subscriber Line technology.

Firewalls

A firewall is a network device for controlling network security and access rules. Firewalls are typically configured to reject access requests from unrecognized sources while allowing actions from recognized ones. The vital role firewalls play in network security grows in parallel with the constant increase in cyber attacks.

Network Structure

Network topology is the layout or organizational hierarchy of interconnected nodes of a computer network. Different network topologies can affect throughput, but reliability is often more critical. With many technologies, such as bus networks, a single failure can cause the network to fail entirely. In general the more interconnections there are, the more robust the network is; but the more expensive it is to install.

Common Layouts

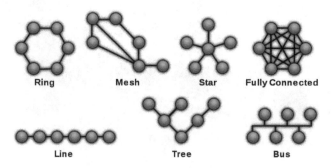

Common network topologies

Common layouts are:

- A bus network: all nodes are connected to a common medium along this medium. This was the layout used in the original Ethernet, called 10BASE5 and 10BASE2.

- A star network: all nodes are connected to a special central node. This is the typical layout found in a Wireless LAN, where each wireless client connects to the central Wireless access point.

- A ring network: each node is connected to its left and right neighbour node, such that all nodes are connected and that each node can reach each other node by traversing nodes left- or rightwards. The Fiber Distributed Data Interface (FDDI) made use of such a topology.

- A mesh network: each node is connected to an arbitrary number of neighbours in such a way that there is at least one traversal from any node to any other.

- A fully connected network: each node is connected to every other node in the network.

- A tree network: nodes are arranged hierarchically.

Note that the physical layout of the nodes in a network may not necessarily reflect the network topology. As an example, with FDDI, the network topology is a ring (actually two counter-rotating rings), but the physical topology is often a star, because all neighboring connections can be routed via a central physical location.

Overlay Network

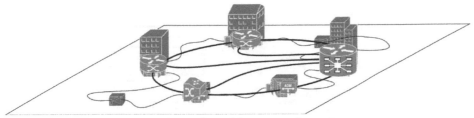

A sample overlay network

An overlay network is a virtual computer network that is built on top of another network. Nodes in the overlay network are connected by virtual or logical links. Each link corresponds to a path, perhaps through many physical links, in the underlying network. The topology of the overlay network may (and often does) differ from that of the underlying one. For example, many peer-to-peer networks are overlay networks. They are organized as nodes of a virtual system of links that run on top of the Internet.

Overlay networks have been around since the invention of networking when computer systems were connected over telephone lines using modems, before any data network existed.

The most striking example of an overlay network is the Internet itself. The Internet itself was initially built as an overlay on the telephone network. Even today, each Internet node can communicate with virtually any other through an underlying mesh of sub-networks of wildly different topologies and technologies. Address resolution and routing are the means that allow mapping of a fully connected IP overlay network to its underlying network.

Another example of an overlay network is a distributed hash table, which maps keys to nodes in the network. In this case, the underlying network is an IP network, and the overlay network is a table (actually a map) indexed by keys.

Overlay networks have also been proposed as a way to improve Internet routing, such as through quality of service guarantees to achieve higher-quality streaming media. Previous proposals such as IntServ, DiffServ, and IP Multicast have not seen wide acceptance largely because they require modification of all routers in the network. On the other hand, an overlay network can be incrementally deployed on end-hosts running the overlay protocol software, without cooperation from Internet service providers. The overlay network has no control over how packets are routed in the underlying network between two overlay nodes, but it can control, for example, the sequence of overlay nodes that a message traverses before it reaches its destination.

For example, Akamai Technologies manages an overlay network that provides reliable, efficient content delivery (a kind of multicast). Academic research includes end system multicast, resilient routing and quality of service studies, among others.

Communications protocols

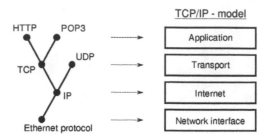

The TCP/IP model or Internet layering scheme and its relation to common protocols often layered on top of it.

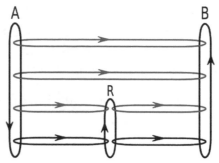

Message flows (A-B) in the presence of a router (R), red flows are effective communication paths, black paths are the actual paths.

A communications protocol is a set of rules for exchanging information over network links. In a protocol stack, each protocol leverages the services of the protocol below it. An important example of a protocol stack is HTTP (the World Wide Web protocol) running over TCP over IP (the Internet protocols) over IEEE 802.11 (the Wi-Fi protocol). This stack is used between the wireless router and the home user's personal computer when the user is surfing the web.

Whilst the use of protocol layering is today ubiquitous across the field of computer networking, it has been historically criticized by many researchers for two principal reasons. Firstly, abstracting the protocol stack in this way may cause a higher layer to duplicate functionality of a lower layer, a prime example being error recovery on both a per-link basis and an end-to-end basis. Secondly, it is common that a protocol implementation at one layer may require data, state or addressing information that is only present at another layer, thus defeating the point of separating the layers in the first place. For example, TCP uses the ECN field in the IPv4 header as an indication of congestion; IP is a network layer protocol whereas TCP is a transport layer protocol.

Communication protocols have various characteristics. They may be connection-oriented or connectionless, they may use circuit mode or packet switching, and they may use hierarchical addressing or flat addressing.

There are many communication protocols, a few of which are described below.

IEEE 802

IEEE 802 is a family of IEEE standards dealing with local area networks and metropolitan area networks. The complete IEEE 802 protocol suite provides a diverse set of networking capabilities. The protocols have a flat addressing scheme. They operate mostly at levels 1 and 2 of the OSI model.

For example, MAC bridging (IEEE 802.1D) deals with the routing of Ethernet packets using a Spanning Tree Protocol. IEEE 802.1Q describes VLANs, and IEEE 802.1X defines a port-based Network Access Control protocol, which forms the basis for the authentication mechanisms used in VLANs (but it is also found in WLANs) – it is what the home user sees when the user has to enter a "wireless access key".

Ethernet

Ethernet, sometimes simply called *LAN*, is a family of protocols used in wired LANs, described by a set of standards together called IEEE 802.3 published by the Institute of Electrical and Electronics Engineers.

Wireless LAN

Wireless LAN, also widely known as WLAN or WiFi, is probably the most well-known member of the IEEE 802 protocol family for home users today. It is standarized by IEEE 802.11 and shares many properties with wired Ethernet.

Internet Protocol Suite

The Internet Protocol Suite, also called TCP/IP, is the foundation of all modern networking. It offers connection-less as well as connection-oriented services over an inherently unreliable network traversed by data-gram transmission at the Internet protocol (IP) level. At its core, the protocol suite defines the addressing, identification, and routing specifications for Internet Protocol Version 4 (IPv4) and for IPv6, the next generation of the protocol with a much enlarged addressing capability.

SONET/SDH

Synchronous optical networking (SONET) and Synchronous Digital Hierarchy (SDH) are standardized multiplexing protocols that transfer multiple digital bit streams over optical fiber using lasers. They were originally designed to transport circuit mode communications from a variety of different sources, primarily to support real-time, uncompressed, circuit-switched voice encoded in PCM (Pulse-Code Modulation) format. However, due to its protocol neutrality and transport-oriented features, SONET/SDH also was the obvious choice for transporting Asynchronous Transfer Mode (ATM) frames.

Asynchronous Transfer Mode

Asynchronous Transfer Mode (ATM) is a switching technique for telecommunication networks. It uses asynchronous time-division multiplexing and encodes data into small, fixed-sized cells. This differs from other protocols such as the Internet Protocol Suite or Ethernet that use variable sized packets or frames. ATM has similarity with both circuit and packet switched networking. This makes it a good choice for a network that must handle both traditional high-throughput data traffic, and real-time, low-latency content such as voice and video. ATM uses a connection-oriented model in which a virtual circuit must be established between two endpoints before the actual data exchange begins.

While the role of ATM is diminishing in favor of next-generation networks, it still plays a role in the last mile, which is the connection between an Internet service provider and the home user.

Cellular Standards

There are a number of different digital cellular standards, including: Global System for Mobile Communications (GSM), General Packet Radio Service (GPRS), cdmaOne, CDMA2000, Evolution-Data Optimized (EV-DO), Enhanced Data Rates for GSM Evolution (EDGE), Universal Mobile Telecommunications System (UMTS), Digital Enhanced Cordless Telecommunications (DECT), Digital AMPS (IS-136/TDMA), and Integrated Digital Enhanced Network (iDEN).

Geographic Scale

A network can be characterized by its physical capacity or its organizational purpose. Use of the network, including user authorization and access rights, differ accordingly.

Nanoscale Network

A nanoscale communication network has key components implemented at the nanoscale including message carriers and leverages physical principles that differ from macroscale communication mechanisms. Nanoscale communication extends communication to very small sensors and actuators such as those found in biological systems and also tends to operate in environments that would be too harsh for classical communication.

Personal Area Network

A personal area network (PAN) is a computer network used for communication among computer and different information technological devices close to one person. Some examples of devices that are used in a PAN are personal computers, printers, fax machines, telephones, PDAs, scanners, and even video game consoles. A PAN may include wired and wireless devices. The reach of a PAN typically extends to 10 meters. A wired

PAN is usually constructed with USB and FireWire connections while technologies such as Bluetooth and infrared communication typically form a wireless PAN.

Local Area Network

A local area network (LAN) is a network that connects computers and devices in a limited geographical area such as a home, school, office building, or closely positioned group of buildings. Each computer or device on the network is a node. Wired LANs are most likely based on Ethernet technology. Newer standards such as ITU-T G.hn also provide a way to create a wired LAN using existing wiring, such as coaxial cables, telephone lines, and power lines.

The defining characteristics of a LAN, in contrast to a wide area network (WAN), include higher data transfer rates, limited geographic range, and lack of reliance on leased lines to provide connectivity. Current Ethernet or other IEEE 802.3 LAN technologies operate at data transfer rates up to 100 Gbit/s, standarized by IEEE in 2010. Currently, 400 Gbit/s Ethernet is being developed.

A LAN can be connected to a WAN using a router.

Home Area Network

A home area network (HAN) is a residential LAN used for communication between digital devices typically deployed in the home, usually a small number of personal computers and accessories, such as printers and mobile computing devices. An important function is the sharing of Internet access, often a broadband service through a cable TV or digital subscriber line (DSL) provider.

Storage Area Network

A storage area network (SAN) is a dedicated network that provides access to consolidated, block level data storage. SANs are primarily used to make storage devices, such as disk arrays, tape libraries, and optical jukeboxes, accessible to servers so that the devices appear like locally attached devices to the operating system. A SAN typically has its own network of storage devices that are generally not accessible through the local area network by other devices. The cost and complexity of SANs dropped in the early 2000s to levels allowing wider adoption across both enterprise and small to medium-sized business environments.

Campus Area Network

A campus area network (CAN) is made up of an interconnection of LANs within a limited geographical area. The networking equipment (switches, routers) and transmission media (optical fiber, copper plant, Cat5 cabling, etc.) are almost entirely owned by the campus tenant / owner (an enterprise, university, government, etc.).

For example, a university campus network is likely to link a variety of campus buildings to connect academic colleges or departments, the library, and student residence halls.

Backbone Network

A backbone network is part of a computer network infrastructure that provides a path for the exchange of information between different LANs or sub-networks. A backbone can tie together diverse networks within the same building, across different buildings, or over a wide area.

For example, a large company might implement a backbone network to connect departments that are located around the world. The equipment that ties together the departmental networks constitutes the network backbone. When designing a network backbone, network performance and network congestion are critical factors to take into account. Normally, the backbone network's capacity is greater than that of the individual networks connected to it.

Another example of a backbone network is the Internet backbone, which is the set of wide area networks (WANs) and core routers that tie together all networks connected to the Internet.

Metropolitan Area Network

A Metropolitan area network (MAN) is a large computer network that usually spans a city or a large campus.

Wide Area Network

A wide area network (WAN) is a computer network that covers a large geographic area such as a city, country, or spans even intercontinental distances. A WAN uses a communications channel that combines many types of media such as telephone lines, cables, and air waves. A WAN often makes use of transmission facilities provided by common carriers, such as telephone companies. WAN technologies generally function at the lower three layers of the OSI reference model: the physical layer, the data link layer, and the network layer.

Enterprise Private Network

An enterprise private network is a network that a single organization builds to interconnect its office locations (e.g., production sites, head offices, remote offices, shops) so they can share computer resources.

Virtual Private Network

A virtual private network (VPN) is an overlay network in which some of the links between nodes are carried by open connections or virtual circuits in some larger network (e.g., the Internet) instead of by physical wires. The data link layer protocols of the virtual network are said to be tunneled through the larger network when this is the case. One common application is secure communications through the public Internet, but a VPN need not have explicit security features, such as authentication or content encryption. VPNs, for example, can be used to separate the traffic of different user communities over an underlying network with strong security features.

VPN may have best-effort performance, or may have a defined service level agreement (SLA) between the VPN customer and the VPN service provider. Generally, a VPN has a topology more complex than point-to-point.

Global Area Network

A global area network (GAN) is a network used for supporting mobile across an arbitrary number of wireless LANs, satellite coverage areas, etc. The key challenge in mobile communications is handing off user communications from one local coverage area to the next. In IEEE Project 802, this involves a succession of terrestrial wireless LANs.

Organizational Scope

Networks are typically managed by the organizations that own them. Private enterprise networks may use a combination of intranets and extranets. They may also provide network access to the Internet, which has no single owner and permits virtually unlimited global connectivity.

Intranet

An intranet is a set of networks that are under the control of a single administrative entity. The intranet uses the IP protocol and IP-based tools such as web browsers and file transfer applications. The administrative entity limits use of the intranet to its authorized users. Most commonly, an intranet is the internal LAN of an organization. A large intranet typically has at least one web server to provide users with organizational information. An intranet is also anything behind the router on a local area network.

Extranet

An extranet is a network that is also under the administrative control of a single organization, but supports a limited connection to a specific external network. For example, an organization may provide access to some aspects of its intranet to share data with its business partners or customers. These other entities are not necessarily trusted from a security standpoint. Network connection to an extranet is often, but not always, implemented via WAN technology.

Internetwork

An internetwork is the connection of multiple computer networks via a common routing technology using routers.

Internet

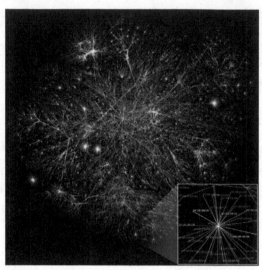

Partial map of the Internet based on the January 15, 2005 data found on opte.org. Each line is drawn between two nodes, representing two IP addresses. The length of the lines are indicative of the delay between those two nodes. This graph represents less than 30% of the Class C networks reachable.

The Internet is the largest example of an internetwork. It is a global system of interconnected governmental, academic, corporate, public, and private computer networks. It is based on the networking technologies of the Internet Protocol Suite. It is the successor of the Advanced Research Projects Agency Network (ARPANET) developed by DARPA of the United States Department of Defense. The Internet is also the communications backbone underlying the World Wide Web (WWW).

Participants in the Internet use a diverse array of methods of several hundred documented, and often standardized, protocols compatible with the Internet Protocol Suite and an addressing system (IP addresses) administered by the Internet Assigned Numbers Authority and address registries. Service providers and large enterprises exchange information about the reachability of their address spaces through the Border Gateway Protocol (BGP), forming a redundant worldwide mesh of transmission paths.

Darknet

A darknet is an overlay network, typically running on the internet, that is only accessible through specialized software. A darknet is an anonymizing network where connections are made only between trusted peers — sometimes called "friends" (F2F) — using non-standard protocols and ports.

Darknets are distinct from other distributed peer-to-peer networks as sharing is anonymous (that is, IP addresses are not publicly shared), and therefore users can communicate with little fear of governmental or corporate interference.

Routing

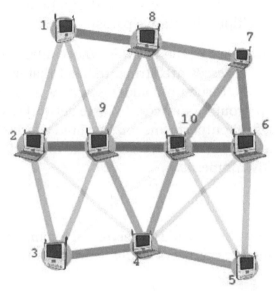

Routing calculates good paths through a network for information to take. For example, from node 1 to node 6 the best routes are likely to be 1-8-7-6 or 1-8-10-6, as this has the thickest routes.

Routing is the process of selecting network paths to carry network traffic. Routing is performed for many kinds of networks, including circuit switching networks and packet switched networks.

In packet switched networks, routing directs packet forwarding (the transit of logically addressed network packets from their source toward their ultimate destination) through intermediate nodes. Intermediate nodes are typically network hardware devices such as routers, bridges, gateways, firewalls, or switches. General-purpose computers can also forward packets and perform routing, though they are not specialized hardware and may suffer from limited performance. The routing process usually directs forwarding on the basis of routing tables, which maintain a record of the routes to various network destinations. Thus, constructing routing tables, which are held in the router's memory, is very important for efficient routing.

There are usually multiple routes that can be taken, and to choose between them, different elements can be considered to decide which routes get installed into the routing table, such as (sorted by priority):

1. *Prefix-Length*: where longer subnet masks are preferred (independent if it is within a routing protocol or over different routing protocol)

2.   *Metric*: where a lower metric/cost is preferred (only valid within one and the same routing protocol)

3.   *Administrative distance*: where a lower distance is preferred (only valid between different routing protocols)

Most routing algorithms use only one network path at a time. Multipath routing techniques enable the use of multiple alternative paths.

Routing, in a more narrow sense of the term, is often contrasted with bridging in its assumption that network addresses are structured and that similar addresses imply proximity within the network. Structured addresses allow a single routing table entry to represent the route to a group of devices. In large networks, structured addressing (routing, in the narrow sense) outperforms unstructured addressing (bridging). Routing has become the dominant form of addressing on the Internet. Bridging is still widely used within localized environments.

Network Service

Network services are applications hosted by servers on a computer network, to provide some functionality for members or users of the network, or to help the network itself to operate.

The World Wide Web, E-mail, printing and network file sharing are examples of well-known network services. Network services such as DNS (Domain Name System) give names for IP and MAC addresses (people remember names like "nm.lan" better than numbers like "210.121.67.18"), and DHCP to ensure that the equipment on the network has a valid IP address.

Services are usually based on a service protocol that defines the format and sequencing of messages between clients and servers of that network service.

Network Performance

Quality of Service

Depending on the installation requirements, network performance is usually measured by the quality of service of a telecommunications product. The parameters that affect this typically can include throughput, jitter, bit error rate and latency.

The following list gives examples of network performance measures for a circuit-switched network and one type of packet-switched network, viz. ATM:

- Circuit-switched networks: In circuit switched networks, network performance is synonymous with the grade of service. The number of rejected calls is a measure of how well the network is performing under heavy traffic loads. Other types of performance measures can include the level of noise and echo.

- ATM: In an Asynchronous Transfer Mode (ATM) network, performance can be measured by line rate, quality of service (QoS), data throughput, connect time, stability, technology, modulation technique and modem enhancements.

There are many ways to measure the performance of a network, as each network is different in nature and design. Performance can also be modelled instead of measured. For example, state transition diagrams are often used to model queuing performance in a circuit-switched network. The network planner uses these diagrams to analyze how the network performs in each state, ensuring that the network is optimally designed.

Network Congestion

Network congestion occurs when a link or node is carrying so much data that its quality of service deteriorates. Typical effects include queueing delay, packet loss or the blocking of new connections. A consequence of these latter two is that incremental increases in offered load lead either only to small increase in network throughput, or to an actual reduction in network throughput.

Network protocols that use aggressive retransmissions to compensate for packet loss tend to keep systems in a state of network congestion—even after the initial load is reduced to a level that would not normally induce network congestion. Thus, networks using these protocols can exhibit two stable states under the same level of load. The stable state with low throughput is known as *congestive collapse*.

Modern networks use congestion control and congestion avoidance techniques to try to avoid congestion collapse. These include: exponential backoff in protocols such as 802.11's CSMA/CA and the original Ethernet, window reduction in TCP, and fair queueing in devices such as routers. Another method to avoid the negative effects of network congestion is implementing priority schemes, so that some packets are transmitted with higher priority than others. Priority schemes do not solve network congestion by themselves, but they help to alleviate the effects of congestion for some services. An example of this is 802.1p. A third method to avoid network congestion is the explicit allocation of network resources to specific flows. One example of this is the use of Contention-Free Transmission Opportunities (CFTXOPs) in the ITU-T G.hn standard, which provides high-speed (up to 1 Gbit/s) Local area networking over existing home wires (power lines, phone lines and coaxial cables).

For the Internet RFC 2914 addresses the subject of congestion control in detail.

Network Resilience

Network resilience is "the ability to provide and maintain an acceptable level of service in the face of faults and challenges to normal operation."

Network Security

Network security consists of provisions and policies adopted by the network administrator to prevent and monitor unauthorized access, misuse, modification, or denial of the computer network and its network-accessible resources. Network security is the authorization of access to data in a network, which is controlled by the network administrator. Users are assigned an ID and password that allows them access to information and programs within their authority. Network security is used on a variety of computer networks, both public and private, to secure daily transactions and communications among businesses, government agencies and individuals.

Network Surveillance

Network surveillance is the monitoring of data being transferred over computer networks such as the Internet. The monitoring is often done surreptitiously and may be done by or at the behest of governments, by corporations, criminal organizations, or individuals. It may or may not be legal and may or may not require authorization from a court or other independent agency.

Computer and network surveillance programs are widespread today, and almost all Internet traffic is or could potentially be monitored for clues to illegal activity.

Surveillance is very useful to governments and law enforcement to maintain social control, recognize and monitor threats, and prevent/investigate criminal activity. With the advent of programs such as the Total Information Awareness program, technologies such as high speed surveillance computers and biometrics software, and laws such as the Communications Assistance For Law Enforcement Act, governments now possess an unprecedented ability to monitor the activities of citizens.

However, many civil rights and privacy groups—such as Reporters Without Borders, the Electronic Frontier Foundation, and the American Civil Liberties Union—have expressed concern that increasing surveillance of citizens may lead to a mass surveillance society, with limited political and personal freedoms. Fears such as this have led to numerous lawsuits such as *Hepting v. AT&T*. The hacktivist group Anonymous has hacked into government websites in protest of what it considers "draconian surveillance".

End to End Encryption

End-to-end encryption (E2EE) is a digital communications paradigm of uninterrupted protection of data traveling between two communicating parties. It involves the originating party encrypting data so only the intended recipient can decrypt it, with no dependency on third parties. End-to-end encryption prevents intermediaries, such as Internet providers or application service providers, from discovering or tampering with communications. End-to-end encryption generally protects both confidentiality and integrity.

Examples of end-to-end encryption include PGP for email, OTR for instant messaging, ZRTP for telephony, and TETRA for radio.

Typical server-based communications systems do not include end-to-end encryption. These systems can only guarantee protection of communications between clients and servers, not between the communicating parties themselves. Examples of non-E2EE systems are Google Talk, Yahoo Messenger, Facebook, and Dropbox. Some such systems, for example LavaBit and SecretInk, have even described themselves as offering "end-to-end" encryption when they do not. Some systems that normally offer end-to-end encryption have turned out to contain a back door that subverts negotiation of the encryption key between the communicating parties, for example Skype or Hushmail.

The end-to-end encryption paradigm does not directly address risks at the communications endpoints themselves, such as the technical exploitation of clients, poor quality random number generators, or key escrow. E2EE also does not address traffic analysis, which relates to things such as the identities of the end points and the times and quantities of messages that are sent.

Views of Networks

Users and network administrators typically have different views of their networks. Users can share printers and some servers from a workgroup, which usually means they are in the same geographic location and are on the same LAN, whereas a Network Administrator is responsible to keep that network up and running. A community of interest has less of a connection of being in a local area, and should be thought of as a set of arbitrarily located users who share a set of servers, and possibly also communicate via peer-to-peer technologies.

Network administrators can see networks from both physical and logical perspectives. The physical perspective involves geographic locations, physical cabling, and the network elements (e.g., routers, bridges and application layer gateways) that interconnect via the transmission media. Logical networks, called, in the TCP/IP architecture, subnets, map onto one or more transmission media. For example, a common practice in a campus of buildings is to make a set of LAN cables in each building appear to be a common subnet, using virtual LAN (VLAN) technology.

Both users and administrators are aware, to varying extents, of the trust and scope characteristics of a network. Again using TCP/IP architectural terminology, an intranet is a community of interest under private administration usually by an enterprise, and is only accessible by authorized users (e.g. employees). Intranets do not have to be connected to the Internet, but generally have a limited connection. An extranet is an extension of an intranet that allows secure communications to users outside of the intranet (e.g. business partners, customers).

Unofficially, the Internet is the set of users, enterprises, and content providers that are interconnected by Internet Service Providers (ISP). From an engineering viewpoint, the Internet is the set of subnets, and aggregates of subnets, which share the registered IP address space and exchange information about the reachability of those IP addresses using the Border Gateway Protocol. Typically, the human-readable names of servers are translated to IP addresses, transparently to users, via the directory function of the Domain Name System (DNS).

Over the Internet, there can be business-to-business (B2B), business-to-consumer (B2C) and consumer-to-consumer (C2C) communications. When money or sensitive information is exchanged, the communications are apt to be protected by some form of communications security mechanism. Intranets and extranets can be securely superimposed onto the Internet, without any access by general Internet users and administrators, using secure Virtual Private Network (VPN) technology.

Network Technologies

There is no generally accepted taxonomy into which all computer networks fit, but two dimensions stand out as important: Transmission Technology and Scale. The classifications based on these two basic approaches are considered in this section.

Classification Based on Transmission Technology

Computer networks can be broadly categorized into two types based on transmission technologies:

- Broadcast networks
- Point-to-point networks

Broadcast Networks

Broadcast network have a single communication channel that is shared by all the machines on the network as shown in figures. All the machines on the network receive short messages, called packets in certain contexts, sent by any machine. An address field within the packet specifies the intended recipient. Upon receiving a packet, machine checks the address field. If packet is intended for itself, it processes the packet; if packet is not intended for itself it is simply ignored.

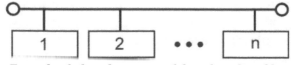

Example of a broadcast network based on shared bus

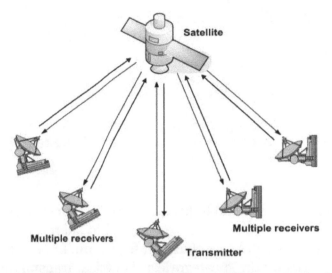

Example of a broadcast network based on satellite communication

This system generally also allows possibility of addressing the packet to all destinations (all nodes on the network). When such a packet is transmitted and received by all the machines on the network. This mode of operation is known as *Broadcast Mode*. Some Broadcast systems also supports transmission to a sub-set of machines, something known as *Multicasting*.

Point-to-Point Networks

A network based on point-to-point communication is shown in figure. The end devices that wish to communicate are called *stations*. The switching devices are called *nodes*. Some Nodes connect to other nodes and some to attached stations. It uses FDM or TDM for node-to-node communication. There may exist multiple paths between a source-destination pair for better network reliability. The switching nodes are not concerned with the contents of data. Their purpose is to provide a switching facility that will move data from node to node until they reach the destination.

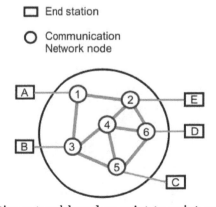

Communication network based on point-to-point communication

As a general rule (although there are many exceptions), smaller, geographically localized networks tend to use broadcasting, whereas larger networks normally use are point-to-point communication.

Classification Based on Scale

Alternative criteria for classifying networks are their scale. They are divided into Local Area (LAN), Metropolitan Area Network (MAN) and Wide Area Networks (WAN).

Local Area Network (LAN)

LAN is usually privately owned and links the devices in a single office, building or campus of up to few kilometers in size. These are used to share resources (may be hardware or software resources) and to exchange information. LANs are distinguished from other kinds of networks by three categories: their size, transmission technology and topology.

LANs are restricted in size, which means that their worst-case transmission time is bounded and known in advance. Hence this is more reliable as compared to MAN and WAN. Knowing this bound makes it possible to use certain kinds of design that would not otherwise be possible. It also simplifies network management.

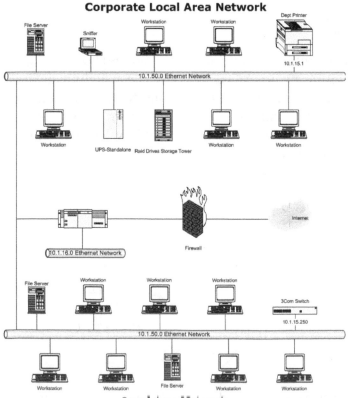

Local Area Network

LAN typically used transmission technology consisting of single cable to which all machines are connected. Traditional LANs run at speeds of 10 to 100 Mbps (but now much higher speeds can be achieved). The most common LAN topologies are bus, ring and star. A typical LAN is shown in the above figure.

Metropolitan Area Networks (MAN)

MAN is designed to extend over the entire city. It may be a single network as a cable TV network or it may be means of connecting a number of LANs into a larger network so that resources may be shared as shown in figure. For example, a company can use a MAN to connect the LANs in all its offices in a city. MAN is wholly owned and operated by a private company or may be a service provided by a public company.

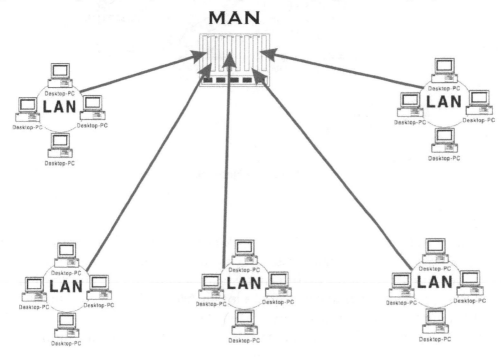

Metropolitan Area Networks (MAN)

The main reason for distinguishing MANs as a special category is that a standard has been adopted for them. It is DQDB (Distributed Queue Dual Bus) or IEEE 802.6.

Wide Area Network (WAN)

WAN provides long-distance transmission of data, voice, image and information over large geographical areas that may comprise a country, continent or even the whole world. In contrast to LANs, WANs may utilize public, leased or private communication devices, usually in combinations, and can therefore span an unlimited number of miles as shown in figure. A WAN that is wholly owned and used by a single company is often referred to as *enterprise network*.

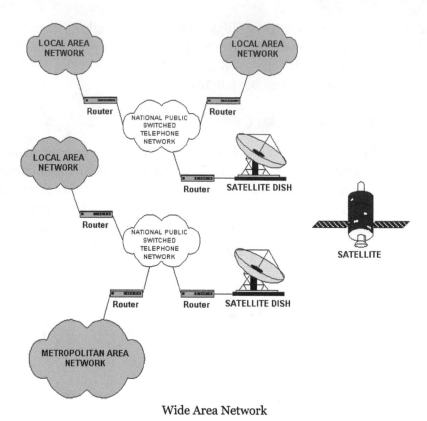

Wide Area Network

The Internet

Internet is a collection of networks or network of networks. Various networks such as LAN and WAN connected through suitable hardware and software to work in a seamless manner. Schematic diagram of the Internet is shown in figure. It allows various applications such as e-mail, file transfer, remote log-in, World Wide Web, Multimedia, etc run across the internet. The basic difference between WAN and Internet is that WAN is owned by a single organization while internet is not so. But with the time the line between WAN and Internet is shrinking, and these terms are sometimes used interchangeably.

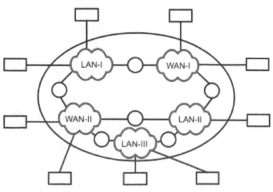

Internet – network of networks

Applications

In a short period of time computer networks have become an indispensable part of business, industry, entertainment as well as a common-man's life. These applications have changed tremendously from time and the motivation for building these networks are all essentially economic and technological.

Initially, computer network was developed for defense purpose, to have a secure communication network that can even withstand a nuclear attack. After a decade or so, companies, in various fields, started using computer networks for keeping track of inventories, monitor productivity, communication between their different branch offices located at different locations. For example, Railways started using computer networks by connecting their nationwide reservation counters to provide the facility of reservation and enquiry from any where across the country.

And now after almost two decades, computer networks have entered a new dimension; they are now an integral part of the society and people. In 1990s, computer network started delivering services to private individuals at home. These services and motivation for using them are quite different. Some of the services are access to remote information, person-person communication, and interactive entertainment. So, some of the applications of computer networks that we can see around us today are as follows:

Marketing and sales: Computer networks are used extensively in both marketing and sales organizations. Marketing professionals use them to collect, exchange, and analyze data related to customer needs and product development cycles. Sales application includes teleshopping, which uses order-entry computers or telephones connected to order processing network, and online-reservation services for hotels, airlines and so on.

Financial services: Today's financial services are totally depended on computer networks. Application includes credit history searches, foreign exchange and investment services, and electronic fund transfer, which allow user to transfer money without going into a bank (an automated teller machine is an example of electronic fund transfer, automatic pay-check is another).

Manufacturing: Computer networks are used in many aspects of manufacturing including manufacturing process itself. Two of them that use network to provide essential services are computer-aided design (CAD) and computer-assisted manufacturing (CAM), both of which allow multiple users to work on a project simultaneously.

Directory services: Directory services allow list of files to be stored in central location to speed worldwide search operations.

Information services: A Network information service includes bulletin boards and data banks. A World Wide Web site offering technical specification for a new product is an information service.

Electronic data interchange (EDI): EDI allows business information, including documents such as purchase orders and invoices, to be transferred without using paper.

Electronic mail: probably it's the most widely used computer network application.

Teleconferencing: Teleconferencing allows conference to occur without the participants being in the same place. Applications include simple text conferencing (where participants communicate through their normal keyboards and monitor) and video conferencing where participants can even see as well as talk to other fellow participants. Different types of equipments are used for video conferencing depending on what quality of the motion you want to capture (whether you want just to see the face of other fellow participants or do you want to see the exact facial expression).

Voice over IP: Computer networks are also used to provide voice communication. This kind of voice communication is pretty cheap as compared to the normal telephonic conversation.

Video on demand: Future services provided by the cable television networks may include video on request where a person can request for a particular movie or any clip at anytime he wish to see.

Layering Concepts

Network architectures define the standards and techniques for designing and building communication systems for computers and other devices. In the past, vendors developed their own architectures and required that other vendors conform to this architecture if they wanted to develop compatible hardware and software. There are proprietary network architectures such as IBM's SNA (Systems Network Architecture) and there are open architectures like the OSI (Open Systems Interconnection) model defined by the International Organization for Standardization. The previous strategy, where the computer network is designed with the hardware as the main concern and software is afterthought, no longer works. Network software is now highly *structured*.

To reduce the design complexity, most of the networks are organized as a series of layers or levels, each one build upon one below it. The basic idea of a layered architecture is *to divide the design into small pieces*. Each layer adds to the services provided by the lower layers in such a manner that the highest layer is provided a full set of services to manage communications and run the applications. The benefits of the layered models are modularity and clear interfaces, i.e. open architecture and comparability between the different providers' components.

A basic principle is to ensure independence of layers by defining services provided by each layer to the next higher layer without defining how the services are to be performed. This permits changes in a layer without affecting other layers. Prior to the use of layered protocol architectures, simple changes such as adding one terminal type to the list of those supported by an architecture often required changes to essentially all communications software at a site. The number of layers, functions and contents of each layer differ from network to network. However in all networks, the purpose of each layer is to offer certain services to higher layers, shielding those layers from the details of how the services are actually implemented.

The basic elements of a layered model are services, protocols and interfaces. A *service* is a set of actions that a layer offers to another (higher) layer. *Protocol* is a set of rules that a layer uses to exchange information with a peer entity. These rules concern both the contents and the order of the messages used. Between the layers service interfaces are defined. The messages from one layer to another are sent through those interfaces.

In an n-layer architecture, layer n on one machine carries on conversation with the layer n on other machine. The rules and conventions used in this conversation are collectively known as the *layer-n protocol*. Basically, a protocol is an agreement between the communicating parties on how communication is to proceed. Violating the protocol will make communication more difficult, if not impossible. A five-layer architecture is shown in figure, the entities comprising the corresponding layers on different machines are called *peers*. In other words, it is the peers that communicate using protocols. In reality, no data is transferred from layer n on one machine to layer n of another machine. Instead, each layer passes data and control information to the layer immediately below it, until the lowest layer is reached. Below layer-1 is the physical layer through which actual communication occurs. The peer process abstraction is crucial to all network design. Using it, the un-manageable tasks of designing the complete network can be broken into several smaller, manageable, design problems, namely design of individual layers.

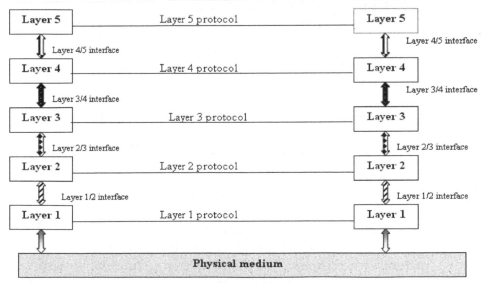

Basic five layer architecture

Between each pair of adjacent layers there is an interface. The *interface* defines which primitives operations and services the lower layer offers to the upper layer adjacent to it. When network designer decides how many layers to include in the network and what each layer should do, one of the main considerations is defining clean interfaces between adjacent layers. Doing so, in turns requires that each layer should perform well-defined functions. In addition to minimize the amount of information passed between layers, clean-cut interface also makes it simpler to replace the implementation of one layer with a completely different implementation, because all what is required of new implementation is that it offers same set of services to its upstairs neighbor as the old implementation (that is what a layer provides and how to use that service from it is more important than knowing how exactly it implements it).

A set of layers and protocols is known as network architecture. The specification of architecture must contain enough information to allow an implementation to write the program or build the hardware for each layer so that it will correctly obey the appropriate protocol. Neither the details of implementation nor the specification of interface is a part of network architecture because these are hidden away inside machines and not visible from outside. It is not even necessary that the interface on all machines in a network be same, provided that each machine can correctly use all protocols. A list of protocols used by a certain system, one protocol per layer, is called protocol stack.

OSI Model

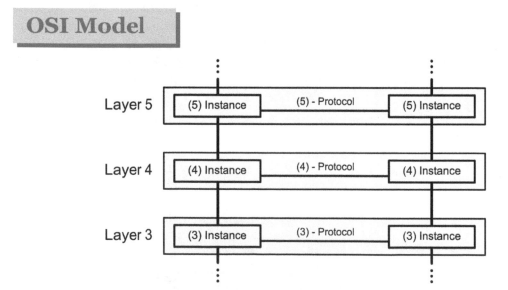

Communication in the OSI-Model (example with layers 3 to 5)

The Open Systems Interconnection model (OSI model) is a conceptual model that characterizes and standardizes the communication functions of a telecommunication or computing system without regard to their underlying internal structure and technology. Its goal is the interoperability of diverse communication systems with standard protocols. The model partitions a communication system into abstraction layers. The original version of the model defined seven layers.

A layer serves the layer above it and is served by the layer below it. For example, a layer that provides error-free communications across a network provides the path needed by applications above it, while it calls the next lower layer to send and receive packets that comprise the contents of that path. Two instances at the same layer are visualized as connected by a *horizontal* connection in that layer.

The model is a product of the Open Systems Interconnection project at the International Organization for Standardization (ISO), maintained by the identification ISO/ IEC 7498-1.

History

In the late 1970s, one project was administered by the International Organization for Standardization (ISO), while another was undertaken by the International Telegraph and Telephone Consultative Committee, or CCITT (the abbreviation is from the French version of the name). These two international standards bodies each developed a document that defined similar networking models.

In 1983, these two documents were merged to form a standard called The Basic Reference Model for Open Systems Interconnection. The standard is usually referred to as the Open Systems Interconnection Reference Model, the OSI Reference Model, or simply the OSI model. It was published in 1984 by both the ISO, as standard ISO 7498, and the renamed CCITT (now called the Telecommunications Standardization Sector of the International Telecommunication Union or ITU-T) as standard X.200.

OSI had two major components, an *abstract model* of networking, called the Basic Reference Model or seven-layer model, and a set of specific protocols.

The concept of a seven-layer model was provided by the work of Charles Bachman at Honeywell Information Services. Various aspects of OSI design evolved from experiences with the ARPANET, NPLNET, EIN, CYCLADES network and the work in IFIP WG6.1. The new design was documented in ISO 7498 and its various addenda. In this model, a networking system was divided into layers. Within each layer, one or more entities implement its functionality. Each entity interacted directly only with the layer immediately beneath it, and provided facilities for use by the layer above it.

Protocols enable an entity in one host to interact with a corresponding entity at the same layer in another host. Service definitions abstractly described the functionality provided to an (N)-layer by an (N-1) layer, where N was one of the seven layers of protocols operating in the local host.

The OSI standards documents are available from the ITU-T as the X.200-series of recommendations. Some of the protocol specifications were also available as part of the

ITU-T X series. The equivalent ISO and ISO/IEC standards for the OSI model were available from ISO, not all are free of charge.

Description of OSI layers

The recommendation X.200 describes seven layers, labeled 1 to 7. Layer 1 is the lowest layer in this model.

OSI Model			
Layer		**Protocol data unit (PDU)**	**Function**
Host layers	7. Application	Data	High-level APIs, including resource sharing, remote file access
	6. Presentation		Translation of data between a networking service and an application; including character encoding, data compression and encryption/decryption
	5. Session		Managing communication sessions, i.e. continuous exchange of information in the form of multiple back-and-forth transmissions between two nodes
	4. Transport	Segment (TCP) / Datagram (UDP)	Reliable transmission of data segments between points on a network, including segmentation, acknowledgement and multiplexing
Media layers	3. Network	Packet	Structuring and managing a multi-node network, including addressing, routing and traffic control
	2. Data link	Frame	Reliable transmission of data frames between two nodes connected by a physical layer
	1. Physical	Bit	Transmission and reception of raw bit streams over a physical medium

At each level N, two entities at the communicating devices (layer N *peers*) exchange protocol data units (PDUs) by means of a layer N *protocol*. Each PDU contains a payload, called the service data unit (SDU), along with protocol-related headers or footers.

Data processing by two communicating OSI-compatible devices is done as such:

1.   The data to be transmitted is composed at the topmost layer of the transmitting device (layer N) into a *protocol data unit (PDU)*.

2.   The *PDU* is passed to layer *N-1*, where it is known as the *service data unit (SDU)*.

3.   At layer *N-1* the *SDU* is concatenated with a header, a footer, or both, producing a *layer N-1 PDU*. It is then passed to layer *N-2*.

4.   The process continues until reaching the lowermost level, from which the data is transmitted to the receiving device.

5. At the receiving device the data is passed from the lowest to the highest layer as a series of *SDU*s while being successively stripped from each layer's header or footer, until reaching the topmost layer, where the last of the data is consumed.

Some orthogonal aspects, such as management and security, involve all of the layers. These services are aimed at improving the CIA triad - confidentiality, integrity, and availability - of the transmitted data. In practice, the availability of a communication service is determined by the interaction between network design and network management protocols. Appropriate choices for both of these are needed to protect against denial of service.

Layer 1: Physical Layer

The physical layer defines the electrical and physical specifications of the data connection. It defines the relationship between a device and a physical transmission medium (e.g., a copper or fiber optical cable, radio frequency). This includes the layout of pins, voltages, line impedance, cable specifications, signal timing and similar characteristics for connected devices and frequency (5 GHz or 2.4 GHz etc.) for wireless devices. It is responsible for transmission and reception of unstructured raw data in a physical medium. It may define transmission mode as simplex, half duplex, and full duplex. It defines the network topology as bus, mesh, or ring being some of the most common.

The physical layer of Parallel SCSI operates in this layer, as do the physical layers of Ethernet and other local-area networks, such as token ring, FDDI, ITU-T G.hn, and IEEE 802.11 (Wi-Fi), as well as personal area networks such as Bluetooth and IEEE 802.15.4.

The physical layer is the layer of low-level networking equipment, such as some hubs, cabling, and repeaters. The physical layer is never concerned with protocols or other such higher-layer items. Examples of hardware in this layer are network adapters, repeaters, network hubs, modems, and fiber media converters.

Layer 2: Data Link Layer

The data link layer provides node-to-node data transfer—a link between two directly connected nodes. It detects and possibly corrects errors that may occur in the physical layer. It defines the protocol to establish and terminate a connection between two physically connected devices. It also defines the protocol for flow control between them.

IEEE 802 divides the data link layer into two sublayers:

- Media access control (MAC) layer – responsible for controlling how devices in a network gain access to a medium and permission to transmit data.

- Logical link control (LLC) layer – responsible for identifying network layer protocols and then encapsulating them and controls error checking and frame synchronization.

The MAC and LLC layers of IEEE 802 networks such as 802.3 Ethernet, 802.11 Wi-Fi, and 802.15.4 ZigBee operate at the data link layer.

The Point-to-Point Protocol (PPP) is a data link layer protocol that can operate over several different physical layers, such as synchronous and asynchronous serial lines.

The ITU-T G.hn standard, which provides high-speed local area networking over existing wires (power lines, phone lines and coaxial cables), includes a complete data link layer that provides both error correction and flow control by means of a selective-repeat sliding-window protocol.

Layer 3: Network Layer

The network layer provides the functional and procedural means of transferring variable length data sequences (called datagrams) from one node to another connected to the same "network". A network is a medium to which many nodes can be connected, on which every node has an *address* and which permits nodes connected to it to transfer messages to other nodes connected to it by merely providing the content of a message and the address of the destination node and letting the network find the way to deliver the message to the destination node, possibly routing it through intermediate nodes. If the message is too large to be transmitted from one node to another on the data link layer between those nodes, the network may implement message delivery by splitting the message into several fragments at one node, sending the fragments independently, and reassembling the fragments at another node. It may, but need not, report delivery errors.

Message delivery at the network layer is not necessarily guaranteed to be reliable; a network layer protocol may provide reliable message delivery, but it need not do so.

A number of layer-management protocols, a function defined in the *management annex*, ISO 7498/4, belong to the network layer. These include routing protocols, multicast group management, network-layer information and error, and network-layer address assignment. It is the function of the payload that makes these belong to the network layer, not the protocol that carries them.

Layer 4: Transport Layer

The transport layer provides the functional and procedural means of transferring variable-length data sequences from a source to a destination host via one or more networks, while maintaining the quality of service functions.

An example of a transport-layer protocol in the standard Internet stack is Transmission Control Protocol (TCP), usually built on top of the Internet Protocol (IP).

The transport layer controls the reliability of a given link through flow control, segmentation/desegmentation, and error control. Some protocols are state- and connection-oriented. This means that the transport layer can keep track of the segments and re-transmit those that fail. The transport layer also provides the acknowledgement of the successful data transmission and sends the next data if no errors occurred. The transport layer creates packets out of the message received from the application layer. Packetizing is a process of dividing the long message into smaller messages.

OSI defines five classes of connection-mode transport protocols ranging from class 0 (which is also known as TP0 and provides the fewest features) to class 4 (TP4, designed for less reliable networks, similar to the Internet). Class 0 contains no error recovery, and was designed for use on network layers that provide error-free connections. Class 4 is closest to TCP, although TCP contains functions, such as the graceful close, which OSI assigns to the session layer. Also, all OSI TP connection-mode protocol classes provide expedited data and preservation of record boundaries. Detailed characteristics of TP0-4 classes are shown in the following table:

Feature name	TP0	TP1	TP2	TP3	TP4
Connection-oriented network	Yes	Yes	Yes	Yes	Yes
Connectionless network	No	No	No	No	Yes
Concatenation and separation	No	Yes	Yes	Yes	Yes
Segmentation and reassembly	Yes	Yes	Yes	Yes	Yes
Error recovery	No	Yes	Yes	Yes	Yes
Reinitiate connection[a]	No	Yes	No	Yes	No
Multiplexing / demultiplexing over single virtual circuit	No	No	Yes	Yes	Yes
Explicit flow control	No	No	Yes	Yes	Yes
Retransmission on timeout	No	No	No	No	Yes
Reliable transport service	No	Yes	No	Yes	Yes
[a] If an excessive number of PDUs are unacknowledged.					

An easy way to visualize the transport layer is to compare it with a post office, which deals with the dispatch and classification of mail and parcels sent. Do remember, however, that a post office manages the outer envelope of mail. Higher layers may have the equivalent of double envelopes, such as cryptographic presentation services that can be read by the addressee only. Roughly speaking, tunneling protocols operate at the transport layer, such as carrying non-IP protocols such as IBM's SNA or Novell's IPX over an IP network, or end-to-end encryption with IPsec. While Generic Routing Encapsulation (GRE) might seem to be a network-layer protocol, if the encapsulation of the payload takes place only at endpoint, GRE becomes closer to a transport protocol that uses IP headers but contains complete frames or packets to deliver to an endpoint. L2TP carries PPP frames inside transport packet.

Although not developed under the OSI Reference Model and not strictly conforming to the OSI definition of the transport layer, the Transmission Control Protocol (TCP) and the User Datagram Protocol (UDP) of the Internet Protocol Suite are commonly categorized as layer-4 protocols within OSI.

Layer 5: Session Layer

The session layer controls the dialogues (connections) between computers. It establishes, manages and terminates the connections between the local and remote application. It provides for full-duplex, half-duplex, or simplex operation, and establishes checkpointing, adjournment, termination, and restart procedures. The OSI model made this layer responsible for graceful close of sessions, which is a property of the Transmission Control Protocol, and also for session checkpointing and recovery, which is not usually used in the Internet Protocol Suite. The session layer is commonly implemented explicitly in application environments that use remote procedure calls.

Layer 6: Presentation Layer

The presentation layer establishes context between application-layer entities, in which the application-layer entities may use different syntax and semantics if the presentation service provides a mapping between them. If a mapping is available, presentation service data units are encapsulated into session protocol data units, and passed down the protocol stack.

This layer provides independence from data representation (e.g., encryption) by translating between application and network formats. The presentation layer transforms data into the form that the application accepts. This layer formats and encrypts data to be sent across a network. It is sometimes called the syntax layer.

The original presentation structure used the Basic Encoding Rules of Abstract Syntax Notation One (ASN.1), with capabilities such as converting an EBCDIC-coded text file to an ASCII-coded file, or serialization of objects and other data structures from and to XML.

Layer 7: Application Layer

The application layer is the OSI layer closest to the end user, which means both the OSI application layer and the user interact directly with the software application. This layer interacts with software applications that implement a communicating component. Such application programs fall outside the scope of the OSI model. Application-layer functions typically include identifying communication partners, determining resource availability, and synchronizing communication. When identifying communication partners, the application layer determines the identity and availability of communication partners for an application with data to transmit. When determining resource availability, the application layer must decide whether sufficient network resources for the requested communication are available.

Cross-layer Functions

Cross-layer functions are services that are not tied to a given layer, but may affect more than one layer. Examples include the following:

- Security service (telecommunication) as defined by ITU-T X.800 recommendation.

- Management functions, i.e. functions that permit to configure, instantiate, monitor, terminate the communications of two or more entities: there is a specific application-layer protocol, common management information protocol (CMIP) and its corresponding service, common management information service (CMIS), they need to interact with every layer in order to deal with their instances.

- Multiprotocol Label Switching (MPLS) operates at an OSI-model layer that is generally considered to lie between traditional definitions of layer 2 (data link layer) and layer 3 (network layer), and thus is often referred to as a "layer-2.5" protocol. It was designed to provide a unified data-carrying service for both circuit-based clients and packet-switching clients which provide a datagram-based service model. It can be used to carry many different kinds of traffic, including IP packets, as well as native ATM, SONET, and Ethernet frames.

- ARP is used to translate IPv4 addresses (OSI layer 3) into Ethernet MAC addresses (OSI layer 2).

- Domain Name Service is an Application Layer service which is used to look up the IP address of a given domain name. Once a reply is received from the DNS server, it is then possible to form a Layer 3 connection to the third-party host.

- Cross MAC and PHY Scheduling is essential in wireless networks because of the time varying nature of wireless channels. By scheduling packet transmission only in favorable channel conditions, which requires the MAC layer to obtain channel state information from the PHY layer, network throughput can be significantly improved and energy waste can be avoided.

Interfaces

Neither the OSI Reference Model nor OSI protocols specify any programming interfaces, other than deliberately abstract service specifications. Protocol specifications precisely define the interfaces between different computers, but the software interfaces inside computers, known as network sockets are implementation-specific.

For example, Microsoft Windows' Winsock, and Unix's Berkeley sockets and System V Transport Layer Interface, are interfaces between applications (layer 5 and above) and the transport (layer 4). NDIS and ODI are interfaces between the media (layer 2) and the network protocol (layer 3).

Interface standards, except for the physical layer to media, are approximate implementations of OSI service specifications.

Comparison with TCP/IP model

The design of protocols in the TCP/IP model of the Internet does not concern itself with strict hierarchical encapsulation and layering. RFC 3439 contains a section entitled "Layering considered harmful". TCP/IP does recognize four broad layers of functionality which are derived from the operating scope of their contained protocols: the scope of the software application; the end-to-end transport connection; the internetworking range; and the scope of the direct links to other nodes on the local network.

Despite using a different concept for layering than the OSI model, these layers are often compared with the OSI layering scheme in the following way:

- The Internet application layer includes the OSI application layer, presentation layer, and most of the session layer.

- Its end-to-end transport layer includes the graceful close function of the OSI session layer as well as the OSI transport layer.

- The internetworking layer (Internet layer) is a subset of the OSI network layer.

- The link layer includes the OSI data link layer and sometimes the physical layers, as well as some protocols of the OSI's network layer.

These comparisons are based on the original seven-layer protocol model as defined in ISO 7498, rather than refinements in such things as the internal organization of the network layer document.

The presumably strict layering of the OSI model as it is usually described does not present contradictions in TCP/IP, as it is permissible that protocol usage does not follow the hierarchy implied in a layered model. Such examples exist in some routing protocols (e.g., OSPF), or in the description of tunneling protocols, which provide a link layer for an application, although the tunnel host protocol might well be a transport or even an application-layer protocol in its own right.

Characteristics of the OSI Layers

The seven layers of the OSI reference model can be divided into two categories: upper layers and lower layers as shown in figure.

The upper layers of the OSI model deal with application issues and generally are implemented only in software. The highest layer, the application layer, is closest to the end user. Both users and application layer processes interact with software applications that contain a communications component. The term upper layer is sometimes used to refer to any layer above another layer in the OSI model.

The lower layers of the OSI model handle data transport issues. The physical layer and the data link layer are implemented in hardware and software. The lowest layer, the physical layer, is closest to the physical network medium (the network cabling, for example) and is responsible for actually placing information on the medium.

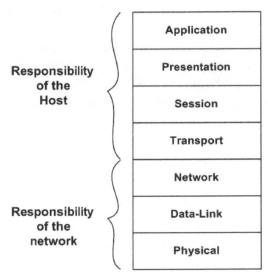

Two sets of layers make up the OSI layers

Protocols

The OSI model provides a conceptual framework for communication between computers, but the model itself is not a method of communication. Actual communication is made possible by using communication protocols. In the context of data networking, a protocol *is a formal set of rules and conventions that governs how computers exchange information over a network medium.* A protocol implements the functions of one or more of the OSI layers.

A wide variety of communication protocols exist. Some of these protocols include LAN protocols, WAN protocols, network protocols, and routing protocols. LAN protocols operate at the physical and data link layers of the OSI model and define communication over various LAN media. WAN protocols operate at the lowest three layers of the OSI model and define communication over the various wide-area media. Routing protocols are network layer protocols that are responsible for exchanging information between routers so that the routers can select the proper path for network traffic. Finally, network protocols are the various upper-layer protocols that exist in a given protocol suite.

Many protocols rely on others for operation. For example, many routing protocols use network protocols to exchange information between routers. This concept of building upon the layers already in existence is the foundation of the OSI model.

OSI Model and Communication between Systems

Information being transferred from a software application in one computer system to a software application in another must pass through the OSI layers. For example, if a software application in System A has information to transmit to a software application in System B, the application program in System A will pass its information to the application layer (Layer 7) of System A. The application layer then passes the information to the presentation layer (Layer 6), which relays the data to the session layer (Layer 5), and so on down to the physical layer (Layer 1). At the physical layer, the information is placed on the physical network medium and is sent across the medium to System B. The physical layer of System B removes the information from the physical medium, and then its physical layer passes the information up to the data link layer (Layer 2), which passes it to the network layer (Layer 3), and so on, until it reaches the application layer (Layer 7) of System B. Finally, the application layer of System B passes the information to the recipient application program to complete the communication process.

Interaction between OSI Model Layers

A given layer in the OSI model generally communicates with three other OSI layers: the layer directly above it, the layer directly below it, and its peer layer in other networked computer systems. The data link layer in System A, for example, communicates with the network layer of System A, the physical layer of System A, and the data link layer in System B. Figure illustrates this example.

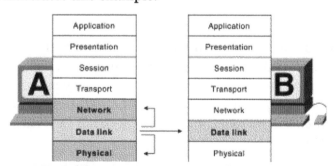

OSI Model Layers Communicate with Other Layers

Services and Service Access Points

One OSI layer communicates with another layer to make use of the services provided by the second layer. The services provided by adjacent layers help a given OSI layer communicate with its peer layer in other computer systems. Three basic elements are involved in layer services: the service user, the service provider, and the service access point (SAP).

In this context, the service user is the OSI layer that requests services from an adjacent OSI layer. The service provider is the OSI layer that provides services to service users. OSI layers can provide services to multiple service users. The SAP is a conceptual location at which one OSI layer can request the services of another OSI layer.

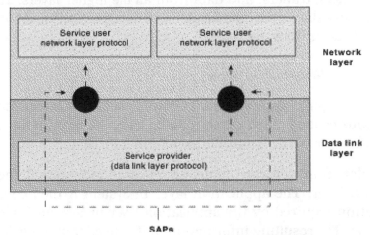

Service Users, Providers, and SAPs interact at the Network and Data Link Layers

OSI Model Layers and Information Exchange

The seven OSI layers use various forms of control information to communicate with their peer layers in other computer systems. This control information consists of specific requests and instructions that are exchanged between peer OSI layers.

Control information typically takes one of two forms: headers and trailers. Headers are prepended to data that has been passed down from upper layers. Trailers are appended to data that has been passed down from upper layers. An OSI layer is not required to attach a header or a trailer to data from upper layers.

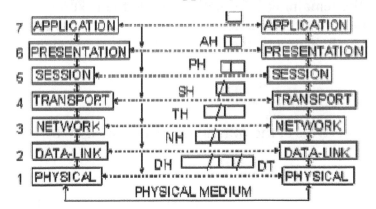

Headers and Data can be encapsulated during Information exchange

Headers, trailers, and data are relative concepts, depending on the layer that analyzes the information unit. At the network layer, for example, an information unit consists of a Layer 3 header and data. At the data link layer, however, all the information passed down by the network layer (the Layer 3 header and the data) is treated as data.

In other words, the data portion of an information unit at a given OSI layer potentially can contain headers, trailers, and data from all the higher layers. This is known as encapsulation. Figure shows how the header and data from one layer are encapsulated into the header of the next lowest layer.

Information Exchange Process

The information exchange process occurs between peer OSI layers. Each layer in the source system adds control information to data, and each layer in the destination system analyzes and removes the control information from that data.

If system A has data from software application to send to System B, the data is passed to the application layer. The application layer in System A then communicates any control information required by the application layer in System B by pre-pending a header to the data. The resulting information unit (a header and the data) is passed to the presentation layer, which pre-pends its own header containing control information intended for the presentation layer in System B. The information unit grows in size as each layer pre-pends its own header (and, in some cases, a trailer) that contains control information to be used by its peer layer in System B. At the physical layer, the entire information unit is placed onto the network medium.

The physical layer in System B receives the information unit and passes it to the data link layer. The data link layer in System B then reads the control information contained in the header pre-pended by the data link layer in System A. The header is then removed, and the remainder of the information unit is passed to the network layer. Each layer performs the same actions: The layer reads the header from its peer layer, strips it off, and passes the remaining information unit to the next highest layer. After the application layer performs these actions, the data is passed to the recipient software application in System B, in exactly the form in which it was transmitted by the application in System A.

Functions of the OSI Layers

Functions of different layers of the OSI model are presented in this section.

Physical Layer

The physical layer is concerned with transmission of raw bits over a communication channel. It specifies the mechanical, electrical and procedural network interface specifications and the physical transmission of bit streams over a transmission medium connecting two pieces of communication equipment. In simple terns, the physical layer decides the following:

- Number of pins and functions of each pin of the network connector (Mechanical)

- Signal Level, Data rate (Electrical)

- Whether simultaneous transmission in both directions

- Establishing and breaking of connection

- Deals with physical transmission

There exist a variety of physical layer protocols such as RS-232C, Rs-449 standards developed by Electronics Industries Association (EIA).

Data Link Layer

The goal of the data link layer is to provide reliable, efficient communication between adjacent machines connected by a single communication channel. Specifically:

1. Group the physical layer bit stream into units called frames. Note that frames are nothing more than ``packets" or ``messages". By convention, we shall use the term ``frames" when discussing DLL packets.

2. Sender calculates the checksum and sends checksum together with data. The checksum allows the receiver to determine when a frame has been damaged in transit or received correctly.

3. Receiver recomputes the checksum and compares it with the received value. If they differ, an error has occurred and the frame is discarded.

4. Error control protocol returns a positive or negative acknowledgment to the sender. A positive acknowledgment indicates the frame was received without errors, while a negative acknowledgment indicates the opposite.

5. Flow control prevents a fast sender from overwhelming a slower receiver. For example, a supercomputer can easily generate data faster than a PC can consume it.

6. In general, data link layer provides service to the network layer. The network layer wants to be able to send packets to its neighbors without worrying about the details of getting it there in one piece.

Design Issues

Below are the some of the important design issues of the data link layer:

a) Reliable Delivery:

Frames are delivered to the receiver reliably and in the same order as generated by the sender. Connection state keeps track of sending order and which frames require retransmission. For example, receiver state includes which frames have been received, which ones have not, etc.

b)   Best Effort: The receiver does not return acknowledgments to the sender, so the sender has no way of knowing if a frame has been successfully delivered.

When would such a service be appropriate?

1.   When higher layers can recover from errors with little loss in performance. That is, when errors are so infrequent that there is little to be gained by the data link layer performing the recovery. It is just as easy to have higher layers deal with occasional loss of packet.

2.   For real-time applications requiring ``better never than late" semantics. Old data may be worse than no data.

c)   Acknowledged Delivery

The receiver returns an acknowledgment frame to the sender indicating that a data frame was properly received. This sits somewhere between the other two in that the sender keeps connection state, but may not necessarily retransmit unacknowledged frames. Likewise, the receiver may hand over received packets to higher layer in the order in which they arrive, regardless of the original sending order. Typically, each frame is assigned a unique sequence number, which the receiver returns in an acknowledgment frame to indicate which frame the ACK refers to. The sender must retransmit unacknowledged (e.g., lost or damaged) frames.

d)   Framing

The DLL translates the physical layer's raw bit stream into discrete units (messages) called frames. How can the receiver detect frame boundaries? Various techniques are used for this: Length Count, Bit Stuffing, and Character stuffing.

e)   Error Control

Error control is concerned with insuring that all frames are eventually delivered (possibly in order) to a destination. To achieve this, three items are required: Acknowledgements, Timers, and Sequence Numbers.

f)   Flow Control

Flow control deals with throttling the speed of the sender to match that of the receiver. Usually, this is a dynamic process, as the receiving speed depends on such changing factors as the load, and availability of buffer space.

Link Management

In some cases, the data link layer service must be ``opened" before use:

- The data link layer uses open operations for allocating buffer space, control blocks, agreeing on the maximum message size, etc.

- Synchronize and initialize send and receive sequence numbers with its peer at the other end of the communications channel.

Error Detection and Correction

In data communication, error may occur because of various reasons including attenuation, noise. Moreover, error usually occurs as bursts rather than independent, single bit errors. For example, a burst of lightning will affect a set of bits for a short time after the lightning strike. Detecting and correcting errors requires redundancy (i.e., sending additional information along with the data).

There are two types of attacks against errors:

- Error Detecting Codes: Include enough redundancy bits to detect errors and use ACKs and retransmissions to recover from the errors. Example: parity encoding.

- Error Correcting Codes: Include enough redundancy to detect and correct errors. Examples: CRC checksum, MD5.

Network Layer

The basic purpose of the network layer is to provide an end-to-end communication capability in contrast to machine-to-machine communication provided by the data link layer. This end-to-end is performed using two basic approaches known as connection-oriented or connectionless network-layer services.

Four issues:

1. Interface between the host and the network (the network layer is typically the boundary between the host and subnet)

2. Routing

3. Congestion and deadlock

4. Internetworking (A path may traverse different network technologies (e.g., Ethernet, point-to-point links, etc.)

Network Layer Interface

There are two basic approaches used for sending packets, which is a group of bits that includes data plus source and destination addresses, from node to node called *virtual circuit* and *datagram* methods. These are also referred to as *connection-oriented* and *connectionless* network-layer services. In virtual circuit approach, a *route*, which consists of logical connection, is first established between two users. During this establishment phase, the two users not only agree to set up a connection between them but also decide upon the quality of service to be associated with the connection. The well-known virtual-circuit protocol is the ISO and CCITT *X.25* specification. The datagram is a self-contained message unit, which contains sufficient information for routing from the source node to the destination node without dependence on previous message interchanges between them. In contrast to the virtual-circuit method, where a fixed path is explicitly set up before message transmission, sequentially transmitted messages can follow completely different paths. The datagram method is analogous to the postal system and the virtual-circuit method is analogous to the telephone system.

Overview of Other Network Layer Issues:

The network layer is responsible for routing packets from the source to destination. The *routing algorithm* is the piece of software that decides where a packet goes next (e.g., which output line, or which node on a broadcast channel).

For connectionless networks, the routing decision is made for each datagram. For connection-oriented networks, the decision is made once, at circuit setup time.

Routing Issues:

The routing algorithm must deal with the following issues:

- Correctness and simplicity: networks are never taken down; individual parts (e.g., links, routers) may fail, but the whole network should not.

- Stability: if a link or router fails, how much time elapses before the remaining routers recognize the topology change? (Some never do.)

- Fairness and optimality: an inherently intractable problem. Definition of optimality usually doesn't consider fairness. Do we want to maximize channel usage? Minimize average delay?

When we look at routing in detail, we'll consider both adaptive--those that take current traffic and topology into consideration--and non-adaptive algorithms.

Congestion

The network layer also must deal with congestion:

- When more packets enter an area than can be processed, delays increase and performance decreases. If the situation continues, the subnet may have no alternative but to discard packets.

- If the delay increases, the sender may (incorrectly) retransmit, making a bad situation even worse.

- Overall, performance degrades because the network is using (wasting) resources processing packets that eventually get discarded.

Internetworking

Finally, when we consider internetworking -- connecting different network technologies together -- one finds the same problems, only worse:

- Packets may travel through many different networks

- Each network may have a different frame format

- Some networks may be connectionless, other connection oriented

Routing

Routing is concerned with the question: Which line should router J use when forwarding a packet to router K?

There are two types of algorithms:

- Adaptive algorithms use such dynamic information as current topology, load, delay, etc. to select routes.

- In non-adaptive algorithms, routes never change once initial routes have been selected. Also called static routing.

Obviously, adaptive algorithms are more interesting, as non-adaptive algorithms don't even make an attempt to handle failed links.

Transport Layer

The transport level provides end-to-end communication between processes executing on different machines. Although the services provided by a transport protocol are similar to those provided by a data link layer protocol, there are several important differences between the transport and lower layers:

1. User Oriented. Application programmers interact directly with the transport layer, and from the programmers perspective, the transport layer is the ``network''. Thus, the transport layer should be oriented more towards user services than simply reflect what the underlying layers happen to provide. (Similar to the beautification principle in operating systems.)

2. Negotiation of Quality and Type of Services. The user and transport protocol may need to negotiate as to the quality or type of service to be provided. Examples? A user may want to negotiate such options as: throughput, delay, protection, priority, reliability, etc.

3. Guarantee Service. The transport layer may have to overcome service deficiencies of the lower layers (e.g. providing reliable service over an unreliable network layer).

4. Addressing becomes a significant issue. That is, now the user must deal with it; before it was buried in lower levels.

Two solutions:

- Use well-known addresses that rarely if ever change, allowing programs to ``wire in" addresses. For what types of service does this work? While this works for services that are well established (e.g., mail, or telnet), it doesn't allow a user to easily experiment with new services.

- Use a name server. Servers register services with the name server, which clients contact to find the transport address of a given service.

In both cases, we need a mechanism for mapping high-level service names into low-level encoding that can be used within packet headers of the network protocols. In its general parts: have transport addresses be a combination of machine address and local process on that machine.

5. Storage capacity of the subnet. Assumptions valid at the data link layer do not necessarily hold at the transport Layer. Specifically, the subnet may buffer messages for a potentially long time, and an ``old" packet may arrive at a destination at unexpected times.

6. We need a dynamic flow control mechanism. The data link layer solution of reallocating buffers is inappropriate because a machine may have hundreds of connections sharing a single physical link. In addition, appropriate settings for the flow control parameters depend on the communicating end points (e.g., Cray supercomputers vs. PCs), not on the protocol used.

Don't send data unless there is room. Also, the network layer/data link layer solution of simply not acknowledging frames for which the receiver has no space is unacceptable. Why? In the data link case, the line is not being used for anything else; thus retransmissions are inexpensive. At the transport level, end-to-end retransmissions are needed, which wastes resources by sending the same packet over the same links multiple times. If the receiver has no buffer space, the sender should be prevented from sending data.

7. Deal with congestion control. In connectionless Internets, transport protocols must exercise congestion control. When the network becomes congested, they must reduce rate at which they insert packets into the subnet, because the subnet has no way to prevent itself from becoming overloaded.

8. Connection establishment. Transport level protocols go through three phases: establishing, using, and terminating a connection. For data gram-oriented protocols, opening a connection simply allocates and initializes data structures in the operating system kernel.

Connection oriented protocols often exchanges messages that negotiate options with the remote peer at the time a connection are opened. Establishing a connection may be tricky because of the possibility of old or duplicate packets.

Finally, although not as difficult as establishing a connection, terminating a connection presents subtleties too. For instance, both ends of the connection must be sure that all the data in their queues have been delivered to the remote application.

Session Layer

This layer allows users on different machines to establish session between them. A session allows ordinary data transport but it also provides enhanced services useful in some applications. A session may be used to allow a user to log into a remote time-sharing machine or to transfer a file between two machines. Some of the session related services are:

1. This layer manages *Dialogue Control*. Session can allow traffic to go in both direction at the same time, or in only one direction at one time.

2. *Token management*. For some protocols, it is required that both sides don't attempt same operation at the same time. To manage these activities, the session layer provides tokens that can be exchanged. Only one side that is holding token can perform the critical operation. This concept can be seen as entering into a critical section in operating system using semaphores.

3. *Synchronization*. Consider the problem that might occur when trying to transfer a 4-hour file transfer with a 2-hour mean time between crashes. After each transfer was aborted, the whole transfer has to start again and again would probably fail. To Eliminate this problem, Session layer provides a way to insert checkpoints into data streams, so that after a crash, only the data transferred after the last checkpoint have to be repeated.

Presentation Layer

This layer is concerned with Syntax and Semantics of the information transmitted, unlike other layers, which are interested in moving data reliably from one machine to other. Few of the services that Presentation layer provides are:

1. Encoding data in a standard agreed upon way.

2. It manages the abstract data structures and converts from representation used inside computer to network standard representation and back.

Application Layer

The application layer consists of what most users think of as programs. The application does the actual work at hand. Although each application is different, some applications are so useful that they have become standardized. The Internet has defined standards for:

- File transfer (FTP): Connect to a remote machine and send or fetch an arbitrary file. FTP deals with authentication, listing a directory contents, ASCII or binary files, etc.

- Remote login (telnet): A remote terminal protocol that allows a user at one site to establish a TCP connection to another site, and then pass keystrokes from the local host to the remote host.

- Mail (SMTP): Allow a mail delivery agent on a local machine to connect to a mail delivery agent on a remote machine and deliver mail.

- News (NNTP): Allows communication between a news server and a news client.

- Web (HTTP): Base protocol for communication on the World Wide Web.

References

- Mansfield-Devine, Steve (December 2009). "Darknets". Computer Fraud & Security. 2009 (12): 4–6. doi:10.1016/S1361-3723(09)70150-2

- "ITU-T Recommendataion X.800 (03/91), Security architecture for Open Systems Interconnection for CCITT applications". ITU. Retrieved 14 August 2015

- International Organization for Standardization (1989-11-15). "ISO/IEC 7498-4:1989 -- Information technology -- Open Systems Interconnection -- Basic Reference Model: Naming and addressing". ISO Standards Maintenance Portal. ISO Central Secretariat. Retrieved 2015-08-17

- Walter Goralski. The Illustrated Network: How TCP/IP Works in a Modern Network (PDF). Morgan Kaufmann. p. 26. ISBN 978-0123745415

- Wood, Jessica (2010). "The Darknet: A Digital Copyright Revolution" (PDF). Richmond Journal of Law and Technology. 16 (4). Retrieved 25 October 2011

- "Internetworking Technology Handbook - Internetworking Basics [Internetworking]". Cisco. 15 January 2014. Retrieved 14 August 2015

- Telecommunications Magazine Online, Americas January 2003, Issue Highlights, Online Exclusive: Broadband Access Maximum Performance, Retrieved on February 13, 2005

- Miao, Guowang; Song, Guocong (2014). Energy and spectrum efficient wireless network design. Cambridge University Press. ISBN 1107039886

- "Anonymous hacks UK government sites over 'draconian surveillance' ", Emil Protalinski, ZDNet, 7 April 2012, retrieved 12 March 2013

- "Bigger Monster, Weaker Chains: The Growth of an American Surveillance Society" (PDF). American Civil Liberties Union. January 15, 2003. Retrieved March 13, 2009

Data Transmission in Computer Networks

Ideal cable types allow for large amounts of data to be transferred along longer distances. A coaxial cable has an inner tubular insulator layer and a tubular conducting shield. Broadband coaxial cables allow for a typical bandwith of 300 MHz. The major components of data communication systems are discussed in this section.

Transmission Medium

A transmission medium is a material substance (solid, liquid, gas, or plasma) that can propagate energy waves. For example, the transmission medium for sounds is usually air, but solids and liquids may also act as transmission media for sound.

The absence of a material medium in vacuum may also constitute a transmission medium for electromagnetic waves such as light and radio waves. While material substance is not required for electromagnetic waves to propagate, such waves are usually affected by the transmission media they pass through, for instance by absorption or by reflection or refraction at the interfaces between media.

The term transmission medium also refers to a technical device that employs the material substance to transmit or guide waves. Thus, an optical fiber or a copper cable is a transmission medium. Not only this but also is able to guide the transmission of networks.

A transmission medium can be classified as a:

- *Linear medium*, if different waves at any particular point in the medium can be superposed;
- *Bounded medium*, if it is finite in extent, otherwise *unbounded medium*;
- *Uniform medium* or *homogeneous medium*, if its physical properties are unchanged at different points;
- *Isotropic medium*, if its physical properties are the same in different directions.

Electromagnetic radiation can be transmitted through an optical medium, such as optical fiber, or through twisted pair wires, coaxial cable, or dielectric-slab waveguides. It may also pass through any physical material that is transparent to the specific wavelength, such as water, air, glass, or concrete. Sound is, by definition, the vibration of matter, so it requires a physical medium for transmission, as do other kinds of mechanical waves and heat energy. Historically, science incorporated various aether theories to explain the transmission medium. However, it is now known that electromagnetic waves do not require a physical transmission medium, and so can travel through the "vacuum" of free space. Regions of the insulative vacuum can become conductive for electrical conduction through the presence of free electrons, holes, or ions.

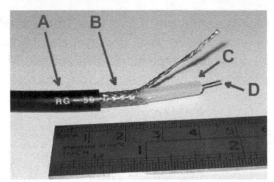

Coaxial cable, one example of a transmission medium

Telecommunications

A physical medium in data communications is the transmission path over which a signal propagates.

Many transmission media are used as communications channel.

For telecommunications purposes in the United States, Federal Standard 1037C, transmission media are classified as one of the following:

- Guided (or bounded)—waves are guided along a solid medium such as a transmission line.

- Wireless (or unguided)—transmission and reception are achieved by means of an antenna.

One of the most common physical medias used in networking is copper wire. Copper wire to carry signals to long distances using relatively low amounts of power. The unshielded twisted pair (UTP) is eight strands of copper wire, organized into four pairs.

Another example of a physical medium is optical fiber, which has emerged as the most commonly used transmission medium for long-distance communications. Optical fiber is a thin strand of glass that guides light along its length. Four major factors favor optical fiber over copper- data rates, distance, installation, and costs. Optical fiber can carry huge amounts of data compared to copper. It can be run for hundreds of miles without the need for signal repeaters, in turn, reducing maintenance costs and improving the reliability of the communication system because repeaters are a common source of network failures. Glass is lighter than copper allowing for less need for specialized heavy-lifting equipment when installing long-distance optical fiber. Optical fiber for indoor applications cost approximately a dollar a foot, the same as copper.

Multimode and single mode are two types of commonly used optical fiber. Multimode fiber uses LEDs as the light source and can carry signals over shorter distances, about 2 kilometers. Single mode can carry signals over distances of tens of miles.

Wireless media may carry surface waves or skywaves, either longitudinally or transversely, and are so classified.

In both communications, communication is in the form of electromagnetic waves. With guided transmission media, the waves are guided along a physical path; examples of guided media include phone lines, twisted pair cables, coaxial cables, and optical fibers. Unguided transmission media are methods that allow the transmission of data without the use of physical means to define the path it takes. Examples of this include microwave, radio or infrared. Unguided media provide a means for transmitting electromagnetic waves but do not guide them; examples are propagation through air, vacuum and seawater.

The term direct link is used to refer to the transmission path between two devices in which signals propagate directly from transmitters to receivers with no intermediate devices, other than amplifiers or repeaters used to increase signal strength. This term can apply to both guided and unguided media.

Types of Transmissions

A transmission may be simplex, half-duplex, or full-duplex.

In simplex transmission, signals are transmitted in only one direction; one station is a transmitter and the other is the receiver. In the half-duplex operation, both stations may transmit, but only one at a time. In full duplex operation, both stations may transmit simultaneously. In the latter case, the medium is carrying signals in both directions at same time.

There are two types of transmission media: guided and unguided.

Guided Media:

- Unshielded Twisted Pair (UTP)

- Shielded Twisted Pair

- Coaxial Cable

- Optical Fiber

- hub

Unguided Media: Transmission media then looking at analysis of using them unguided transmission media is data signals that flow through the air. They are not guided or bound to a channel to follow. Following are unguided media used for data communication:

- Radio Transmission
- Microwave

Digital Encoding

Transmission and reception of data typically is performed in four steps.

1. The data is coded as binary numbers at the sender end

2. A carrier signal is modulated as specified by the binary representation of the data

3. At the receiving end, the incoming signal is demodulated into the respective binary numbers

4. Decoding of the binary numbers is performed

Guided Transmission Media

Twisted Pair

Twisted pair cabling is a type of wiring in which two conductors of a single circuit are twisted together for the purposes of canceling out electromagnetic interference (EMI) from external sources; for instance, electromagnetic radiation from unshielded twisted pair (UTP) cables, and crosstalk between neighboring pairs. It was invented by Alexander Graham Bell.

Explanation

In balanced pair operation, the two wires carry equal and opposite signals, and the destination detects the difference between the two. This is known as differential mode transmission. Noise sources introduce signals into the wires by coupling of electric or magnetic fields and tend to couple to both wires equally. The noise thus produces a common-mode signal which is canceled at the receiver when the difference signal is taken.

This method starts to fail when the noise source is close to the signal wires; the closer wire will couple with the noise more strongly and the common-mode rejection of the receiver will fail to eliminate it. This problem is especially apparent in telecommunication cables where pairs in the same cable lie next to each other for many miles. One pair can induce crosstalk in another and it is additive along the length of the cable. Twisting the pairs counters this effect as on each half twist the wire nearest to the noise-source is exchanged.

Providing the interfering source remains uniform, or nearly so, over the distance of a single twist, the induced noise will remain common-mode. Differential signaling also reduces electromagnetic radiation from the cable, along with the associated attenuation allowing for greater distance between exchanges.

The twist rate (also called *pitch* of the twist, usually defined in twists per meter) makes up part of the specification for a given type of cable. When nearby pairs have equal twist rates, the same conductors of the different pairs may repeatedly lie next to each other, partially undoing the benefits of differential mode. For this reason it is commonly specified that, at least for cables containing small numbers of pairs, the twist rates must differ.

In contrast to shielded or foiled twisted pair (typically F/UTP or S/FTP cable shielding), UTP (unshielded twisted pair) cable is not surrounded by any shielding. UTP is the primary wire type for telephone usage and is very common for computer networking, especially as patch cables or temporary network connections due to the high flexibility of the cables.

History

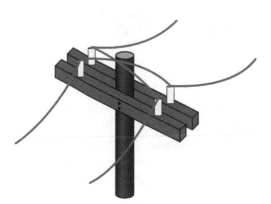

Wire transposition on top of pole

The earliest telephones used telegraph lines, or open-wire single-wire earth return circuits. In the 1880s electric trams were installed in many cities, which induced noise into these circuits. Lawsuits being unavailing, the telephone companies converted to balanced circuits, which had the incidental benefit of reducing attenuation, hence increasing range.

As electrical power distribution became more commonplace, this measure proved inadequate. Two wires, strung on either side of cross bars on utility poles, shared the route with electrical power lines. Within a few years, the growing use of electricity again brought an increase of interference, so engineers devised a method called wire transposition, to cancel out the interference.

In wire transposition, the wires exchange position once every several poles. In this way, the two wires would receive similar EMI from power lines. This represented an early implementation of twisting, with a twist rate of about four twists per kilometre, or six per mile. Such open-wire balanced lines with periodic transpositions still survive today in some rural areas.

Twisted-pair cabling was invented by Alexander Graham Bell in 1881. By 1900, the entire American telephone line network was either twisted pair or open wire with transposition to guard against interference. Today, most of the millions of kilometres of twisted pairs in the world are outdoor landlines, owned by telephone companies, used for voice service, and only handled or even seen by telephone workers.

Unshielded Twisted Pair (UTP)

Cross-section of cable with several unshielded twisted pairs

UTP cables are found in many Ethernet networks and telephone systems. For indoor telephone applications, UTP is often grouped into sets of 25 pairs according to a standard 25-pair color code originally developed by AT&T Corporation. A typical subset of these colors (white/blue, blue/white, white/orange, orange/white) shows up in most UTP cables. The cables are typically made with copper wires measured at 22 or 24 American Wire Gauge (AWG), with the colored insulation typically made from an insulator such as polyethylene or FEP and the total package covered in a polyethylene jacket.

For urban outdoor telephone cables containing hundreds or thousands of pairs, the cable is divided into small but identical bundles. Each bundle consists of twisted pairs that have different twist rates. The bundles are in turn twisted together to make up the cable. Pairs having the same twist rate within the cable can still experience some degree of crosstalk. Wire pairs are selected carefully to minimize crosstalk within a large cable.

UTP cable is also the most common cable used in computer networking. Modern Ethernet, the most common data networking standard, can use UTP cables. Twisted pair cabling is often used in data networks for short and medium length connections because of its relatively lower costs compared to optical fiber and coaxial cable.

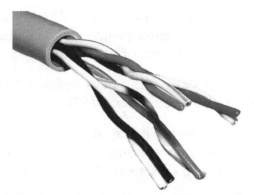

Unshielded twisted pair cable with different twist rates

UTP is also finding increasing use in video applications, primarily in security cameras. Many cameras include a UTP output with screw terminals; UTP cable bandwidth has improved to match the baseband of television signals. As UTP is a balanced transmission line, a balun is needed to connect to unbalanced equipment, for example any using BNC connectors and designed for coaxial cable.

Cable Shielding

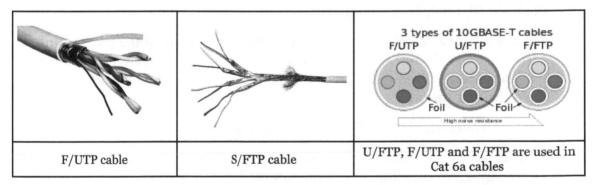

F/UTP cable	S/FTP cable	U/FTP, F/UTP and F/FTP are used in Cat 6a cables

Twisted-pair cables are often shielded in an attempt to prevent electromagnetic interference. Shielding provides an electrically conductive barrier to attenuate electromagnetic waves external to the shield, and provides a conduction path by which induced currents can be circulated and returned to the source, via ground reference connection.

This shielding can be applied to individual pairs or quads, or to the collection of pairs. Individual pairs are foiled, while overall cable may use braided screen, foil, or braiding with foil.

When shielding is applied to the collection of pairs, this is usually referred to as screening, but different vendors and authors use "screening", "shielding", and "STP" inconsistently to denote various shielded cable types.

ISO/IEC 11801:2002 (Annex E) attempts to internationally standardize the various designations for shielded cables by using combinations of three letters - U for unshielded, S for braided shielding (in outer layer only), and F for foiled shielding - to explicitly indicate the type of screen for overall cable protection and for individual pairs or quads, using a two-part abbreviation in the form of *x/xTP*.

Shielded Cat 5e, Cat 6/6$_A$, and Cat 8/8.1 cables typically have F/UTP construction, while shielded Cat 7/7$_A$ and Cat 8.2 cables use S/FTP construction.

Because the shielding is made of metal, it may also serve as a ground. Usually a shielded twisted pair cable has a special grounding wire added called a drain wire which is electrically connected to the shield or screen. The drain wire simplifies connection to ground at the connectors.

Common shield construction types used include:

Individual shield (U/FTP)

> Individual shielding with aluminum foil for each twisted pair or quad. Common names: pair in metal foil, shielded twisted pair, screened twisted pair. This type of shielding protects cable from external EMI entering or exiting the cable and also protects neighboring pairs from crosstalk.

Overall shield (F/UTP, S/UTP, and SF/UTP)

> Overall foil, braided shield or braiding with foil across all of the pairs within the 100 ohm twisted pair cable. Common names: foiled twisted pair, shielded twisted pair, screened twisted pair. This type of shielding helps prevent EMI from entering or exiting the cable.

Individual and overall shield (F/FTP, S/FTP, and SF/FTP)

> Individual shielding using foil between the twisted pair sets, and also an outer foil and/or braided shielding. Common names: fully shielded twisted pair, screened foiled twisted pair, shielded foiled twisted pair, screened shielded twisted pair, shielded screened twisted pair. This type of shielding helps prevent EMI from entering or exiting the cable and also protects neighboring pairs from crosstalk.

An early example of shielded twisted-pair is IBM STP-A, which was a two-pair 150 ohm S/FTP cable defined in 1985 by the IBM Cabling System specifications, and used with token ring or FDDI networks.

Common industry abbreviations for cable construction			
Industry acronyms	**ISO/IEC 11801** name	Cable shielding	Pair shielding
UTP	U/UTP	None	None
STP, ScTP, PiMF	U/FTP	None	Foil
FTP, STP, ScTP	F/UTP	Foil	None

Common industry abbreviations for cable construction			
Industry acronyms	**ISO/IEC 11801** name	Cable shielding	Pair shielding
STP, ScTP	S/UTP	Braiding	None
SFTP, S-FTP, STP	SF/UTP	Braiding, foil	None
FFTP	F/FTP	Foil	Foil
SSTP, SFTP, STP PiMF	S/FTP	Braiding	Foil
SSTP, SFTP	SF/FTP	Braiding, foil	Foil

The code before the slash designates the shielding for the cable itself, while the code after the slash determines the shielding for the individual pairs:

U = unshielded

F = foil shielding

S = braided shielding (outer layer only)

TP = twisted pair

TQ = twisted pair, individual shielding in quads

Common Types

Name	Typical construction	Bandwidth	Applications	Notes
Level 1		0.4 MHz	Telephone and modem lines	Not described in EIA/TIA recommendations. Unsuitable for modern systems.
Level 2		4 MHz	Older terminal systems, e.g. IBM 3270	Not described in EIA/TIA recommendations. Unsuitable for modern systems.
Cat 3	UTP	16 MHz	10BASE-T and 100BASE-T4 Ethernet	Described in EIA/TIA-568. Unsuitable for speeds above 16 Mbit/s. Now mainly for telephone cables
Cat 4	UTP	20 MHz	16 Mbit/s Token Ring	Not commonly used
Cat 5	UTP	100 MHz	100BASE-TX & 1000BASE-T Ethernet	Common for current LANs. Superseded by Cat5e, but most Cat5 cable meets Cat5e standards.
Cat 5e	UTP	100 MHz	100BASE-TX & 1000BASE-T Ethernet	Enhanced Cat5. Common for current LANs. Same construction as Cat5, but with better testing standards.
Cat 6	UTP	250 MHz	10GBASE-T Ethernet	ISO/IEC 11801 2nd Ed. (2002), ANSI/TIA 568-B.2-1. Most commonly installed cable in Finland according to the 2002 standard EN 50173-1.

Cat 6$_A$	F/UTP, U/FTP	500 MHz	10GBASE-T Ethernet	Adds cable shielding. ISO/IEC 11801 2nd Ed. Am. 2. (2008), ANSI/TIA-568-C.1 (2009)
Cat 7	S/FTP, F/FTP	600 MHz	10GBASE-T Ethernet or POTS/CAT-V/1000BASE-T over single cable	Fully shielded cable. ISO/IEC 11801 2nd Ed. (2002)
Cat 7$_A$	S/FTP, F/FTP	1000 MHz	10GBASE-T Ethernet or POTS/CAT-V/1000BASE-T over single cable	Uses all four pairs. ISO/IEC 11801 2nd Ed. Am. 2. (2008)
Cat 8/8.1	F/UTP, U/FTP	1600-2000 MHz	40GBASE-T Ethernet or POTS/CAT-V/1000BASE-T over single cable	In development (ANSI/TIA-568-C.2-1, ISO/IEC 11801 3rd Ed.)
Cat 8.2	S/FTP, F/FTP	1600-2000 MHz	40GBASE-T Ethernet or POTS/CAT-V/1000BASE-T over single cable	In development (ISO/IEC 11801 3rd Ed.)

Solid-core Cable vs. Stranded Cable

A solid-core cable uses one solid wire per conductor and in a four pair cable there would be a total of eight solid wires. Stranded conductor uses multiple wires wrapped around each other in each conductor and in a four pair with seven strands per conductor cable, there would be a total of 56 wires (2 per pair × 4 pairs × 7 strands).

Solid core cable is intended for permanently installed runs. It is less flexible than stranded cable and is more prone to failure if repeatedly flexed. Stranded cable is used for fly leads at patch panel and for connections from wall-ports to end devices, as it resists cracking of the conductors.

Connectors need to be designed differently for solid core than for stranded. Use of a connector with the wrong cable type is likely to lead to unreliable cabling. Plugs designed for solid and stranded core are readily available, and some vendors even offer plugs designed for use with both types. The punch-down blocks on patch-panel and wall-port jacks are designed for use with solid core cable.

Advantages

- Electrical noise going into or coming from the cable can be prevented.
- Crosstalk is minimized.
- Cheapest form of cable available for networking purposes.
- Easy to handle and install.

Disadvantages

- Deformation: twisted pair's susceptibility to electromagnetic interference greatly depends on the pair twisting schemes (sometimes patented by the manufacturers) staying intact during the installation. As a result, twisted pair cables usually have stringent requirements for maximum pulling tension as well as minimum bend radius. This fragility of twisted pair cables makes the installation practices an important part of ensuring the cable's performance.

- Delay skew: different pairs within the cable have different delays, due to different twist rates used to minimize crosstalk between the pairs. This can degrade image quality when multiple pairs are used to carry components of a video signal. Low skew cable is available to mitigate this problem.

- Imbalance: differences between the two wires in a pair can cause coupling between the common mode and the differential mode. Differential to common mode conversion produces common mode currents that can cause external interference and can produce common mode signals in other pairs. Common mode to differential mode conversion can produce differential mode signals from common mode interference from other pairs or external sources. Imbalance can be caused by asymmetry between the two conductors of the pair from each other and in relationship to other wires and the shield. Some sources of asymmetry are differences in conductor diameter and insulation thickness. In telephone jargon, the common mode is called *longitudinal* and the differential mode is called *metallic*.

Less Common Variants

Loaded twisted pair

> A twisted pair that has intentionally added inductance, formerly common practice on telecommunication lines. The added inductors are known as load coils and reduce attenuation for voiceband frequencies but increase it on higher frequencies. Load coils reduce distortion in voiceband on very long lines. In this context a line without load coils is referred to as an unloaded line.

Bonded twisted pair

> A twisted pair variant in which the pairs are individually bonded to increase robustness of the cable. Pioneered by Belden, it means the electrical specifications of the cable are maintained despite rough handling.

Twisted ribbon cable

> A variant of standard ribbon cable in which adjacent pairs of conductors are bonded and twisted together. The twisted pairs are then lightly bonded to each other

in a ribbon format. Periodically along the ribbon there are short sections with no twisting to enable connectors and PCB headers to be terminated using the usual ribbon cable IDC techniques.

Coaxial cable

Coaxial cable, or coax, is a type of cable that has an inner conductor surrounded by a tubular insulating layer, surrounded by a tubular conducting shield. Many coaxial cables also have an insulating outer sheath or jacket. The term coaxial comes from the inner conductor and the outer shield sharing a geometric axis. Coaxial cable was invented by English engineer and mathematician Oliver Heaviside, who patented the design in 1880.

Coaxial cable differs from other shielded cable used for carrying lower-frequency signals, in that the dimensions of the cable are controlled to give a precise, constant conductor spacing, which is needed for it to function efficiently as a transmission line.

Applications

Coaxial cable is used as a transmission line for radio frequency signals. Its applications include feedlines connecting radio transmitters and receivers with their antennas, computer network (Internet) connections, digital audio (S/PDIF), and distributing cable television signals. One advantage of coaxial over other types of radio transmission line is that in an ideal coaxial cable the electromagnetic field carrying the signal exists only in the space between the inner and outer conductors. This allows coaxial cable runs to be installed next to metal objects such as gutters without the power losses that occur in other types of transmission lines. Coaxial cable also provides protection of the signal from external electromagnetic interference.

Description

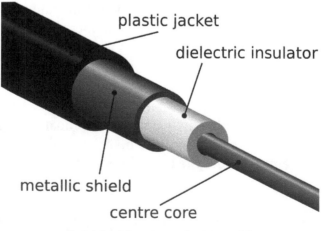

Coaxial cable cutaway (not to scale)

Coaxial cable conducts electrical signal using an inner conductor (usually a solid copper, stranded copper or copper plated steel wire) surrounded by an insulating layer and all enclosed by a shield, typically one to four layers of woven metallic braid and metallic tape. The cable is protected by an outer insulating jacket. Normally, the shield is kept at ground potential and a signal carrying voltage is applied to the center conductor. The advantage of coaxial design is that electric and magnetic fields are restricted to the dielectric with little leakage outside the shield. Conversely, electric and magnetic fields outside the cable are largely kept from interfering with signals inside the cable. Larger diameter cables and cables with multiple shields have less leakage. This property makes coaxial cable a good choice for carrying weak signals that cannot tolerate interference from the environment or for stronger electrical signals that must not be allowed to radiate or couple into adjacent structures or circuits.

Common applications of coaxial cable include video and CATV distribution, RF and microwave transmission, and computer and instrumentation data connections.

The characteristic impedance of the cable (Z_0) is determined by the dielectric constant of the inner insulator and the radii of the inner and outer conductors. A controlled cable characteristic impedance is important because the source and load impedance should be matched to ensure maximum power transfer and minimum standing wave ratio. Other important properties of coaxial cable include attenuation as a function of frequency, voltage handling capability, and shield quality.

Construction

Coaxial cable design choices affect physical size, frequency performance, attenuation, power handling capabilities, flexibility, strength, and cost. The inner conductor might be solid or stranded; stranded is more flexible. To get better high-frequency performance, the inner conductor may be silver-plated. Copper-plated steel wire is often used as an inner conductor for cable used in the cable TV industry.

The insulator surrounding the inner conductor may be solid plastic, a foam plastic, or air with spacers supporting the inner wire. The properties of dielectric control some electrical properties of the cable. A common choice is a solid polyethylene (PE) insulator, used in lower-loss cables. Solid Teflon (PTFE) is also used as an insulator. Some coaxial lines use air (or some other gas) and have spacers to keep the inner conductor from touching the shield.

Many conventional coaxial cables use braided copper wire forming the shield. This allows the cable to be flexible, but it also means there are gaps in the shield layer, and the inner dimension of the shield varies slightly because the braid cannot be flat. Sometimes the braid is silver-plated. For better shield performance, some cables have a double-layer shield. The shield might be just two braids, but it is more common now to have a thin foil shield covered by a wire braid. Some cables may invest in more than two shield layers, such as "quad-shield", which uses four alternating layers of foil and braid. Other shield designs sacrifice flexibility for better performance; some shields are a solid metal tube. Those cables cannot be bent sharply, as the shield will kink, causing losses in the cable.

For high-power radio-frequency transmission up to about 1 GHz, coaxial cable with a solid copper outer conductor is available in sizes of 0.25 inch upward. The outer conductor is rippled like a bellows to permit flexibility and the inner conductor is held in position by a plastic spiral to approximate an air dielectric.

Coaxial cables require an internal structure of an insulating (dielectric) material to maintain the spacing between the center conductor and shield. The dielectric losses increase in this order: Ideal dielectric (no loss), vacuum, air, polytetrafluoroethylene (PTFE), polyethylene foam, and solid polyethylene. A low relative permittivity allows for higher-frequency usage. An inhomogeneous dielectric needs to be compensated by a non-circular conductor to avoid current hot-spots.

While many cables have a solid dielectric, many others have a foam dielectric that contains as much air or other gas as possible to reduce the losses by allowing the use of a larger diameter center conductor. Foam coax will have about 15% less attenuation but some types of foam dielectric can absorb moisture—especially at its many surfaces — in humid environments, significantly increasing the loss. Supports shaped like stars or spokes are even better but more expensive and very susceptible to moisture infiltration. Still more expensive were the air-spaced coaxials used for some inter-city communications in the mid-20th century. The center conductor was suspended by polyethylene discs every few centimeters. In some low-loss coaxial cables such as the RG-62 type, the inner conductor is supported by a spiral strand of polyethylene, so that an air space exists between most of the conductor and the inside of the jacket. The lower dielectric constant of air allows for a greater inner diameter at the same impedance and a greater outer diameter at the same cutoff frequency, lowering ohmic losses. Inner conductors are sometimes silver-plated to smooth the surface and reduce losses due to skin effect. A rough surface prolongs the path for the current and concentrates the current at peaks and, thus, increases ohmic losses.

The insulating jacket can be made from many materials. A common choice is PVC, but some applications may require fire-resistant materials. Outdoor applications may require the jacket resist ultraviolet light, oxidation, rodent damage, or direct burial. Flooded coaxial cables use a water blocking gel to protect the cable from water infiltration through minor cuts in the jacket. For internal chassis connections the insulating jacket may be omitted.

Signal Propagation

Twin-lead transmission lines have the property that the electromagnetic wave propagating down the line extends into the space surrounding the parallel wires. These lines have low loss, but also have undesirable characteristics. They cannot be bent, tightly twisted, or otherwise shaped without changing their characteristic impedance, causing reflection of the signal back toward the source. They also cannot be buried or run along or attached to anything conductive, as the extended fields will induce currents in the nearby conductors causing unwanted radiation and detuning of the line. Coaxial lines largely solve this problem by confining virtually all of the electromagnetic wave to the area inside the cable. Coaxial lines can therefore be bent and moderately twisted without negative effects, and they can be strapped to conductive supports without inducing unwanted currents in them.

In radio-frequency applications up to a few gigahertz, the wave propagates primarily in the transverse electric magnetic (TEM) mode, which means that the electric and magnetic fields are both perpendicular to the direction of propagation. However, above a certain cutoff frequency, transverse electric (TE) or transverse magnetic (TM) modes can also propagate, as they do in a waveguide. It is usually undesirable to transmit signals above the cutoff frequency, since it may cause multiple modes with different phase velocities to propagate, interfering with each other. The outer diameter is roughly inversely proportional to the cutoff frequency. A propagating surface-wave mode that does not involve or require the outer shield but only a single central conductor also exists in coax but this mode is effectively suppressed in coax of conventional geometry and common impedance. Electric field lines for this [TM] mode have a longitudinal component and require line lengths of a half-wavelength or longer.

Coaxial cable may be viewed as a type of waveguide. Power is transmitted through the radial electric field and the circumferential magnetic field in the TEM00 transverse mode. This is the dominant mode from zero frequency (DC) to an upper limit determined by the electrical dimensions of the cable.

Connectors

A male F-type connector used with common RG-6 cable

A male N-type connector

The ends of coaxial cables usually terminate with connectors. Coaxial connectors are designed to maintain a coaxial form across the connection and have the same impedance as the attached cable. Connectors are usually plated with high-conductivity metals such as silver or tarnish-resistant gold. Due to the skin effect, the RF signal is only carried by the plating at higher frequencies and does not penetrate to the connector body. Silver however tarnishes quickly and the silver sulfide that is produced is poorly conductive, degrading connector performance, making silver a poor choice for this application.

Important parameters

Coaxial cable is a particular kind of transmission line, so the circuit models developed for general transmission lines are appropriate.

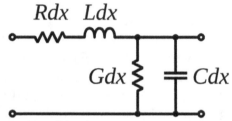

Schematic representation of the elementary components of a transmission line.

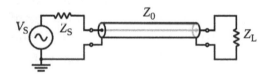

Schematic representation of a coaxial transmission line, showing the characteristic impedance .

Physical Parameters

In the following section, these symbols are used:

- Length of the cable, h.

- Outside diameter of inner conductor, d.

- Inside diameter of the shield, D.

- Dielectric constant of the insulator, ϵ. The dielectric constant is often quoted as the relative dielectric constant ϵ_r referred to the dielectric constant of free space $\epsilon_0 : \epsilon = \epsilon_r \epsilon_0$. When the insulator is a mixture of different dielectric materials (e.g., polyethylene foam is a mixture of polyethylene and air), then the term effective dielectric constant ϵ_{eff} is often used.

- Magnetic permeability of the insulator, $\imath$. Permeability is often quoted as the relative permeability $\imath_r$ referred to the permeability of free space $\imath_0 : \imath = \imath_r \imath_0$. The relative permeability will almost always be 1.

Fundamental Electrical Parameters

- Shunt capacitance per unit length, in farads per metre.

$$\left(\frac{C}{h}\right) = \frac{2\pi\epsilon}{\ln(D/d)} = \frac{2\pi\epsilon_0\epsilon_r}{\ln(D/d)}$$

- Series inductance per unit length, in henrys per metre.

$$\left(\frac{L}{h}\right) = \frac{\mu}{2\pi}\ln(D/d) = \frac{\mu_0\mu_r}{2\pi}\ln(D/d)$$

- Series resistance per unit length, in ohms per metre. The resistance per unit length is just the resistance of inner conductor and the shield at low frequencies. At higher frequencies, skin effect increases the effective resistance by confining the conduction to a thin layer of each conductor.

- Shunt conductance per unit length, in siemens per metre. The shunt conductance is usually very small because insulators with good dielectric properties are used (a very low loss tangent). At high frequencies, a dielectric can have a significant resistive loss.

Derived electrical parameters

- Characteristic impedance in ohms (Ω). The complex impedance Z of an infinite length of transmission line is:

$$Z = \sqrt{\frac{R+sL}{G+sC}}$$

Where R is the resistance per unit length, L is the inductance per unit length, G is the conductance per unit length of the dielectric, C is the capacitance per unit length, and $s = j\omega = j2\pi f$ is the frequency. The "per unit length" dimensions cancel out in the impedance formula.

At very low frequencies ($s\approx 0$), the two reactive terms are negligible, so the impedance is real-valued and looks like

$$Z_{DC} = \sqrt{\frac{R}{G}}.$$

With increasing frequency, the reactive components take effect and the impedance of the line is complex-valued.

At higher frequences, the reactive terms usually dominate R and G, and the cable impedance again becomes real-valued. That value is Z_0, the *characteristic impedance* of the cable:

$$Z_0 = \sqrt{\frac{sL}{sC}} = \sqrt{\frac{L}{C}}.$$

Assuming the dielectric properties of the material inside the cable do not vary appreciably over the operating range of the cable, the characteristic impedance is frequency independent above about five times the shield cutoff frequency. For typical coaxial cables, the shield cutoff frequency is 600 (RG-6A) to 2,000 Hz (RG-58C).

The parameters L and C are determined from the ratio of the inner (d) and outer (D) diameters and the dielectric constant (ε). The characteristic impedance is given by

$$Z_0 = \frac{1}{2\pi}\sqrt{\frac{\mu}{\epsilon}}\ln\frac{D}{d} \approx \frac{60\Omega}{\sqrt{\epsilon_r}}\ln\frac{D}{d} \approx \frac{138\Omega}{\sqrt{\epsilon_r}}\log_{10}\frac{D}{d}$$

- Attenuation (loss) per unit length, in decibels per meter. This is dependent on the loss in the dielectric material filling the cable, and resistive losses in the center conductor and outer shield. These losses are frequency dependent, the losses becoming higher as the frequency increases. Skin effect losses in the conductors can be reduced by increasing the diameter of the cable. A cable with twice the diameter will have half the skin effect resistance. Ignoring dielectric and other losses, the larger cable would halve the dB/meter loss. In designing a system, engineers consider not only the loss in the cable but also the loss in the connectors.

- Velocity of propagation, in meters per second. The velocity of propagation depends on the dielectric constant and permeability (which is usually 1).

$$v = \frac{1}{\sqrt{\epsilon\mu}} = \frac{c}{\sqrt{\epsilon_r\mu_r}}$$

- Single-mode band. In coaxial cable, the dominant mode (the mode with the lowest cutoff frequency) is the TEM mode, which has a cutoff frequency of zero; it propagates all the way down to d.c. The mode with the next lowest cutoff is the TE_{11} mode. This mode has one 'wave' (two reversals of polarity) in going around the circumference of the cable. To a good approximation, the condition for the TE_{11} mode to propagate is that the wavelength in the dielectric is no longer than the average circumference of the insulator; that is that the frequency is at least

$$f_c \approx \frac{1}{\pi\left(\dfrac{D+d}{2}\right)\sqrt{\mu\epsilon}} = \frac{c}{\pi\left(\dfrac{D+d}{2}\right)\sqrt{\mu_r\epsilon_r}}.$$

Hence, the cable is single-mode from to d.c. up to this frequency, and might in practice be used up to 90% of this frequency.

- Peak Voltage. The peak voltage is set by the breakdown voltage of the insulator. One website gives:

$$V_p = 1150 \, S_{mils} \, d_{in} \, \log_{10} \left(\frac{D}{d} \right)$$

where

S_{mils} is the insulator's breakdown voltage in volts per mil

d_{in} is the inner diameter in inches

The 1150 factor converts inches (diameter) to mils (radius) and $\log_{10}$ to ln.

The above expression may be rewritten as

$$V_p = 0.5 \, S \, d \, \ln \left(\frac{D}{d} \right)$$

where

S is the insulator's breakdown voltage in volts per meter

d is the inner diameter in meters

The calculated peak voltage is often reduced by a safety factor.

Choice of Impedance

The best coaxial cable impedances in high-power, high-voltage, and low-attenuation applications were experimentally determined at Bell Laboratories in 1929 to be 30, 60, and 77 Ω, respectively. For a coaxial cable with air dielectric and a shield of a given inner diameter, the attenuation is minimized by choosing the diameter of the inner conductor to give a characteristic impedance of 76.7 Ω. When more common dielectrics are considered, the best-loss impedance drops down to a value between 52–64 Ω. Maximum power handling is achieved at 30 Ω.

The approximate impedance required to match a centre-fed dipole antenna in free space (i.e., a dipole without ground reflections) is 73 Ω, so 75 Ω coax was commonly used for connecting shortwave antennas to receivers. These typically involve such low levels of RF power that power-handling and high-voltage breakdown characteristics are unimportant when compared to attenuation. Likewise with CATV, although many broadcast TV installations and CATV headends use 300 Ω folded dipole antennas to receive off-the-air signals, 75 Ω coax makes a convenient 4:1 balun transformer for these as well as possessing low attenuation.

The arithmetic mean between 30 Ω and 77 Ω is 53.5 Ω; the geometric mean is 48 Ω. The selection of 50 Ω as a compromise between power-handling capability and attenuation is in general cited as the reason for the number. 50 Ω also works out tolerably well because it corresponds approximately to the drive impedance (ideally 36 ohms) of a quarter-wave monopole, mounted on a less than optimum ground plane such as a vehicle roof. The match is better at low frequencies, such as for CB Radio around 27 MHz, where the roof dimensions are much less than a quarter wavelength, and relatively poor at higher frequencies, VHF and UHF, where the roof dimensions may be several wavelengths. The match is at best poor, because the antenna drive impedance, due to the imperfect ground plane, is reactive rather than purely resistive, and so a 36 ohm coaxial cable would not match properly either. Installations which need exact matching will use some kind of matching circuit at the base of the antenna, or elsewhere, in conjunction with a carefully chosen (in terms of wavelength) length of coaxial, such that a proper match is achieved, which will be only over a fairly narrow frequency range.

RG-62 is a 93 Ω coaxial cable originally used in mainframe computer networks in the 1970s and early 1980s (it was the cable used to connect IBM 3270 terminals to IBM 3274/3174 terminal cluster controllers). Later, some manufacturers of LAN equipment, such as Datapoint for ARCNET, adopted RG-62 as their coaxial cable standard. The cable has the lowest capacitance per unit-length when compared to other coaxial cables of similar size. Capacitance is the enemy of square-wave data transmission (in particular, it slows down edge transitions), and this is a much more important factor for baseband digital data transmission than power handling or attenuation.

All of the components of a coaxial system should have the same impedance to avoid internal reflections at connections between components. Such reflections may cause signal attenuation and ghosting TV picture display; multiple reflections may cause the original signal to be followed by more than one echo. In analog video or TV systems, this causes ghosting in the image. Reflections also introduce standing waves, which cause increased losses and can even result in cable dielectric breakdown with high-power transmission. Briefly, if a coaxial cable is open, the termination has nearly infinite resistance, this causes reflections; if the coaxial cable is short-circuited, the termination resistance is nearly zero, there will be reflections with the opposite polarity. Reflection will be nearly eliminated if the coaxial cable is terminated in a pure resistance equal to its impedance.

Issues

Signal Leakage

Signal leakage is the passage of electromagnetic fields through the shield of a cable and occurs in both directions. Ingress is the passage of an outside signal into the cable and can result in noise and disruption of the desired signal. Egress is the passage of signal intended to remain within the cable into the outside world and can result in a weaker signal at the end of the cable and radio frequency interference to nearby devices. Severe leakage usually results from improperly installed connectors or faults in the cable shield.

For example, in the United States, signal leakage from cable television systems is regulated by the FCC, since cable signals use the same frequencies as aeronautical and radionavigation bands. CATV operators may also choose to monitor their networks for leakage to prevent ingress. Outside signals entering the cable can cause unwanted noise and picture ghosting. Excessive noise can overwhelm the signal, making it useless.

An ideal shield would be a perfect conductor with no holes, gaps, or bumps connected to a perfect ground. However, a smooth solid highly conductive shield would be heavy, inflexible, and expensive. Such coax is used for straight line feeds to commercial radio broadcast towers. More economical cables must make compromises between shield efficacy, flexibility, and cost, such as the corrugated surface of flexible hardline, flexible braid, or foil shields. Since shields cannot be perfect conductors, current flowing on the inside of the shield produces an electromagnetic field on the outer surface of the shield.

Consider the skin effect. The magnitude of an alternating current in a conductor decays exponentially with distance beneath the surface, with the depth of penetration being proportional to the square root of the resistivity. This means that, in a shield of finite thickness, some small amount of current will still be flowing on the opposite surface of the conductor. With a perfect conductor (i.e., zero resistivity), all of the current would flow at the surface, with no penetration into and through the conductor. Real cables have a shield made of an imperfect, although usually very good, conductor, so there must always be some leakage.

The gaps or holes, allow some of the electromagnetic field to penetrate to the other side. For example, braided shields have many small gaps. The gaps are smaller when using a foil (solid metal) shield, but there is still a seam running the length of the cable. Foil becomes increasingly rigid with increasing thickness, so a thin foil layer is often surrounded by a layer of braided metal, which offers greater flexibility for a given cross-section.

Signal leakage can be severe if there is poor contact at the interface to connectors at either end of the cable or if there is a break in the shield.

To greatly reduce signal leakage into or out of the cable, by a factor of 1000, or even 10,000, superscreened cables are often used in critical applications, such as for neutron flux counters in nuclear reactors.

Ground Loops

A continuous current, even if small, along the imperfect shield of a coaxial cable can cause visible or audible interference. In CATV systems distributing analog signals the potential difference between the coaxial network and the electrical grounding system of a house can cause a visible "hum bar" in the picture. This appears as a wide horizontal distortion bar in the picture that scrolls slowly upward. Such differences in potential can be reduced by proper bonding to a common ground at the house.

Noise

External fields create a voltage across the inductance of the outside of the outer conductor between sender and receiver. The effect is less when there are several parallel cables, as this reduces the inductance and, therefore, the voltage. Because the outer conductor carries the reference potential for the signal on the inner conductor, the receiving circuit measures the wrong voltage.

Transformer Effect

The transformer effect is sometimes used to mitigate the effect of currents induced in the shield. The inner and outer conductors form the primary and secondary winding of the transformer, and the effect is enhanced in some high-quality cables that have an outer layer of mu-metal. Because of this 1:1 transformer, the aforementioned voltage across the outer conductor is transformed onto the inner conductor so that the two voltages can be cancelled by the receiver. Many sender and receivers have means to reduce the leakage even further. They increase the transformer effect by passing the whole cable through a ferrite core one or more times.

Common Mode Current and Radiation

Common mode current occurs when stray currents in the shield flow in the same direction as the current in the center conductor, causing the coax to radiate.

Most of the shield effect in coax results from opposing currents in the center conductor and shield creating opposite magnetic fields that cancel, and thus do not radiate. The same effect helps ladder line. However, ladder line is extremely sensitive to surrounding metal objects, which can enter the fields before they completely cancel. Coax does not have this problem, since the field is enclosed in the shield. However, it is still possible for a field to form between the shield and other connected objects, such as the antenna the coax feeds. The current formed by the field between the antenna and the coax shield would flow in the same direction as the current in the center conductor, and thus not be canceled. Energy would radiate from the coax itself, affecting the radiation pattern of the antenna. With sufficient power this could be a hazard to people near the cable. A properly placed and properly sized balun can prevent common mode radiation in coax. An isolating transformer or blocking capacitor can be used to couple a coaxial cable to equipment, where it is desirable to pass radio-frequency signals but to block direct current or low-frequency power.

Uses

Short coaxial cables are commonly used to connect home video equipment, in ham radio setups, and in measurement electronics. While formerly common for implementing computer networks, in particular Ethernet ("thick" 10BASE5 and "thin" 10BASE2), twisted pair cables have replaced them in most applications except in the growing consumer cable modem market for broadband Internet access.

Long distance coaxial cable was used in the 20th century to connect radio networks, television networks, and Long Distance telephone networks though this has largely been superseded by later methods (fibre optics, T1/E1, satellite).

Shorter coaxials still carry cable television signals to the majority of television receivers, and this purpose consumes the majority of coaxial cable production. In 1980s and early 1990s coaxial cable was also used in computer networking, most prominently in Ethernet networks, where it was later in late 1990s to early 2000s replaced by UTP cables in North America and STP cables in Western Europe, both with 8P8C modular connectors.

Micro coaxial cables are used in a range of consumer devices, military equipment, and also in ultra-sound scanning equipment.

The most common impedances that are widely used are 50 or 52 ohms, and 75 ohms, although other impedances are available for specific applications. The 50 / 52 ohm cables are widely used for industrial and commercial two-way radio frequency applications (including radio, and telecommunications), although 75 ohms is commonly used for broadcast television and radio.

Coax cable is often used to carry data/signals from an antenna to a receiver—from a satellite dish to a satellite receiver, from a television antenna to a television receiver, from a radio mast to a radio receiver, etc. In many cases, the same single coax cable carries power in the opposite direction, to the antenna, to power the low-noise amplifier. In some cases a single coax cable carries (unidirectional) power and bidirectional data/signals, as in DiSEqC.

Types

Hard line

Hard line is used in broadcasting as well as many other forms of radio communication. It is a coaxial cable constructed using round copper, silver or gold tubing or a combination of such metals as a shield. Some lower-quality hard line may use aluminum shielding, aluminum however is easily oxidized and unlike silver oxide, aluminum oxide drastically loses effective conductivity. Therefore, all connections must be air and water tight. The center conductor may consist of solid copper, or copper-plated aluminum. Since skin effect is an issue with RF, copper plating provides sufficient surface for an effective conductor. Most varieties of hardline used for external chassis or when exposed to the elements have a PVC jacket; however, some internal applications may omit the insulation jacket. Hard line can be very thick, typically at least a half inch or 13 mm and up to several times that, and has low loss even at high power. These large-scale hard lines are almost always used in the connection between a transmitter on the ground and the antenna or aerial on a tower. Hard line may also be known by trade-marked names such as Heliax (CommScope), or Cablewave (RFS/Cablewave). Larger varieties of hardline may have a center conductor that is constructed from either rigid or corrugated copper tubing. The dielectric in hard line may consist of polyethylene foam, air, or a pressurized gas such as nitrogen or desiccated air (dried air). In gas-charged lines, hard plastics such as nylon are used as spacers to separate the inner and outer conductors. The addition of these gases into the dielectric space reduces moisture contamination, provides a stable dielectric constant, and provides a reduced risk of internal arcing. Gas-filled hardlines are usually used on high-power RF transmitters such as television or radio broadcasting, military transmitters, and high-power amateur radio applications but may also be used on some critical lower-power applications such as those in the microwave bands. However, in the microwave region, *waveguide* is more often used than hard line for transmitter-to-antenna, or antenna-to-receiver applications. The various shields used in hardline also differ; some forms use rigid tubing, or pipe, others may use a corrugated tubing, which makes bending easier, as well as reduces kinking when the cable is bent to conform. Smaller varieties of hard line may be used internally in some high-frequency applications, in particular in equipment within the microwave range, to reduce interference between stages of the device.

1 ⅝ in (41 mm) flexible line   1-5/8" Heliax coaxial cable

Radiating

Radiating or leaky cable is another form of coaxial cable which is constructed in a similar fashion to hard line, however it is constructed with tuned slots cut into the shield.

These slots are tuned to the specific RF wavelength of operation or tuned to a specific radio frequency band. This type of cable is to provide a tuned bi-directional "desired" leakage effect between transmitter and receiver. It is often used in elevator shafts, US Navy Ships, underground transportation tunnels and in other areas where an antenna is not feasible. One example of this type of cable is Radiax (CommScope).

RG-6

RG-6 is available in four different types designed for various applications. In addition, the core may be copper clad steel (CCS) or bare solid copper (BC). "Plain" or "house" RG-6 is designed for indoor or external house wiring. "Flooded" cable is infused with waterblocking gel for use in underground conduit or direct burial. "Messenger" may contain some waterproofing but is distinguished by the addition of a steel messenger wire along its length to carry the tension involved in an aerial drop from a utility pole. "Plenum" cabling is expensive and comes with a special Teflon-based outer jacket designed for use in ventilation ducts to meet fire codes. It was developed since the plastics used as the outer jacket and inner insulation in many "Plain" or "house" cabling gives off poison gas when burned.

Triaxial Cable

Triaxial cable or triax is coaxial cable with a third layer of shielding, insulation and sheathing. The outer shield, which is earthed (grounded), protects the inner shield from electromagnetic interference from outside sources.

Twin-axial Cable

Twin-axial cable or twinax is a balanced, twisted pair within a cylindrical shield. It allows a nearly perfect differential signal which is *both* shielded *and* balanced to pass through. Multi-conductor coaxial cable is also sometimes used.

Semi-rigid

Semi-Rigid coax assembly

Semi-rigid cable is a coaxial form using a solid copper outer sheath. This type of coax offers superior screening compared to cables with a braided outer conductor, especially at higher frequencies. The major disadvantage is that the cable, as its name implies, is not very flexible, and is not intended to be flexed after initial forming.

Semi-Rigid coax installed in an Agilent N9344C 20GHz spectrum analyser

Conformable cable is a flexible reformable alternative to semi-rigid coaxial cable used where flexibility is required. Conformable cable can be stripped and formed by hand without the need for specialized tools, similar to standard coaxial cable.

Rigid line

Rigid line is a coaxial line formed by two copper tubes maintained concentric every other meter using PTFE-supports. Rigid lines can not be bent, so they often need elbows. Interconnection with rigid line is done with an inner bullet/inner support and a flange or connection kit. Typically rigid lines are connected using standardised EIA RF Connectors whose bullet and flange sizes match the standard line diameters, for each outer diameter either 75 or 50ohm inner tubes can be obtained. Rigid line is commonly used indoors for interconnection between high power transmitters and other RF-components, but more rugged rigid line with weatherproof flanges is used outdoors on antenna masts, etc. In the interests of saving weight and costs, on masts and similar structures the outer line is often aluminium, and special care must be taken to prevent corrosion. With a flange connector it is also possible to go from rigid line to hard line. Many broadcasting antennas and antenna splitters use the flanged rigid line interface even when connecting to flexible coaxial cables and hard line. Rigid line is produced in a number of different sizes:

Size	Outer conductor		Inner conductor	
	Outer diameter (not flanged)	Inner diameter	Outer diameter	Inner diameter
7/8"	22.2 mm	20 mm	8.7 mm	7.4 mm
1 5/8"	41.3 mm	38.8 mm	16.9 mm	15.0 mm
3 1/8"	79.4 mm	76.9 mm	33.4 mm	31.3 mm
4 1/2"	106 mm	103 mm	44.8 mm	42.8 mm
6 1/8"	155.6 mm	151.9 mm	66.0 mm	64.0 mm

Cables Used in the UK

At the start of analogue satellite TV broadcasts in the UK by BskyB, a 75 ohm cable referred to as *RG6* was used. This cable had a 1 mm copper core, air-spaced polyethylene dielectric and copper braid on an aluminium foil shield. When installed outdoors without protection, the cable was affected by UV radiation, which cracked the PVC outer sheath and allowed moisture ingress. The combination of copper, aluminium, moisture and air caused rapid corrosion, sometimes resulting in a 'snake swallowed an egg' appearance. Consequently, despite the higher cost, the RG6 cable was dropped in favour of CT100 when BSKYB launched its digital broadcasts.

From around 1999 to 2005 (when CT100 manufacturer Raydex went out of business), CT100 remained the 75 ohm cable of choice for satellite TV and especially BskyB. It had an air-spaced polyethylene dielectric, a 1 mm solid copper core and copper braid on copper foil shield. CT63 was a thinner cable in 'shotgun' style, meaning that it was two cables moulded together and was used mainly by BskyB for the twin connection required by the *Sky+* satellite TV receiver, which incorporated a hard drive recording system and a second, independent tuner.

In 2005, these cables were replaced by WF100 and WF65, respectively, manufactured by Webro and having a similar construction but a foam dielectric that provided the same electrical performance as air-spaced but was more robust and less likely to be crushed.

At the same time, with the price of copper steadily rising, the original RG6 was dropped in favour of a construction that used a copper-clad steel core and aluminium braid on aluminium foil. Its lower price made it attractive to aerial installers looking for a replacement for the so-called *low-loss* cable traditionally used for UK terrestrial aerial installations. This cable had been manufactured with a decreasing number of strands of braid, as the price of copper increased, such that the shielding performance of cheaper brands had fallen to as low as 40 percent. With the advent of digital terrestrial transmissions in the UK, this low-loss cable was no longer suitable.

The new RG6 still performed well at high frequencies because of the skin effect in the copper cladding. However, the aluminium shield had a high DC resistance and the steel core an even higher one. The result is that this type of cable could not reliably be used in satellite TV installations, where it was required to carry a significant amount of current, because the voltage drop affected the operation of the low noise block downconverter (LNB) on the dish.

A problem with all the aforementioned cables, when passing current, is that electrolytic corrosion can occur in the connections unless moisture and air are excluded. Consequently, various solutions to exclude moisture have been proposed. The first was to seal the connection by wrapping it with self-amalgamating rubberised tape, which bonds to itself when activated by stretching. The second proposal, by the American Channel Master company (now owned by Andrews corp.) at least as early as 1999, was to apply silicone grease to the wires making connection. The third proposal was to fit a self-sealing plug to the cable. All of these methods are reasonably successful if implemented correctly.

Interference and Troubleshooting

Coaxial cable insulation may degrade, requiring replacement of the cable, especially if it has been exposed to the elements on a continuous basis. The shield is normally grounded, and if even a single thread of the braid or filament of foil touches the center conductor, the signal will be shorted causing significant or total signal loss. This most often occurs at improperly installed end connectors and splices. Also, the connector or splice must be properly attached to the shield, as this provides the path to ground for the interfering signal.

Despite being shielded, interference can occur on coaxial cable lines. Susceptibility to interference has little relationship to broad cable type designations (e.g. RG-59, RG-6) but is strongly related to the composition and configuration of the cable's shielding. For cable television, with frequencies extending well into the UHF range, a foil shield is normally provided, and will provide total coverage as well as high effectiveness against high-frequency interference. Foil shielding is ordinarily accompanied by a tinned copper or aluminum braid shield, with anywhere from 60 to 95% coverage. The braid is important to shield effectiveness because (1) it is more effective than foil at preventing low-frequency interference, (2) it provides higher conductivity to ground than foil, and (3) it makes attaching a connector easier and more reliable. "Quad-shield" cable, using two low-coverage aluminum braid shields and two layers of foil, is often used in situations involving troublesome interference, but is less effective than a single layer of foil and single high-coverage copper braid shield such as is found on broadcast-quality precision video cable.

In the United States and some other countries, cable television distribution systems use extensive networks of outdoor coaxial cable, often with in-line distribution amplifiers. Leakage of signals into and out of cable TV systems can cause interference to cable subscribers and to over-the-air radio services using the same frequencies as those of the cable system.

Base Band Coaxial

With "coax", the medium consists of a copper core surrounded by insulating material and a braided outer conductor as shown in figure. The term *base band* indicates digital transmission (as opposed to *broadband* analog).

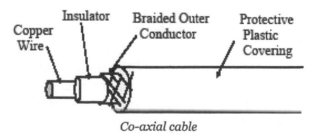

Co-axial cable

Physical connection consists of metal pin touching the copper core. There are two common ways to connect to a coaxial cable:

1. With *vampire taps*, a metal pin is inserted into the copper core. A special tool drills a hole into the cable, removing a small section of the insulation, and a special connector is screwed into the hole. The tap makes contact with the copper core.

2. With a *T*-junction, the cable is cut in half, and both halves connect to the T-junction. A T-connector is analogous to the signal splitters used to hook up multiple TVs to the same cable wire.

Characteristics: Co-axial cable has superior frequency characteristics compared to twisted-pair and can be used for both analog and digital signaling. In baseband LAN, the data rates lies in the range of 1 KHz to 20 MHz over a distance in the range of 1 Km. Co-axial cables typically have a diameter of 3/8". Coaxial cables are used both for *baseband* and *broadband* communication. For broadband CATV application coaxial cable of 1/2" diameter and 75 Ω impedance is used. This cable offers bandwidths of 300 to 400 MHz facilitating high-speed data communication with low bit-error rate. In broadband signaling, signal propagates only in one direction, in contrast to propagation in both directions in baseband signaling. Broadband cabling uses either dual-cable scheme or single-cable scheme with a headend to facilitate flow of signal in one direction. Because of the shielded, concentric construction, co-axial cable is less susceptible to interference and cross talk than the twisted-pair. For long distance communication, repeaters are needed for every kilometer or so. Data rate depends on physical properties of cable, but 10 Mbps is typical.

Use: One of the most popular use of co-axial cable is in cable TV (CATV) for the distribution of TV signals. Another importance use of co-axial cable is in LAN.

Broadband Coaxial

The term *broadband* refers to analog transmission over coaxial cable. (Note, however, that the telephone folks use broadband to refer to any channel wider than 4 kHz). The technology:

- Typically bandwidth of 300 MHz, total data rate of about 150 Mbps.

- Operates at distances up to 100 km (metropolitan area!).

- Uses analog signaling.

- Technology used in cable television. Thus, it is already available at sites such as universities that may have TV classes.

- Total available spectrum typically divided into smaller channels of 6 MHz each. That is, to get more than 6MHz of bandwidth, you have to use two smaller channels and somehow combine the signals.

- Requires amplifiers to boost signal strength; because amplifiers are one way, data flows in only one direction.

Two types of systems have emerged:

1.   Dual cable systems use two cables, one for transmission in each direction:

     o   One cable is used for receiving data.

     o   Second cable used to communicate with *headend*. When a node wishes to transmit data, it sends the data to a special node called the *headend*. The headend then resends the data on the first cable. Thus, the headend acts as a root of the tree, and all data must be sent to the root for redistribution to the other nodes.

2.   *Midsplit* systems divide the raw channel into two smaller channels, with each sub channel having the same purpose as above.

Which is better, broadband or base band? There is rarely a simple answer to such questions. Base band is simple to install, interfaces are inexpensive, but doesn't have the same range. Broadband is more complicated, more expensive, and requires regular adjustment by a trained technician, but offers more services (e.g., it carries audio and video too).

Fiber Optics

In fiber optic technology, the medium consists of a hair-width strand of silicon or glass, and the signal consists of pulses of light. For instance, a pulse of light means ``1", lack of pulse means ``0". It has a cylindrical shape and consists of three concentric sections: the *core*, the *cladding*, and the *jacket* as shown in figure.

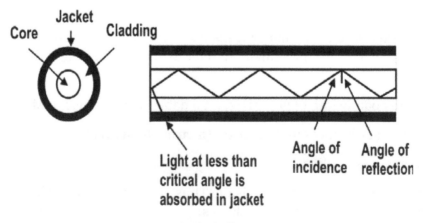

Optical Fiber

The core, innermost section consists of a single solid dielectric cylinder of diameter d1 and of refractive index n1. The core is surrounded by a solid dielectric cladding of refractive index n2 that is less than n1. As a consequence, the light is propagated through multiple total internal reflection. The core material is usually made of ultra pure fused silica or glass and the cladding is either made of glass or plastic. The cladding is surrounded by a jacket made of plastic. The jacket is used to protect against moisture, abrasion, crushing and other environmental hazards.

Three components are required:

1. Fiber medium: Current technology carries light pulses for tremendous distances (e.g., 100s of kilometers) with virtually no signal loss.

2. Light source: typically a Light Emitting Diode (LED) or laser diode. Running current through the material generates a pulse of light.

3. A photo diode light detector, which converts light pulses into electrical signals.

Advantages:

1. Very high data rate, low error rate. 1000 Mbps (1 Gbps) over distances of kilometers common. Error rates are so low they are almost negligible.

2. Difficult to tap, which makes it hard for unauthorized taps as well. This is responsible for higher reliability of this medium.

How difficult is it to prevent coax taps? Very difficult indeed, unless one can keep the entire cable in a locked room!

3. Much thinner (per logical phone line) than existing copper circuits. Because of its thinness, phone companies can replace thick copper wiring with fibers having much more capacity for same volume. This is important because it means that aggregate phone capacity can be upgraded without the need for finding more physical space to hire the new cables.

4. Not susceptible to electrical interference (lightning) or corrosion (rust).

5. Greater repeater distance than coax.

Disadvantages:

1. Difficult to tap. It really is point-to-point technology. In contrast, tapping into coax is trivial. No special training or expensive tools or parts are required.

2. One-way channel. Two fibers needed to get full duplex (both ways) communication.

Optical Fiber works in three different types of modes (or we can say that we have 3 types of communication using Optical fiber). Optical fibers are available in two varieties; *Multi-Mode Fiber (MMF)* and *Single-Mode Fiber (SMF)*. For multi-mode fiber the core and cladding diameter lies in the range 50-200μm and 125-400μm, respectively. Whereas in single-mode fiber, the core and cladding diameters lie in the range 8-12μm and 125μm, respectively. Single-mode fibers are also known as Mono-Mode Fiber. Moreover, both single-mode and multi-mode fibers can have two types; *step index* and *graded index*. In the former case the refractive index of the core is uniform throughout and at the core cladding boundary there is an abrupt change in refractive index. In the later case, the refractive index of the core varies radially from the centre to the core-cladding boundary from n1 to n2 in a linear manner. Figure shows the optical fiber transmission modes.

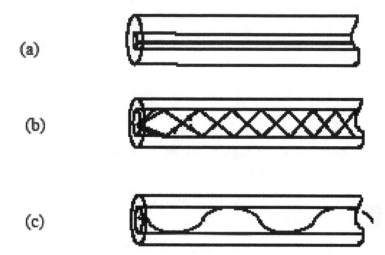

Schematics of three optical fiber types, (a) Single-mode step-index, (b) Multi-mode step-index, and (c) Multi-mode graded-index

Characteristics: Optical fiber acts as a dielectric waveguide that operates at optical frequencies (1014 to 1015 Hz). Three frequency bands centered around 850,1300 and 1500 nanometers are used for best results. When light is applied at one end of the optical fiber core, it reaches the other end by means of total internal reflection because of the choice of refractive index of core and cladding material (n1 > n2). The light source can be either light emitting diode (LED) or injection laser diode (ILD). These semiconductor devices emit a beam of light when a voltage is applied across the device. At the receiving end, a photodiode can be used to detect the signal-encoded light. Either PIN detector or APD (Avalanche photodiode) detector can be used as the light detector.

In a multi-mode fiber, the quality of signal-encoded light deteriorates more rapidly than single-mode fiber, because of interference of many light rays. As a consequence, single-mode fiber allows longer distances without repeater. For multi-mode fiber, the typical maximum length of the cable without a repeater is 2km, whereas for single-mode fiber it is 20km.

Fiber Uses: Because of greater bandwidth (2Gbps), smaller diameter, lighter weight, low attenuation, immunity to electromagnetic interference and longer repeater spacing, optical fiber cables are finding widespread use in long-distance telecommunications. Especially, the single mode fiber is suitable for this purpose. Fiber optic cables are also used in high-speed LAN applications. Multi-mode fiber is commonly used in LAN.

- Long-haul trunks-increasingly common in telephone network (Sprint ads)

- Metropolitan trunks-without repeaters (average 8 miles in length)

- Rural exchange trunks-link towns and villages

- Local loops-direct from central exchange to a subscriber (business or home)

- Local area networks-100Mbps ring networks.

Unguided Transmission

Unguided transmission is used when running a physical cable (either fiber or copper) between two end points is not possible. For example, running wires between buildings is probably not legal if the building is separated by a public street.

Infrared signals typically used for short distances (across the street or within same room),

Microwave signals commonly used for longer distances (10's of km). Sender and receiver use some sort of dish antenna as shown in figure

Communication using Terrestrial Microwave

Difficulties:

1. Weather interferes with signals. For instance, clouds, rain, lightning, etc. may adversely affect communication.

2. Radio transmissions easy to tap. A big concern for companies worried about competitors stealing plans.

3. Signals bouncing off of structures may lead to out-of-phase signals that the receiver must filter out.

Satellite Communication

Satellite communication is based on ideas similar to those used for line-of-sight. A communication satellite is essentially a big microwave repeater or relay station in the sky. Microwave signals from a ground station is picked up by a transponder, amplifies the signal and rebroadcasts it in another frequency, which can be received by ground stations at long distances as shown in figure.

To keep the satellite stationary with respect to the ground based stations, the satellite is placed in a geostationary orbit above the equator at an altitude of about 36,000 km. As the spacing between two satellites on the equatorial plane should not be closer than 40, there can be 360/4 = 90 communication satellites in the sky at a time. A satellite can be used for point-to-point communication between two ground-based stations or it can be used to broadcast a signal received from one station to many ground-based stations as shown in figure. Number of geo-synchronous satellites limited (about 90 total, to minimize interference). International agreements regulate how satellites are used, and how frequencies are allocated. Weather affects certain frequencies. Satellite transmission differs from terrestrial communication in another important way: One-way *propagation delay* is roughly 270 ms. In interactive terms, propagation delay alone inserts a 1 second delay between typing a character and receiving its echo.

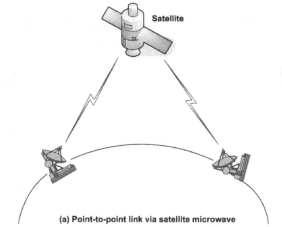

(a) Point-to-point link via satellite microwave

Satellite Microwave Communication: point –to- point

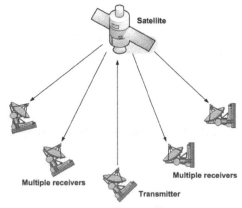

(b) Broadcast link via satellite microwave

Satellite Microwave Communication: Broadcast links

Characteristics: Optimum frequency range for satellite communication is 1 to 10 GHz. The most popular frequency band is referred to as 4/6 band, which uses 3.7 to 4.2 GHz for down link and 5.925 to 6.425 for uplink transmissions. The 500 MHz bandwidth is usually split over a dozen transponders, each with 36 MHz bandwidth. Each 36 MHz bandwidth is shared by time division multiplexing. As this preferred band is already saturated, the next highest band available is referred to as 12/14 GHz. It uses 14 to 14.5GHz for upward transmission and 11.7 to 12.2 GHz for downward transmissions. Communication satellites have several unique properties. The most important is the long communication delay for the round trip (about 270 ms) because of the long distance (about 72,000 km) the signal has to travel between two earth stations. This poses a number of problems, which are to be tackled for successful and reliable communication.

Another interesting property of satellite communication is its broadcast capability. All stations under the downward beam can receive the transmission. It may be necessary to send encrypted data to protect against piracy.

Use: Now-a-days communication satellites are not only used to handle telephone, telex and television traffic over long distances, but are used to support various internet based services such as e-mail, FTP, World Wide Web (WWW), etc. New types of services, based on communication satellites, are emerging.

Comparison/contrast with other technologies:

1. Propagation delay very high. On LANs, for example, propagation time is in nanoseconds -- essentially negligible.

2. One of few alternatives to phone companies for long distances.

3. Uses broadcast technology over a wide area - everyone on earth could receive a message at the same time!

4. Easy to place unauthorized taps into signal.

Satellites have recently fallen out of favor relative to fiber.

However, fiber has one big disadvantage: no one has it coming into their house or building, whereas anyone can place an antenna on a roof and lease a satellite channel.

Microwave Transmission

Microwave transmission is the transmission of information or energy by electromagnetic waves whose wavelengths are measured in small numbers of centimetre; these are called *microwaves*. This part of the radio spectrum ranges across frequencies of roughly 1.0 gigahertz (GHz) to 300 GHz. These correspond to wavelengths from 30 centimeters down to 0.1 cm.

Although an experimental 64 km (40 mile) microwave telecommunication link across the English Channel was demonstrated in 1931, the development of radar in World War II provided the technology for practical exploitation of microwave communication. In the 1950s, large transcontinental *microwave relay* networks, consisting of chains of repeater stations linked by line-of-sight beams of microwaves were built in Europe and America to relay long distance telephone traffic and television programs between cities. Communication satellites which transferred data between ground stations by micro-waves took over much long distance traffic in the 1960s. In recent years there has been an explosive increase in use of the microwave spectrum by new telecommunication technologies such as wireless networks, and direct-broadcast satellites which broadcast television and radio directly into consumers' homes.

Uses

Microwaves are widely used for point-to-point communications because their small wavelength allows conveniently-sized antennas to direct them in narrow beams, which can be pointed directly at the receiving antenna. This allows nearby micro-wave equipment to use the same frequencies without interfering with each other, as lower frequency radio waves do. Another advantage is that the high frequency of microwaves gives the microwave band a very large information-carrying capac-ity; the microwave band has a bandwidth 30 times that of all the rest of the radio spectrum below it. A disadvantage is that microwaves are limited to line of sight propagation; they cannot pass around hills or mountains as lower frequency radio waves can.

Microwave radio transmission is commonly used in point-to-point communication sys-tems on the surface of the Earth, in satellite communications, and in deep space radio communications. Other parts of the microwave radio band are used for radars, radio navigation systems, sensor systems, and radio astronomy.

The next higher part of the radio electromagnetic spectrum, where the frequencies are above 30 GHz and below 100 GHz, are called "millimeter waves" because their wave-lengths are conveniently measured in millimeters, and their wavelengths range from 10 mm down to 3.0 mm. Radio waves in this band are usually strongly attenuated by the Earthly atmosphere and particles contained in it, especially during wet weather. Also, in wide band of frequencies around 60 GHz, the radio waves are strongly atten-uated by molecular oxygen in the atmosphere. The electronic technologies needed in the millimeter wave band are also much more difficult to utilize than those of the mi-crowave band

Wireless transmission of information

- One-way (e.g. television broadcasting) and two-way telecommunication using communications satellite

- Terrestrial microwave relay links in telecommunications networks including backbone or backhaul carriers in cellular networks linking BTS-BSC and BSC-MSC.

A parabolic satellite antenna for Erdfunkstelle Raisting, based in Raisting, Bavaria, Germany.

C band horn-reflector antennas on the roof of a telephone switching center in Seattle, Washington, part of the U.S. AT & T Long Lines microwave relay network.

Wireless transmission of power

- Proposed systems e.g. for connecting solar power collecting satellites to terrestrial power grids.

Microwave Radio Relay

Microwave radio relay is a technology for transmitting digital and analog signals, such as long-distance telephone calls, television programs, and computer data, between two locations on a line of sight radio path. In microwave radio relay, microwaves are transmitted between the two locations with directional antennas, forming a fixed radio connection between the two points. The requirement of a line of sight limits the distance between stations to 30 or 40 miles.

Dozens of microwave dishes on the Heinrich-Hertz-Turm in Germany.

Beginning in the 1950s, networks of microwave relay links, such as the AT & T Long Lines system in the U.S., carried long distance telephone calls and television programs between cities. The first system, dubbed TD-2 and built by AT&T, connected New York and Boston in 1947 with a series of eight radio relay stations. These included long daisy-chained series of such links that traversed mountain ranges and spanned continents. Much of the transcontinental traffic is now carried by cheaper optical fibers and communication satellites, but microwave relay remains important for shorter distances.

Planning

Because the radio waves travel in narrow beams confined to a line-of-sight path from one antenna to the other, they don't interfere with other microwave equipment, so nearby microwave links can use the same frequencies, called frequency reuse. Antennas must be highly directional (high gain); these antennas are installed in elevated locations such as large radio towers in order to be able to transmit across long distances. Typical types of antenna used in radio relay link installations are parabolic antennas, dielectric lens, and horn-reflector antennas, which have a diameter of up to 4 meters. Highly directive antennas permit an economical use of the available frequency spectrum, despite long transmission distances.

Communications tower on Frazier Mountain, Southern California with microwave relay dishes.

Because of the high frequencies used, a line-of-sight path between the stations is required. Additionally, in order to avoid attenuation of the beam an area around the beam called the first Fresnel zone must be free from obstacles. Obstacles in the signal field cause unwanted attenuation. High mountain peak or ridge positions are often ideal

Danish military radio relay node

Obstacles, the curvature of the Earth, the geography of the area and reception issues arising from the use of nearby land (such as in manufacturing and forestry) are important issues to consider when planning radio links. In the planning process, it is essential that "path profiles" are produced, which provide information about the terrain and Fresnel zones affecting the transmission path. The presence of a water surface, such as a lake or river, along the path also must be taken into consideration as it can reflect the beam, and the direct and reflected beam can interfere at the receiving antenna, causing multipath fading. Multipath fades are usually deep only in a small spot and a narrow frequency band, so space and/or frequency diversity schemes can be applied to mitigate these effects.

The effects of atmospheric stratification cause the radio path to bend downward in a typical situation so a major distance is possible as the earth equivalent curvature increases from 6370 km to about 8500 km (a 4/3 equivalent radius effect). Rare events of temperature, humidity and pressure profile versus height, may produce large deviations and distortion of the propagation and affect transmission quality. High intensity rain and snow must also be considered as an impairment factor, especially at frequencies above 10 GHz. All previous factors, collectively known as path loss, make it necessary to compute suitable power margins, in order to maintain the link operative for a high percentage of time, like the standard 99.99% or 99.999% used in 'carrier class' services of most telecommunication operators.

The longest microwave radio relay known up to date crosses the Red Sea with 360 km hop between Jebel Erba (2170m a.s.l., 20°44'46.17"N 36°50'24.65"E, Sudan) and Jebel Dakka (2572m a.s.l., 21° 5'36.89"N 40°17'29.80"E, Saudi Arabia). The link built in 1979 by Telettra allowed to proper transmit 300 telephone channels and 1 TV signal, in the 2 GHz frequency band. (Hop distance is the distance between two microwave stations)

Previous considerations represent typical problems characterizing terrestrial radio links using microwaves for the so-called backbone networks: hop lentghs of few tens of kilometers (typically 10 to 60 km) were largely used until 1990s. Frequency bands below 10 GHz and, above all, the information to be transmitted was a stream containing a fixed capacity block. The target was to supply the requested availability for the whole block (Plesiochronous digital hierarchy, PDH, or Synchronous Digital Hierarchy, SDH). Fading and/or multipath affecting the link for short time period during the day had to be counteracted by the diversity architecture. During 1990s microwave radio links begun widely to be used for urban links in cellular network. Requirements regarding link distances changed to shorter hops (less than 10 km, typically 3 to 5 km) and frequency increased to bands between 11 and 43 GHz and more recently up to 86 GHz (E-band). Furthermore, link planning deals more with intense rainfall and less with multipath, so diversity schemes became less used. Another big change that occurred during the last decade was evolution towards packet radio transmission. Therefore, new countermeasures, such as adaptive modulation, have been adopted.

The emitted power is regulated by norms (EIRP) both for cellular system and microwave. These microwave transmissions use emitted power typically from 30 mW to 0,3 W, radiated by the parabolic antenna on a beam wide round few degrees (1 to 3-4). The microwave channel arrangement is regulated by International Telecommunication Union (ITU-R) or local regulations (ETSI, FCC). In the last decade the dedicated spectrum for each microwave band reaches an extreme overcrowding, forcing efforts towards techniques for increasing the transmission capacity (frequency reuse, Polarization-division multiplexing, XPIC, MIMO).

Production truck used for remote broadcasts by television news has a microwave dish on a retractible telescoping mast to transmit live video back to the studio.

History

In 1931 an Anglo-French consortium headed by Andre C. Clavier demonstrated an experimental microwave relay link across the English Channel using 10 foot (3 m) dishes. Telephony, telegraph and facsimile data was transmitted over the bidirectional 1.7 GHz beams 64 km (40 miles) between Dover, UK and Calais, France. The radiated power, produced by a miniature Barkhausen-Kurz tube located at the dish's focus, was one-half watt. A 1933 military microwave link between airports at St. Inglevert, UK and Lympne, France, a distance of 56 km (35 miles) was followed in 1935 by a 300 MHz telecommunication link, the first commercial microwave relay system.

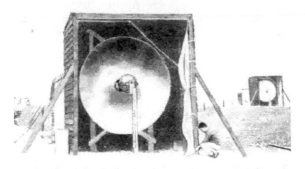

Antennas of 1931 experimental 1.7 GHz microwave relay link across the English Channel. The receiving antenna *(background, right)* was located behind the transmitting antenna to avoid interference.

The development of radar during World War II provided much of the microwave technology which made practical microwave communication links possible, particularly the klystron oscillator and techniques of designing parabolic antennas. Though not commonly known, the US military used both portable and fixed-station microwave communications in the European Theater during World War II.

After the war telephone companies used this technology to build large microwave radio relay networks to carry long distance telephone calls. During the 1950s a unit of the US telephone carrier, AT&T Long Lines, built a transcontinental system of microwave relay links across the US that grew to carry the majority of US long distance telephone traffic, as well as television network signals. The main motivation in 1946 to use microwave radio instead of cable was that a large capacity could be installed quickly and at less cost. It was expected at that time that the annual operating costs for microwave radio would be greater than for cable. There were two main reasons that a large capacity had to be introduced suddenly: Pent up demand for long distance telephone service, because of the hiatus during the war years, and the new medium of television, which needed more bandwidth than radio. The prototype was called TDX and was tested with a connection between New York City and Murray Hill, the location of Bell Laboratories in 1946. The TDX system was set up between New York and Boston in 1947. The TDX was upgraded to the TD2 system, which used [the Morton tube, 416B and later 416C, manufactured by Western electric] in the transmitters, and then later to TD3 that used solid state electronics.

Military microwave relay systems continued to be used into the 1960s, when many of these systems were supplanted with tropospheric scatter or communication satellite systems. When the NATO military arm was formed, much of this existing equipment was transferred to communications groups. The typical communications systems used by NATO during that time period consisted of the technologies which had been developed for use by the telephone carrier entities in host countries. One example from the USA is the RCA CW-20A 1–2 GHz microwave relay system which utilized flexible UHF cable rather than the rigid waveguide required by higher frequency systems, making it ideal for tactical applications. The typical microwave relay installation or portable van had two radio systems (plus backup) connecting two line of sight sites. These radios would often carry 24 telephone channels frequency division multiplexed on the microwave carrier (i.e. Lenkurt 33C FDM). Any channel could be designated to carry up to 18 teletype communications instead. Similar systems from Germany and other member nations were also in use.

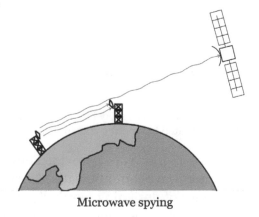

Microwave spying

Long distance microwave relay networks were built in many countries until the 1980s when the technology lost its share of fixed operation to newer technologies such as fiber-optic cable and communication satellites, which offer lower cost per bit.

During the Cold War, the US intelligence agencies, such as the National Security Agency (NSA), were reportedly able to intercept Soviet microwave traffic using satellites such as Rhyolite. Much of the beam of a microwave link passes the receiving antenna and radiates toward the horizon, into space. By positioning a geosynchronous satellite in the path of the beam, the microwave beam can be received.

At the turn of the century, microwave radio relay systems are being used increasingly in portable radio applications. The technology is particularly suited to this application because of lower operating costs, a more efficient infrastructure, and provision of direct hardware access to the portable radio operator.

Microwave Link

A microwave link is a communications system that uses a beam of radio waves in the microwave frequency range to transmit video, audio, or data between two locations, which can be from just a few feet or meters to several miles or kilometers apart. Microwave links are commonly used by television broadcasters to transmit programmes across a country, for instance, or from an outside broadcast back to a studio.

Mobile units can be camera mounted, allowing cameras the freedom to move around without trailing cables. These are often seen on the touchlines of sports fields on Steadicam systems.

Properties of Microwave Links

- Involve line of sight (LOS) communication technology
- Affected greatly by environmental constraints, including rain fade
- Have very limited penetration capabilities through obstacles such as hills, buildings and trees
- Sensitive to high pollen count
- Signals can be degradedduring Solar proton events

Uses of Microwave links

- In communications between satellites and base stations
- As backbone carriers for cellular systems
- In short range indoor communications
- Telecommunications, in linking remote and regional telephone exchanges to larger (main) exchanges without the need for copper/optical fibre lines.

Troposcatter

Terrestrial microwave relay links described above are limited in distance to the visual horizon, about 40 miles. Tropospheric scatter ("troposcatter" or "scatter") was a technology developed in the 1950s allow microwave communication links beyond the horizon, to a range of several hundred kilometers. The transmitter radiates a beam of microwaves into the sky, at a shallow angle above the horizon toward the receiver. As the beam passes through the troposphere a small fraction of the microwave energy is scattered back toward the ground by water vapor and dust in the air. A sensitive receiver beyond the horizon picks up this reflected signal. Signal clarity obtained by this method depends on the weather and other factors, and as a result a high level of technical difficulty is involved in the creation of a reliable over horizon radio relay link. Troposcatter links are therefore only used in special circumstances where satellites and other long distance communication channels cannot be relied on, such as in military communications.

Microwave Power Transmission

Microwave power transmission (MPT) is the use of microwaves to transmit power through outer space or the atmosphere without the need for wires. It is a sub-type of the more general wireless energy transfer methods.

History

Following World War II, which saw the development of high-power microwave emitters known as cavity magnetrons, the idea of using microwaves to transmit power was researched. In 1964, William C. Brown demonstrated a miniature helicopter equipped with a combination antenna and rectifier device called a rectenna. The rectenna converted microwave power into electricity, allowing the helicopter to fly. In principle, the rectenna is capable of very high conversion efficiencies - over 90% in optimal circumstances.

Most proposed MPT systems now usually include a phased array microwave transmitter. While these have lower efficiency levels they have the advantage of being electrically steered using no moving parts, and are easier to scale to the necessary levels that a practical MPT system requires.

Using microwave power transmission to deliver electricity to communities without having to build cable-based infrastructure is being studied at Grand Bassin on Reunion Island in the Indian Ocean.

Common Safety Concerns

The common reaction to microwave transmission is one of concern, as microwaves are generally perceived by the public as dangerous forms of radiation, stemming from the fact that they are used in microwave ovens. While high power microwaves can be painful and dangerous as in the United States Military's Active Denial System, MPT systems are generally proposed to have only low intensity at the rectenna.

Though this would be extremely safe as the power levels would be about equal to the leakage from a microwave oven, and only slightly more than a cell phone, the relatively diffuse microwave beam necessitates a large receiving antenna area for a significant amount of energy to be transmitted.

Research has involved exposing multiple generations of animals to microwave radiation of this or higher intensity, and no health issues have been found.

Proposed Uses

MPT is the most commonly proposed method for transferring energy to the surface of the Earth from solar power satellites or other in-orbit power sources. MPT is occasionally proposed for the power supply in beam-powered propulsion for orbital lift space ships. Even though lasers are more commonly proposed, their low efficiency in light generation and reception has led some designers to opt for microwave based systems.

Current Status

Wireless power transmission (using microwaves) is well proven. Experiments in the tens of kilowatts have been performed at Goldstone in California in 1975 and more recently (1997) at Grand Bassin on Reunion Island. In 2008 a long range transmission experiment successfully transmitted 20 watts 92 miles (148 km) from a mountain on Maui to the main island of Hawaii.

JAXA announced on 12 March 2015 that they wirelessly beamed 1.8 kilowatts 50 meters to a small receiver by converting electricity to microwaves and then back to electricity. This is the standard plan for this type of power. On 12 March 2015 Mitsubishi Heavy Industries demonstrated transmission of 10 kilowatts (kW) of power to a receiver unit located at a distance of 500 meters (m) away.

Transmission Impairments and Channel Capacity

When a signal is transmitted over a communication channel, it is subjected to different types of impairments because of imperfect characteristics of the channel. As a consequence, the received and the transmitted signals are not the same. Outcome of the impairments are manifested in two different ways in analog and digital signals. These impairments introduce random modifications in analog signals leading to distortion. On the other hand, in case of digital signals, the impairments lead to error in the bit values. The impairment can be broadly categorised into the following three types:

- Attenuation and attenuation distortion

- Delay distortion

- Noise

In this lesson these impairments are discussed in detail and possible approaches to overcome these impairments. The concept of channel capacity for both noise-free and noisy channels have also been introduced.

Attenuation

Irrespective of whether a medium is guided or unguided, the strength of a signal falls off with distance. This is known as *attenuation*. In case of guided media, the attenuation is logarithmic, whereas in case of unguided media it is a more complex function of the distance and the material that constitutes the medium.

An important concept in the field of data communications is the use of on unit known as decibel (dB). To define it let us consider the circuit elements shown in figure. The elements can be either a transmission line, an amplifier, an attenuator, a filter, etc. In the figure, a transmission line (between points P1 and P2) is followed by an amplifier (between P2 and P3). The input signal delivers a power P1 at the input of an communication element and the output power is P2. Then the power gain G for this element in decibles is given by G = 10log2 P2/ P1. Here P2/ P1 is referred to as absolute power gain. When P2 > P1, the gain is positive, whereas if P2 < P1, then the power gain is negative and there is a power loss in the circuit element. For P2 = 5mW, P1 = 10mW, the power gain G = 10log 5/10 = 10 × -3 = -3dB is negative and it represents attenuation as a signal passes through the communication element.

Example: Let us consider a transmission line between points 1 and 2 and let the energy strength at point 2 is 1/10 of that of point 1. Then attenuation in dB is 10log10(1/10) = -10 dB. On the other hand, there is an amplifier between points 2 and 3. Let the power is 100 times at point 3 with respect to point 2. Then power gain in dB is 10log10(100/1) = 20 dB, which has a positive sign.

Compensation of attenuation using an amplifier

The attenuation leads to several problems:

Attenuation Distortion: If the strength of the signal is very low, the signal cannot be detected and interpreted properly at the receiving end. The signal strength should be sufficiently high so that the signal can be correctly detected by a receiver in presence of noise in the channel. As shown in figure, an amplifier can be used to compensate the attenuation of the transmission line. So, attenuation decides how far a signal can be sent without amplification through a particular medium.

Attenuation of all frequency components is not same. Some frequencies are passed without attenuation, some are weakened and some are blocked. This dependence of attenuation of a channel on the frequency of a signal leads to a new kind of distortion *attenuation distortion*. As shown in figure, a square wave is sent through a medium and the output is no longer a square wave because of more attenuation of the high-frequency components in the medium.

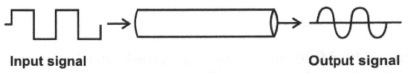

Input signal   **Output signal**

Attenuation distortion of a square wave after passing through a medium.

The effect of attenuation distortion can be reduced with the help of a suitable equalizer circuit, which is placed between the channel and the receiver. The equalizer has opposite attenuation/amplification characteristics of the medium and compensates higher losses of some frequency components in the medium by higher amplification in the equalizer. Attenuation characteristics of three popular transmission media are shown in figure. As shown in the figure, the attenuation of a signal increases exponentially as frequency is increased from KHz range to MHz range. In case of coaxial cable attenuation increases linearly with frequency in the Mhz range. The optical fibre, on the other hand, has attenuation characteristic similar to a band-pass filter and a small frequency band in the THz range can be used for the transmission of signal.

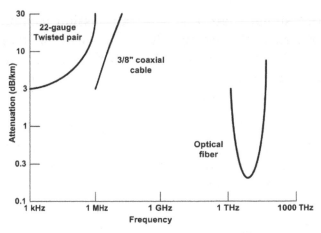

Attenuation of typical guided media

Attenuation characteristics of the popular guided media

Delay Distortion

The velocity of propagation of different frequency components of a signal are different in guided media. This leads to delay distortion in the signal. For a bandlimited signal, the velocity of propagation has been found to be maximum near the center frequency and lower on both sides of the edges of the frequency band. In case of analog signals, the received signal is distorted because of variable delay of different components. In case of digital signals, the problem is much more severe. Some frequency components of one bit position spill over to other bit positions, because of delay distortion. This leads to intersymbol interference, which restricts the maximum bit rate of transmission through a particular transmission medium. The delay distortion can also be neutralised, like attenuation distortion, by using suitable equalizers.

Noise

As signal is transmitted through a channel, undesired signal in the form of noise gets mixed up with the signal, along with the distortion introduced by the transmission media. Noise can be categorised into the following four types:

- Thermal Noise

- Intermodulation Noise

- Cross talk

- Impulse Noise

The *thermal noise* is due to thermal agitation of electrons in a conductor. It is distributed across the entire spectrum and that is why it is also known as *white noise* (as the frequency encompass over a broad range of frequencies).

When more than one signal share a single transmission medium, *intermodulation noise* is generated. For example, two signals f1 and f2 will generate signals of frequencies (f1 + f2) and (f1 - f2), which may interfere with the signals of the same frequencies sent by the transmitter. Intermodulation noise is introduced due to nonlinearity present in any part of the communication system.

Cross talk is a result of bunching several conductors together in a single cable. Signal carrying wires generate electromagnetic radiation, which is induced on other conductors because of close proximity of the conductors. While using telephone, it is a common experience to hear conversation of other people in the background. This is known as *cross talk*.

Impulse noise is irregular pulses or noise spikes of short duration generated by phenomena like lightning, spark due to loose contact in electric circuits, etc. Impulse noise is a primary source of bit-errors in digital data communication. This kind of noise introduces burst errors.

Bandwidth and Channel Capacity

Bandwidth refers to the range of frequencies that a medium can pass without a loss of one-half of the power (-3dB) contained in the signal. Figure shows the bandwidth of a channel. The points Fl and Fh points correspond to −3bB of the maximum amplitude A.

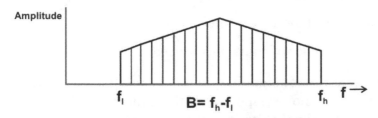

Bandwidth of a channel

Bandwidth of a medium decides the quality of the signal at the other end. A digital signal (usually aperiodic) requires a bandwidth from 0 to infinity. So, it needs a low-pass channel characteristic as shown in figure. On the other hand, a band-pass channel characteristic is required for the transmission of analog signals, as shown in figure.

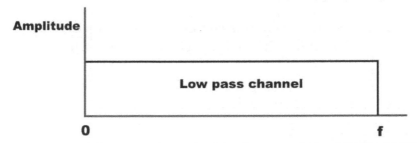

Low-pass channel characteristic required for the transmission of digital signals

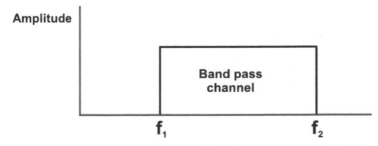

Band-pass channel characteristic required for the transmission of analog signals

Nyquist Bit Rate

The maximum rate at which data can be correctly communicated over a channel in presence of noise and distortion is known as its channel capacity. Consider first a noise-free channel of Bandwidth B. Based on Nyquist formulation it is known that given a bandwidth B of a channel, the maximum data rate that can be carried is 2B. This limitation arises due to the effect of intersymbol interference caused by the frequency components higher than B. If the signal consists of m discrete levels, then Nyquist theorem states:

Maximum data rate C = 2 B log2 m bits/sec,

Where,

C is known as the channel capacity,

B is the bandwidth of the channel

and m is the number of signal levels used.

Baud Rate: The baud rate or signaling rate is defined as the number of distinct symbols transmitted per second, irrespective of the form of encoding. For baseband digital transmission m = 2. So, the maximum baud rate = 1/Element width (in Seconds) = 2B

Bit Rate: The bit rate or information rate I is the actual equivalent number of bits transmitted per second. I = Baud Rate × Bits per Baud

= Baud Rate × N = Baud Rate × log2m

For binary encoding, the bit rate and the baud rate are the same; i.e., I = Baud Rate.

Example: Let us consider the telephone channel having bandwidth B = 4 kHz. Assuming there is no noise, determine channel capacity for the following encoding levels:

(i) 2, and (ii) 128.

Ans: (i) C = 2B = 2×4000 = 8 Kbits/s

(ii) C = 2×4000×log2128 = 8000×7 = 56 Kbits/s

Effects of Noise

When there is noise present in the medium, the limitations of both bandwidth and noise must be considered. A noise spike may cause a given level to be interpreted as a signal of greater level, if it is in positive phase or a smaller level, if it is negative phase. Noise becomes more problematic as the number of levels increases.

Shannon Capacity (Noisy Channel)

In presence of Gaussian band-limited white noise, Shannon-Hartley theorem gives the maximum data rate capacity

$$C = B \: log2 \: (1 + S/N),$$

where S and N are the signal and noise power, respectively, at the output of the channel. This theorem gives an upper bound of the data rate which can be reliably transmitted over a thermal-noise limited channel.

Example: Suppose we have a channel of 3000 Hz bandwidth, we need an S/N ratio (i.e. signal to noise ration, SNR) of 30 dB to have an acceptable bit-error rate. Then, the maximum data rate that we can transmit is 30,000 bps. In practice, because of the presence of different types of noises, attenuation and delay distortions, actual (practical) upper limit will be much lower.

In case of extremely noisy channel, C = 0

Between the Nyquist Bit Rate and the Shannon limit, the result providing the smallest channel capacity is the one that establishes the limit.

Example: A channel has B = 4 KHz. Determine the channel capacity for each of the following signal-to-noise ratios: (a) 20 dB, (b) 30 dB, (c) 40 dB.

Answer: (a) C= B $\log_2$ (1 + S/N) = 4×10³×$\log_2$ (1+100) = 4×10³×3.32×2.004 = 26.6 kbits/s

b) C= B $\log_2$ (1 + S/N) = 4×10³×$\log_2$ (1+1000) = 4×10³×3.32×3.0 = 39.8 kbits/s

(c) C= B $\log_2$ (1 + S/N) = 4×10³×$\log_2$ (1+10000) = 4×10³×3.32×4.0 = 53.1 kbits/s

Example: A channel has B = 4 KHz and a signal-to-noise ratio of 30 dB. Determine maximum information rate for 4-level encoding.

Answer: For B = 4 KHz and 4-level encoding the *Nyquist Bit Rate* is 16 Kbps. Again for B = 4 KHz and S/N of 30 dB the *Shannon capacity* is 39.8 Kbps. The smallest of the two values has to be taken as the Information capacity I = 16 Kbps.

Example: A channel has B = 4 kHz and a signal-to-noise ratio of 30 dB. Determine maximum information rate for 128-level encoding.

Answer: The *Nyquist Bit Rate* for B = 4 kHz and M = 128 levels is 56 kbits/s. Again the *Shannon capacity* for B = 4 kHz and S/N of 30 dB is 39.8 Kbps. The smallest of the two values decides the channel capacity C = 39.8 kbps.

Example: The digital signal is to be designed to permit 160 kbps for a bandwidth of 20 KHz. Determine (a) number of levels and (b) S/N ratio.

(a) Apply *Nyquist Bit Rate* to determine number of levels.

C = 2B $\log_2$ (M),

or 160×10³ = 2×20×10³ $\log_2$ (M),

or M = 2⁴, which means 4bits/baud.

(b) Apply *Shannon capacity* to determine the S/N ratio

C = B $\log_2$ (1+S/N),

or 160×10³ = 20×10³ $\log_2$ (1+S/N) ×10³ $\log_2$ (M) ,

or S/N = 2^8 - 1,

or S/N = 255,

or S/N = 24.07 dB.

References

- Proakis, John G.; Manolakis, Dimitris G. (2007-01-01). Digital Signal Processing. Pearson Prentice Hall. ISBN 9780131873742

- "Analyzing Microwave Spectra Collected by the Solar Radio Burst Locator". Digital.library.unt.edu. 2012-09-24. Retrieved 2012-10-02

- McBee, David Barnett, David Groth, Jim (2004). Cabling : the complete guide to network wiring (3rd ed.). San Francisco: SYBEX. p. 11. ISBN 9780782143317. Retrieved 16 August 2016

- Tamburini, Fabrizio; Mari, Elettra; Sponselli, Anna; Thidé, Bo; Bianchini, Antonio; Romanato, Filippo (2012-01-01). "Encoding many channels on the same frequency through radio vorticity: first experimental test". New Journal of Physics. 14 (3): 033001. ISSN 1367-2630. doi:10.1088/1367-2630/14/3/033001

- Chris C. Bissell and David A. Chapman (1992). Digital Signal Transmission. Cambridge University Press. ISBN 0-521-42557-3

- Brown, W. C. (Raytheon) (December 1965) "Experimental Airborne Microwave Supported Platform" Technical Report NO. RADC-TR- 65- 188, Air Force Systems Command. Retrieved July 9, 2012

- Steven Alan Tretter (1995). Communication System Design Using Dsp Algorithms: With Laboratory Experiments for the TMS320C30. Springer. ISBN 0-306-45032-1

- e, E. E. (August 1931). "Searchlight radio with the new 7 inch waves" (PDF). Radio News. New York: Radio Science Publications. 8 (2): 107–109. Retrieved March 24, 2015

- Reeve, Whitman D. (1995). Subscriber Loop Signaling and Transmission Handbook - Digital (1st ed.). IEEE Press. pp. 215–220. ISBN 0-7803-0440-3

- "Microwaves span the English Channel" (PDF). Short Wave Craft. New York: Popular Book Co. 6 (5): 262. September 1935. Retrieved March 24, 2015

- Nahin, Paul J. (2002). Oliver Heaviside: The Life, Work, and Times of an Electrical Genius of the Victorian Age. ISBN 0-8018-6909-9

- Brown., W. C. (September 1984). "The History of Power Transmission by Radio Waves". Microwave Theory and Techniques, IEEE Transactions on (Volume: 32, Issue: 9 On page(s): 1230-1242). Bibcode:1984ITMTT..32.1230B. ISSN 0018-9480. doi:10.1109/TMTT.1984.1132833

- The ARRL UHF/Microwave Experimenter's Manual, American Radio Relay League, Newington CT USA,1990 ISBN 0-87259-312-6, Chapter 5 Transmission Media pages 5.19 through 5.21

3

Data Link Control in Computer Networks

Data link control devices allow for the transmission of data and the correction of data errors. The transmission from a source is carried through a data terminal equipment (DTE) to data circuit terminal equipment (DCE), which converts data into signals. Since communication channels may sometimes fail to deliver data, the use of error detection and correction helps in guaranteeing data delivery. This chapter has been carefully written to provide an easy understanding of the varied facets of data transmission and link control.

Data Transmission

Data transmission, digital transmission or digital communications is the transfer of data (a digital bit stream or a digitized analog signal) over a point-to-point or point-to-multipoint communication channel. Examples of such channels are copper wires, optical fibers, wireless communication channels, storage media and computer buses. The data are represented as an electromagnetic signal, such as an electrical voltage, radiowave, microwave, or infrared signal.

Analog or analogue transmission is a transmission method of conveying voice, data, image, signal or video information using a continuous signal which varies in amplitude, phase, or some other property in proportion to that of a variable. The messages are either represented by a sequence of pulses by means of a line code (*baseband transmission*), or by a limited set of continuously varying wave forms (*passband transmission*), using a digital modulation method. The passband modulation and corresponding demodulation (also known as detection) is carried out by modem equipment. According to the most common definition of digital signal, both baseband and passband signals representing bit-streams are considered as digital transmission, while an alternative definition only considers the baseband signal as digital, and passband transmission of digital data as a form of digital-to-analog conversion.

Data transmitted may be digital messages originating from a data source, for example a computer or a keyboard. It may also be an analog signal such as a phone call or a video signal, digitized into a bit-stream for example using pulse-code modulation (PCM) or more advanced source coding (analog-to-digital conversion and data compression) schemes. This source coding and decoding is carried out by codec equipment.

Distinction between Related Subjects

Courses and textbooks in the field of *data transmission* as well as *digital transmission* and *digital communications* have similar content.

Digital transmission or data transmission traditionally belongs to telecommunications and electrical engineering. Basic principles of data transmission may also be covered within the computer science/computer engineering topic of data communications, which also includes computer networking or computer communication applications and networking protocols, for example routing, switching and inter-process communication. Although the Transmission control protocol (TCP) involves the term "transmission", TCP and other transport layer protocols are typically *not* discussed in a textbook or course about data transmission, but in computer networking.

The term tele transmission involves the analog as well as digital communication. In most textbooks, the term analog transmission only refers to the transmission of an analog message signal (without digitization) by means of an analog signal, either as a non-modulated baseband signal, or as a passband signal using an analog modulation method such as AM or FM. It may also include analog-over-analog pulse modulatated baseband signals such as pulse-width modulation. In a few books within the computer networking tradition, "analog transmission" also refers to passband transmission of bit-streams using digital modulation methods such as FSK, PSK and ASK. Note that these methods are covered in textbooks named digital transmission or data transmission, for example.

The theoretical aspects of data transmission are covered by information theory and coding theory.

Protocol Layers and Sub-topics

Courses and textbooks in the field of data transmission typically deal with the following OSI model protocol layers and topics:

- Layer 1, the physical layer:
  - Channel coding including
    - Digital modulation schemes
    - Line coding schemes
    - Forward error correction (FEC) codes
  - Bit synchronization
  - Multiplexing
  - Equalization
  - Channel models

- Layer 2, the data link layer:

    o   Channel access schemes, media access control (MAC)

    o   Packet mode communication and Frame synchronization

    o   Error detection and automatic repeat request (ARQ)

    o   Flow control

- Layer 6, the presentation layer:

    o   Source coding (digitization and data compression), and information theory.

    o   Cryptography (may occur at any layer)

Applications and History

Data (mainly but not exclusively informational) has been sent via non-electronic (e.g. optical, acoustic, mechanical) means since the advent of communication. Analog signal data has been sent electronically since the advent of the telephone. However, the first data electromagnetic transmission applications in modern time were telegraphy (1809) and teletypewriters (1906), which are both digital signals. The fundamental theoretical work in data transmission and information theory by Harry Nyquist, Ralph Hartley, Claude Shannon and others during the early 20th century, was done with these applications in mind.

Data transmission is utilized in computers in computer buses and for communication with peripheral equipment via parallel ports and serial ports such as RS-232 (1969), Firewire (1995) and USB (1996). The principles of data transmission are also utilized in storage media for Error detection and correction since 1951.

Data transmission is utilized in computer networking equipment such as modems (1940), local area networks (LAN) adapters (1964), repeaters, hubs, microwave links, wireless network access points (1997), etc.

In telephone networks, digital communication is utilized for transferring many phone calls over the same copper cable or fiber cable by means of Pulse code modulation (PCM), i.e. sampling and digitization, in combination with Time division multiplexing (TDM) (1962). Telephone exchanges have become digital and software controlled, facilitating many value added services. For example, the first AXE telephone exchange was presented in 1976. Since the late 1980s, digital communication to the end user has been possible using Integrated Services Digital Network (ISDN) services. Since the end of the 1990s, broadband access techniques such as ADSL, Cable modems, fiber-to-the-building (FTTB) and fiber-to-the-home (FTTH) have become widespread to small offices and homes. The current tendency is to replace traditional telecommunication services by packet mode communication such as IP telephony and IPTV.

Transmitting analog signals digitally allows for greater signal processing capability.

The ability to process a communications signal means that errors caused by random processes can be detected and corrected. Digital signals can also be sampled instead of continuously monitored. The multiplexing of multiple digital signals is much simpler to the multiplexing of analog signals.

Because of all these advantages, and because recent advances in wideband communication channels and solid-state electronics have allowed scientists to fully realize these advantages, digital communications has grown quickly. Digital communications is quickly edging out analog communication because of the vast demand to transmit computer data and the ability of digital communications to do so.

The digital revolution has also resulted in many digital telecommunication applications where the principles of data transmission are applied. Examples are second-generation (1991) and later cellular telephony, video conferencing, digital TV (1998), digital radio (1999), telemetry, etc.

Data transmission, digital transmission or digital communications is the physical transfer of data (a digital bit stream or a digitized analog signal) over a point-to-point or point-to-multipoint communication channel. Examples of such channels are copper wires, optical fibers, wireless communication channels, storage media and computer buses. The data are represented as an electromagnetic signal, such as an electrical voltage, radiowave, microwave, or infrared signal.

While analog transmission is the transfer of a continuously varying analog signal over an analog channel, digital communications is the transfer of discrete messages over a digital or an analog channel. The messages are either represented by a sequence of pulses by means of a line code (baseband transmission), or by a limited set of continuously varying wave forms (passband transmission), using a digital modulation method. The passband modulation and corresponding demodulation (also known as detection) is carried out by modem equipment. According to the most common definition of digital signal, both baseband and passband signals representing bit-streams are considered as digital transmission, while an alternative definition only considers the baseband signal as digital, and passband transmission of digital data as a form of digital-to-analog conversion.

Data transmitted may be digital messages originating from a data source, for example a computer or a keyboard. It may also be an analog signal such as a phone call or a video signal, digitized into a bit-stream for example using pulse-code modulation (PCM) or more advanced source coding (analog-to-digital conversion and data compression) schemes. This source coding and decoding is carried out by codec equipment.

Serial and Parallel Transmission

In telecommunications, serial transmission is the sequential transmission of signal elements of a group representing a character or other entity of data. Digital serial transmissions are bits sent over a single wire, frequency or optical path sequentially. Because it requires less signal processing and less chances for error than parallel transmission, the transfer rate of each individual path may be faster. This can be used over longer distances as a check digit or parity bit can be sent along it easily.

In telecommunications, parallel transmission is the simultaneous transmission of the signal elements of a character or other entity of data. In digital communications, parallel transmission is the simultaneous transmission of related signal elements over two or more separate paths. Multiple electrical wires are used which can transmit multiple bits simultaneously, which allows for higher data transfer rates than can be achieved with serial transmission. This method is used internally within the computer, for example the internal buses, and sometimes externally for such things as printers, The major issue with this is "skewing" because the wires in parallel data transmission have slightly different properties (not intentionally) so some bits may arrive before others, which may corrupt the message. A parity bit can help to reduce this. However, electrical wire parallel data transmission is therefore less reliable for long distances because corrupt transmissions are far more likely.

Types of Communication Channels

Some communications channel types include:

- Data transmission circuit
- Full-duplex
- Half-duplex
- Multi-drop:
  - Bus network
  - Mesh network
  - Ring network
  - Star network
  - Wireless network
- Point-to-point
- Simplex

Asynchronous and Synchronous Data Transmission

Asynchronous start-stop transmission uses start and stop bits to signify the beginning bit ASCII character would actually be transmitted using 10 bits. For example, "0100 0001" would become "1 0100 0001 0". The extra one (or zero, depending on parity bit) at the start and end of the transmission tells the receiver first that a character is coming and secondly that the character has ended. This method of transmission is used when data are sent intermittently as opposed to in a solid stream. In the previous example the start and stop bits are in bold. The start and stop bits must be of opposite polarity. This allows the receiver to recognize when the second packet of information is being sent.

Synchronous transmission uses no start and stop bits, but instead synchronizes transmission speeds at both the receiving and sending end of the transmission using clock signal(s) built into each component. A continual stream of data is then sent between the two nodes. Due to there being no start and stop bits the data transfer rate is quicker although more errors will occur, as the clocks will eventually get out of sync, and the receiving device would have the wrong time that had been agreed in the protocol for sending/receiving data, so some bytes could become corrupted (by losing bits). Ways to get around this problem include re-synchronization of the clocks and use of check digits to ensure the byte is correctly interpreted and received.

Framing and Synchronization

Normally, units of data transfer are larger than a single analog or digital encoding symbol. It is necessary to recover clock information for both the signal (so we can recover the right number of symbols and recover each symbol as accurately as possible), and obtain synchronization for larger units of data (such as data words and frames). It is necessary to recover the data in words or blocks because this is the only way the receiver process will be able to interpret the data received; for a given bit stream. Depending on the byte boundaries, there will be seven or eight ways to interpret the bit stream as ASCII characters, and these are likely to be very different. So, it is necessary to add other bits to the block that convey control information used in the data link control procedures. The data along with preamble, postamble, and control information forms a frame. This framing is necessary for the purpose of synchronization and other data control functions.

Synchronization

Data sent by a sender in bit-serial form through a medium must be correctly interpreted at the receiving end. This requires that the beginning, the end and logic level and duration of each bit as sent at the transmitting end must be recognized at the receiving end. There are three synchronization levels: *Bit, Character and Frame*. Moreover, to achieve synchronization, two approaches known as *asynchronous* and *synchronous* transmissions are used.

Frame synchronization is the process by which incoming frame alignment signals (i.e., distinctive bit sequences) are identified, i.e. distinguished from data bits, permitting the data bits within the frame to be extracted for decoding or retransmission. The usual practice is to insert, in a dedicated time slot within the frame, a non-information bit that is used for the actual synchronization of the incoming data with the receiver.

In order to receive bits in the first place, the receiver must be able to determine how fast bits are being sent and when it has received a signal symbol. Further, the receiver needs to be able to determine what the relationship of the bits in the received stream have to one another, that is, what the logical units of transfer are, and where each received bit fits into the logical units. We call these logical units *frames*. This means that in addition to bit (or transmission symbol) synchronization, the receiver needs word and frame synchronization.

Synchronous Communication (bit-oriented)

Timing is recovered from the signal itself (by the carrier if the signal is analog, or by regular transitions in the data signal or by a separate clock line if the signal is digital). Scrambling is often used to ensure frequent transitions needed. The data transmitted may be of any bit length, but is often constrained by the frame transfer protocol (data link or MAC protocol).

Bit-oriented framing only assumes that bit synchronization has been achieved by the underlying hardware, and the incoming bit stream is scanned at all possible bit positions for special patterns generated by the sender. The sender uses a special pattern (a flag pattern) to delimit frames (one flag at each end), and has to provide for data transparency by use of bit stuffing. A commonly used flag pattern is HDLC's 01111110 flag as shown in figure. The bit sequence 01111110 is used for both preamble and postamble for the purpose of synchronization. A frame format for bit-oriented synchronous frame is shown in figure. Apart from the flag bits there are control fields. This field contains the commands, responses and sequences numbers used to maintain the data flow accountability of the link, defines the functions of the frame and initiates the logic to control the movement of traffic between sending and receiving stations.

11010001010100000111110010101010

(a)

01111110   11010001010100000110110010101010   **01111110**

Specific pattern   **(b)**   **Specific pattern**
to represent   **to represent**
start of frame   **end of frame**

Bit oriented framing (a) Data to be sent to the peer, (b) Data after being character stuffed.

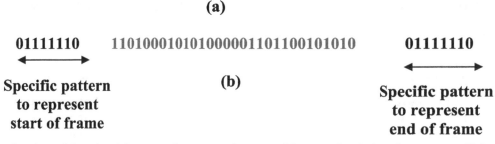

Synchronous frame format

Frame format for synchronous communication

Summary of the approach:

- Initially 1 or 2 synchronization characters are sent

- Data characters are then continuously sent without any extra bits

- At the end, some error detection data is sent

Advantages:

- Much less overhead

- No overhead is incurred except for synchronization characters

Disadvantages:

- No tolerance in clock frequency is allowed

- The clock frequency should be same at both the sending and receiving ends

Bit stuffing: If the flag pattern appears anywhere in the header or data of a frame, then the receiver may prematurely detect the start or end of the received frame. To overcome this problem, the sender makes sure that the frame body it sends has no flags in it at any position (note that since there is no character synchronization, the flag pattern can start at any bit location within the stream). It does this by *bit stuffing*, inserting an extra bit in any pattern that is beginning to look like a flag. In HDLC, whenever 5 consecutive 1's are encountered in the data, a 0 is inserted after the 5th 1, regardless of the next bit in the data as shown in figure. On the receiving end, the bit stream is piped through a shift register as the receiver looks for the flag pattern. If 5 consecutive 1's followed by a 0 is seen, then the 0 is dropped before sending the data on (the receiver destuffs the stream). If 6 1's and a 0 are seen, it is a flag and either the current frame are ended or a new frame is started, depending on the current state of the receiver. If more than 6 consecutive 1's are seen, then the receiver has detected an invalid pattern, and usually the current frame, if any, is discarded.

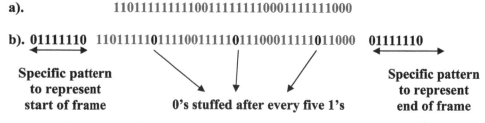

Bit oriented (a) Data to be sent to the peer, (b) Data after being bit stuffed.

With bit stuffing, the boundary between two frames can be unambiguously recognized by the flag pattern. Thus, if receiver loses track of where it is, all it has to do is to scan the input for flag sequence, since they can only occur at frame boundaries and never within data. In addition to receiving the data in logical units called frames, the receiver should have some way of determining if the data has been corrupted or not. If it has been corrupted, it is desirable not only to realize that, but also to make an attempt to obtain the correct data.

Asynchronous Communication (Word-oriented)

In asynchronous communication, small, fixed-length words (usually 5 to 9 bits long) are transferred without any clock line or clock is recovered from the signal itself. Each word has a start bit (usually as a 0) before the first data bit of the word and a stop bit (usually as a 1) after the last data bit of the word, as shown in figure. The receiver's local clock is started when the receiver detects the 1-0 transition of the start bit, and the line is sampled in the middle of the fixed bit intervals (a bit interval is the inverse of the data rate). The sender outputs the bit at the agreed-upon rate, holding the line in the appropriate state for one bit interval for each bit, but using its own local clock to determine the length of these bit intervals. The receiver's clock and the sender's clock may not run at the same speed, so that there is a relative clock drift (this may be caused by variations in the crystals used, temperature, voltage, etc.). If the receiver's clock drifts too much relative to the sender's clock, then the bits may be sampled while the line is in transition from one state to another, causing the receiver to misinterpret the received data. There can be variable amount of gap between two frames as shown in figure.

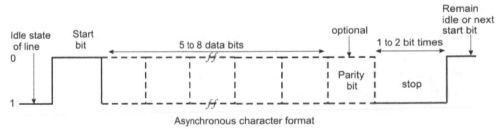

Character or word oriented format for asynchronous mode

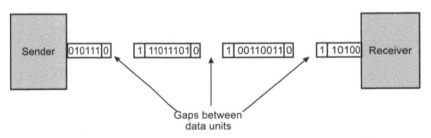

Data units sent with variable gap sent in asynchronous mode

Advantages of asynchronous character oriented mode of communication are summarized below:

- Simple to implement

- Self synchronization; Clock signal need not be sent

- Tolerance in clock frequency is possible

- The bits are sensed in the middle hence ± ½ bit tolerance is provided

This mode of data communication, however, suffers from high overhead incurred in data transmission. Data must be sent in multiples of the data length of the word, and the two or more bits of synchronization overhead compared to the relatively short data length causes the effective data rate to be rather low. For example, 11 bits are required to transmit 8 bits of data. In other words, baud rate (number of signal elements) is higher than data rate.

Character Oriented Framing

The first framing method uses a field in the header to specify the number of characters in the frame. When the data link-layer sees the character count, it knows how many characters follow, and hence where the end of the frame is. This technique is shown in figure for frames of size 6, 4, and 8 characters, respectively. The trouble with this algorithm is that the count can be garbled by a transmission error. For example, if the character count of 4 in the second frame becomes 5, as shown in figure, the destination will get out of synchronization and will be unable to locate the start of next frame. Even if the checksum is incorrect so the destination knows that the frame is bad, it still had no way of telling where the next frame starts. Sending a frame back to the source and asking for retransmission does not help either, since the destination doesn't know how many characters to skip over to the start of retransmission. For this reason the character count method is rarely used.

Character-oriented framing assumes that character synchronization has already been achieved by the hardware. The sender uses special characters to indicate the start and end of frames, and may also use them to indicate header boundaries and to assist the receiver gain character synchronization. Frames must be of an integral character length. Data transparency must be preserved by use of character as shown in figure.

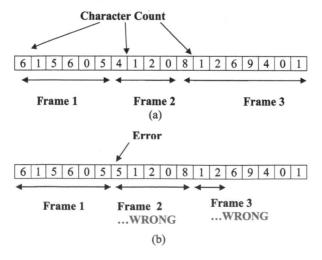

A Character Stream (a) Without error and (b) with error

Most commonly, a DLE (data link escape) character is used to signal that the next character is a control character, with DLE SOH (start of header) used to indicate the start of the frame (it starts with a header), DLE STX (start of text) used to indicate the end of the header and start of the data portion, and DLE ETX (end of text) used to indicate the end of the frame.

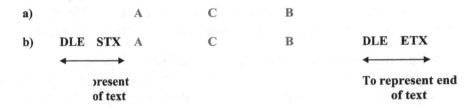

Figure 3.1.13 Character Oriented (a) Data to be send to the peer, (b) Data after being character stuffed

A serious problem occurs with this method when binary data, such as object program are being transmitted. It may easily happen when the characters for DLE STX or DLE ETX occur in the data, which will interfere with the framing. One way to overcome this problem is to use character stuffing discussed below.

Character Stuffing

When a DLE character occurs in the header or the data portion of a frame, the sender must somehow let the receiver know that it is not intended to signal a control character. The sender does this by inserting an extra DLE character after the one occurring inside the frame, so that when the receiver encounters two DLEs in a row, it immediately deletes one and interpret the other as header or data. This is shown in figure. Note that since the receiver has character synchronization, it will not mistake a DLE pattern that crosses a byte boundary as a DLE signal.

a)	DLE DLE	STX ETX	A	DLE	B
b)	DLE DLE	STX ETX	A	DLE	B
c)	DLE DLE	STX ETX	A	DLE	B

Character Stuffing (a). Data send by network layer, (b) Data after being character stuffed by the data link layer. (c) Data passed to the network layer on the receiver side.

The main disadvantage of this method is that it is closely tied to 8-bit characters in general and the ASCII character code in particular. As networks grow, this disadvantage of embedding the character code in framing mechanism becomes more and more obvious, so a new technique had to be developed to allow arbitrary sized character. Bit-oriented frame synchronization and bit stuffing is used that allow data frames to contain an arbitrary number of bits and allow character code with arbitrary number of bits per character.

Data Rate Measures

- The raw data rate (the number of bits that the transmitter can per second without formatting) is only the starting point. There may be overhead for synchronization, for framing, for error checking, for headers and trailers, for retransmissions, etc.

- *Utilization* may mean more than one thing. When dealing with network monitoring and management, it refers to the fraction of the resource actually used (for useful data and for overhead, retransmissions, etc.). In this context, utilization refers to the fraction of the channel that is available for actual data transmission to the next higher layer. It is the ratio of data bits per protocol data unit (PDU) to the total size of the PDU, including synchronization, headers, etc. In other words, it is the ratio of the time spent actually sending useful data to the time it takes to transfer that data and its attendant overhead.

The *effective data rate* at a layer is the net data rate available to the next higher layer. Generally this is the utilization times the raw data rate.

DTE-DCE Interface

As two persons intending to communicate must speak in the same language, for successful communication between two computer systems or between a computer and a peripheral, a natural understanding between the two is essential. In case of two persons a common language known to both of them is used. In case of two computers or a computer and an appliance, this understanding can be ensured with the help of a *standard*, which should be followed by both the parties. Standards are usually recommended by some International bodies, such as, Electronics Industries Association (EIA), The Institution of Electrical and Electronic Engineers (IEEE), etc. The EIA and ITU-T have been involved in developing standards for the DTE-DCE interface known as EIA-232, EIA-442, etc and ITU-T standards are known as V series or X series. The standards should normally define the following four important attributes:

Mechanical: The mechanical attribute concerns the actual physical connection between the two sides. Usually various signal lines are bundled into a cable with a terminator plug, male or female at each end. Each of the systems, between which communication is to be established, provide a plug of opposite gender for connecting the terminator plugs of the cable, thus establishing the physical connection. The mechanical part specifies cables and connectors to be used to link two systems

Electrical: The Electrical attribute relates to the voltage levels and timing of voltage changes. They in turn determine the data rates and distances that can be used for communication. So the electrical part of the standard specifies voltages, Impedances and timing requirements to be satisfied for reliable communication

Functional: Functional attribute pertains to the function to be performed, by associating meaning to the various signal lines. Functions can be typically classified into the broad categories of data control, timing and ground. This component of standard specifies the signal pin assignments and signal definition of each of the pins used for interfacing the devices

Procedural: The procedural attribute specifies the protocol for communication, i.e. the sequence of events that should be followed during data transfer, using the functional characteristic of the interface.

A variety of standards exist, some of the most popular interfaces are presented in this section.

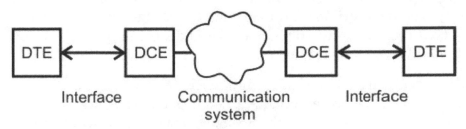

The DTE-DCE interface

The RS-232 C

Most digital data processing devices such as computers and terminals are incapable of transmitting the digital data, which usually is in NRZ-L form, through physical transmission media over long distances. The data processing devices, commonly referred to as *Data Terminal Equipment (DTE)*, utilizes the mediation of another equipment called *Data Circuit communication Equipment (DCE)* to interface with the physical transmission media. An example of a DCE is a MODEM. On the one side, the DCE is responsible for transmitting and receiving bit-serial data in a suitable form for efficient communication through some transmission media such as telephone line. On the other side, the DCE interacts with the DTE by exchanging both data and control information. This is done over a set of wires referred to as interchange circuits. For successful operation of this scheme a high degree of cooperation is required on data processing equipment manufacturers and users, nature of interface between the DTE and DCE. The Electronic Industries Association (EIA) developed the standard RS-232C as an interface between the DTE and DCE as shown in figure. Although developed in 1960, it is still widely used for serial binary data interchange. It specifies all the four attributes mentioned above.

Mechanical: A 25-pin connector (DB-25) or 9-pin connector (DB-9) is commonly used for establishing mechanical connection. In most of the applications, however, fewer number of control lines than specified in the standard are used, as not all the systems require their use. The interface established connection between two types of systems, Data terminal Equipment (DTE) and Data communication Equipment (DCE). The equipment that generates, processes and displays the data is called DTE. Computers and monitors are considered as DTEs. A MODEM, which converts digital data into analog form by modulation and also demodulates analog signal to generate digital data, are considered as data communication equipments (DCEs). Modems are used to establish connection through (Transmission media) analog communication channel, such as a telephone line as shown in figure.

Electrical: The electrical characteristics specify the signaling between DTE and DCE. It uses single-ended, bipolar voltage and unterminated circuit. The single-ended form uses a single conductor to send and another conductor to receive a signal with the voltage reference to a common ground. The bipolar voltage levels are +3 to + 25V for logic 0 and −3 to −25V for logic 1. No termination with a resistor either at input or at output is necessary. The most striking feature is that, the voltage levels are not TTL compatible. This necessitates separate voltage supplies and extra hardware for level conversion from TTL-to-RS 232C and vice versa.

The single-ended unterminated configuration is susceptible to all forms of electromagnetic interference. Noise and cross-talk susceptibility are proportional to the cable length and bandwidth. As a result, the RS-232 C is suitable for serial binary data interchange over a short distance (up to 57 ft) and at low rates (up to 20K baud).

Functional: The functional specification of most of the important lines is given in table. There are two data lines, one for each direction, facilitating full-duplex operation. There are several control and ground lines. The pin number with respect to the connector, abbreviated name and function description of the important lines are given in the table. These nine lines are commonly used.

TABLE: Important RS-232C Pins

Pin No.	Function	Short Name
1	Protective ground	
2	Transmit data to DCE	TxD
3	Receive data from DCE	RxD
4	Request to send to DCE	RTS
5	Clear to send from DCE	CTS
6	Data set ready from DCE	DSR
7	Signal ground	
8	Data carrier detect from DCE	DCD
20	Data terminal ready to DCE	DTR

Procedural: The procedural specification gives the protocol, is the sequence of events to be followed to accomplish data communication.

(i) When a DTE is powered on, after self-test it asserts the Data terminal ready (DTR) signal (pin) to indicate that it is ready to take part in communication. Similarly, when the DCE is powered on and gone through its own self-test, it asserts the Data set Ready (DSR) signal (pin 6) to indicate that it is ready to take part in the communication. When the MODEM detects a carrier on the telephone line, it asserts Data carrier detect (DCD) signal (pin 8).

(ii) When the DTE is ready to send data, it asserts request to send (RTS) signal (pin 4). DCE in turn responds with clear to send (CTS) signal (pin 5), when it is ready to receive data and MODEM start sending carrier over the medium indicating that data transmission is eminent. The CTS signal enables the DTE to start transmission of a data frame.

The procedural specification deals with the legal sequence of events on the action-reaction pair of signal lines. For example, the RTS-CTS control lines form an action-reaction pair. Before sending a data, the DTR-DSR pair should be active and then the DTE asserts the RTS signal. In response to this the modern should generate the CTS signal when ready; thereby indicating that data may be transmitted over the TXD. In this manner the action-reaction pairs of lines allows handshaking needed for asynchronous mode of date communication. It also leads to *flow-control*, the rate at which the two systems can communicate with each other.

Null Modem

In many situations, the distance between two DTEs may be so close that use of modems (DCE), as shown in figure, is unnecessary. In such a case the RS-232 C interface may still be used, but with out the DCEs. A scheme known as null modem is used, in which interconnection is done in such a why that both the DTEs are made to feel as if they have been connected through modems. Essentially, null modem is a cable with two connectors at both ends for interfacing with the DTEs. The reason for this behavior is apparent from the swapping interconnection shown in figure.

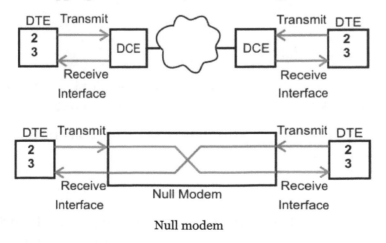

Null modem

Modems

The DCE that is used to interface with the physical transmission media is known as MODEM, derived from MOdulator + DEModulator. The *modulator* converts digital data into an analog signal using ASK, FSK, PSK or QAM modulation techniques. A *demodulator* converts an analog signal back into a digital data. Important Parameters of the modems are the *transmission rate* and Bandwidth (Baud rate). The output of a modem has to match the bandwidth of the bandwidth of the medium, the telephone line as shown in figure.

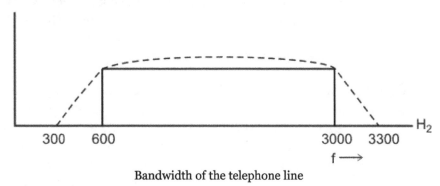

Bandwidth of the telephone line

Error Detection and Correction

In information theory and coding theory with applications in computer science and telecommunication, error detection and correction or error control are techniques that enable reliable delivery of digital data over unreliable communication channels. Many communication channels are subject to channel noise, and thus errors may be introduced during transmission from the source to a receiver. Error detection techniques allow detecting such errors, while error correction enables reconstruction of the original data in many cases.

Definitions

The general definitions of the terms are as follows:

- *Error detection* is the detection of errors caused by noise or other impairments during transmission from the transmitter to the receiver.

- *Error correction* is the detection of errors and reconstruction of the original, error-free data.

History

The modern development of error-correcting codes in 1947 is due to Richard W. Hamming. A description of Hamming's code appeared in Claude Shannon's *A Mathematical Theory of Communication* and was quickly generalized by Marcel J. E. Golay.

Introduction

The general idea for achieving error detection and correction is to add some redundancy (i.e., some extra data) to a message, which receivers can use to check consistency of the delivered message, and to recover data that has been determined to be corrupted. Error-detection and correction schemes can be either systematic or non-systematic: In a systematic scheme, the transmitter sends the original data, and attaches a fixed number of *check bits* (or *parity data*), which are derived from the data bits by some deterministic algorithm. If only error detection is required, a receiver can simply apply the same algorithm to the received data bits and compare its output with the received check bits; if the values do not match, an error has occurred at some point during the transmission. In a system that uses a non-systematic code, the original message is transformed into an encoded message that has at least as many bits as the original message.

Good error control performance requires the scheme to be selected based on the characteristics of the communication channel. Common channel models include memory-less models where errors occur randomly and with a certain probability, and dynamic models where errors occur primarily in bursts. Consequently, error-detecting and correcting codes can be generally distinguished between *random-error-detecting/correcting* and *burst-error-detecting/correcting*. Some codes can also be suitable for a mixture of random errors and burst errors.

If the channel capacity cannot be determined, or is highly variable, an error-detection scheme may be combined with a system for retransmissions of erroneous data. This is known as automatic repeat request (ARQ), and is most notably used in the Internet. An alternate approach for error control is hybrid automatic repeat request (HARQ), which is a combination of ARQ and error-correction coding.

Implementation

Error correction may generally be realized in two different ways:

- *Automatic repeat request (ARQ)* (sometimes also referred to as *backward error correction*): This is an error control technique whereby an error detection scheme is combined with requests for retransmission of erroneous data. Every block of data received is checked using the error detection code used, and if the check fails, retransmission of the data is requested – this may be done repeatedly, until the data can be verified.

- *Forward error correction (FEC)*: The sender encodes the data using an *error-correcting code (ECC)* prior to transmission. The additional information (redundancy) added by the code is used by the receiver to recover the original data. In general, the reconstructed data is what is deemed the "most likely" original data.

ARQ and FEC may be combined, such that minor errors are corrected without retransmission, and major errors are corrected via a request for retransmission: this is called *hybrid automatic repeat-request (HARQ)*.

Error Detection Schemes

Error detection is most commonly realized using a suitable hash function (or checksum algorithm). A hash function adds a fixed-length *tag* to a message, which enables receivers to verify the delivered message by recomputing the tag and comparing it with the one provided.

There exists a vast variety of different hash function designs. However, some are of particularly widespread use because of either their simplicity or their suitability for detecting certain kinds of errors (e.g., the cyclic redundancy check's performance in detecting burst errors).

A random-error-correcting code based on minimum distance coding can provide a strict guarantee on the number of detectable errors, but it may not protect against a preimage attack. A repetition code, described in the section below, is a special case of error-correcting code: although rather inefficient, a repetition code is suitable in some applications of error correction and detection due to its simplicity.

Repetition Codes

A *repetition code* is a coding scheme that repeats the bits across a channel to achieve error-free communication. Given a stream of data to be transmitted, the data are divided into blocks of bits. Each block is transmitted some predetermined number of times. For example, to send the bit pattern "1011", the four-bit block can be repeated three times, thus producing "1011 1011 1011". However, if this twelve-bit pattern was received as "1010 1011 1011" – where the first block is unlike the other two – it can be determined that an error has occurred.

A repetition code is very inefficient, and can be susceptible to problems if the error occurs in exactly the same place for each group (e.g., "1010 1010 1010" in the previous example would be detected as correct). The advantage of repetition codes is that they are extremely simple, and are in fact used in some transmissions of numbers stations.

Parity bits

A *parity bit* is a bit that is added to a group of source bits to ensure that the number of set bits (i.e., bits with value 1) in the outcome is even or odd. It is a very simple scheme that can be used to detect single or any other odd number (i.e., three, five, etc.) of errors in the output. An even number of flipped bits will make the parity bit appear correct even though the data is erroneous.

Extensions and variations on the parity bit mechanism are horizontal redundancy checks, vertical redundancy checks, and "double," "dual," or "diagonal" parity (used in RAID-DP).

Checksums

A *checksum* of a message is a modular arithmetic sum of message code words of a fixed word length (e.g., byte values). The sum may be negated by means of a ones'-complement operation prior to transmission to detect errors resulting in all-zero messages.

Checksum schemes include parity bits, check digits, and longitudinal redundancy checks. Some checksum schemes, such as the Damm algorithm, the Luhn algorithm, and the Verhoeff algorithm, are specifically designed to detect errors commonly introduced by humans in writing down or remembering identification numbers.

Cyclic Redundancy Checks (CRCs)

A *cyclic redundancy check (CRC)* is a non-secure hash function designed to detect accidental changes to digital data in computer networks; as a result, it is not suitable for detecting maliciously introduced errors. It is characterized by specification of what is called a *generator polynomial*, which is used as the divisor in a polynomial long division over a finite field, taking the input data as the dividend, such that the remainder becomes the result.

A cyclic code has favorable properties that make it well suited for detecting burst errors. CRCs are particularly easy to implement in hardware, and are therefore commonly used in digital networks and storage devices such as hard disk drives.

Even parity is a special case of a cyclic redundancy check, where the single-bit CRC is generated by the divisor $x + 1$.

Cryptographic Hash Functions

The output of a *cryptographic hash function*, also known as a *message digest*, can provide strong assurances about data integrity, whether changes of the data are accidental (e.g., due to transmission errors) or maliciously introduced. Any modification to the data will likely be detected through a mismatching hash value. Furthermore, given some hash value, it is infeasible to find some input data (other than the one given) that will yield the same hash value. If an attacker can change not only the message but also the hash value, then a *keyed hash* or message authentication code (MAC) can be used for additional security. Without knowing the key, it is infeasible for the attacker to calculate the correct keyed hash value for a modified message.

Error-correcting Codes

Any error-correcting code can be used for error detection. A code with *minimum Hamming distance, d,* can detect up to $d - 1$ errors in a code word. Using minimum-distance-based error-correcting codes for error detection can be suitable if a strict limit on the minimum number of errors to be detected is desired.

Codes with minimum Hamming distance $d = 2$ are degenerate cases of error-correcting codes, and can be used to detect single errors. The parity bit is an example of a single-error-detecting code.

Error Correction

Automatic Repeat Request (ARQ)

Automatic Repeat Request (ARQ) is an error control method for data transmission that makes use of error-detection codes, acknowledgment and/or negative acknowledgment messages, and timeouts to achieve reliable data transmission. An *acknowledgment* is a message sent by the receiver to indicate that it has correctly received a data frame.

Usually, when the transmitter does not receive the acknowledgment before the timeout occurs (i.e., within a reasonable amount of time after sending the data frame), it retransmits the frame until it is either correctly received or the error persists beyond a predetermined number of retransmissions.

Three types of ARQ protocols are Stop-and-wait ARQ, Go-Back-N ARQ, and Selective Repeat ARQ.

ARQ is appropriate if the communication channel has varying or unknown capacity, such as is the case on the Internet. However, ARQ requires the availability of a back channel, results in possibly increased latency due to retransmissions, and requires the maintenance of buffers and timers for retransmissions, which in the case of network congestion can put a strain on the server and overall network capacity.

For example, ARQ is used on shortwave radio data links in the form of ARQ-E, or combined with multiplexing as ARQ-M.

Error-correcting Code

An error-correcting code (ECC) or forward error correction (FEC) code is a process of adding redundant data, or *parity data*, to a message, such that it can be recovered by a receiver even when a number of errors (up to the capability of the code being used) were introduced, either during the process of transmission, or on storage. Since the receiver does not have to ask the sender for retransmission of the data, a backchannel is not required in forward error correction, and it is therefore suitable for simplex communication such as broadcasting. Error-correcting codes are frequently used in lower-layer communication, as well as for reliable storage in media such as CDs, DVDs, hard disks, and RAM.

Error-correcting codes are usually distinguished between convolutional codes and block codes:

- *Convolutional codes* are processed on a bit-by-bit basis. They are particularly suitable for implementation in hardware, and the Viterbi decoder allows optimal decoding.

- *Block codes* are processed on a block-by-block basis. Early examples of block codes are repetition codes, Hamming codes and multidimensional parity-check codes. They were followed by a number of efficient codes, Reed–Solomon codes being the most notable due to their current widespread use. Turbo codes and low-density parity-check codes (LDPC) are relatively new constructions that can provide almost optimal efficiency.

Shannon's theorem is an important theorem in forward error correction, and describes the maximum information rate at which reliable communication is possible over a channel that has a certain error probability or signal-to-noise ratio (SNR). This strict upper limit is expressed in terms of the channel capacity. More specifically, the theorem says that there exist codes such that with increasing encoding length the probability of error on a discrete memoryless channel can be made arbitrarily small, provided that the code rate is smaller than the channel capacity. The code rate is defined as the fraction k/n of k source symbols and n encoded symbols.

The actual maximum code rate allowed depends on the error-correcting code used, and may be lower. This is because Shannon's proof was only of existential nature, and did not show how to construct codes which are both optimal and have efficient encoding and decoding algorithms.

Hybrid Schemes

Hybrid ARQ is a combination of ARQ and forward error correction. There are two basic approaches:

- Messages are always transmitted with FEC parity data (and error-detection redundancy). A receiver decodes a message using the parity information, and requests retransmission using ARQ only if the parity data was not sufficient for successful decoding (identified through a failed integrity check).

- Messages are transmitted without parity data (only with error-detection information). If a receiver detects an error, it requests FEC information from the transmitter using ARQ, and uses it to reconstruct the original message.

The latter approach is particularly attractive on an erasure channel when using a rateless erasure code.

Applications

Applications that require low latency (such as telephone conversations) cannot use Automatic Repeat Request (ARQ); they must use forward error correction (FEC). By the time an ARQ system discovers an error and re-transmits it, the re-sent data will arrive too late to be any good.

Applications where the transmitter immediately forgets the information as soon as it is sent (such as most television cameras) cannot use ARQ; they must use FEC because when an error occurs, the original data is no longer available. (This is also why FEC is used in data storage systems such as RAID and distributed data store).

Applications that use ARQ must have a return channel; applications having no return channel cannot use ARQ. Applications that require extremely low error rates (such as digital money transfers) must use ARQ. Reliability and inspection engineering also make use of the theory of error-correcting codes.

Internet

In a typical TCP/IP stack, error control is performed at multiple levels:

- Each Ethernet frame carries a CRC-32 checksum. Frames received with incorrect checksums are discarded by the receiver hardware.

- The IPv4 header contains a checksum protecting the contents of the header. Packets with mismatching checksums are dropped within the network or at the receiver.

- The checksum was omitted from the IPv6 header in order to minimize processing costs in network routing and because current link layer technology is assumed to provide sufficient error detection.

- UDP has an optional checksum covering the payload and addressing information from the UDP and IP headers. Packets with incorrect checksums are discarded by the operating system network stack. The checksum is optional under IPv4, only, because the Data-Link layer checksum may already provide the desired level of error protection.

- TCP provides a checksum for protecting the payload and addressing information from the TCP and IP headers. Packets with incorrect checksums are discarded within the network stack, and eventually get retransmitted using ARQ, either explicitly (such as through triple-ack) or implicitly due to a timeout.

Deep-space Telecommunications

Development of error-correction codes was tightly coupled with the history of deep-space missions due to the extreme dilution of signal power over interplanetary distances, and the limited power availability aboard space probes. Whereas early missions sent their data uncoded, starting from 1968 digital error correction was implemented in the form of (sub-optimally decoded) convolutional codes and Reed–Muller codes. The Reed–Muller code was well suited to the noise the spacecraft was subject to (approximately matching a bell curve), and was implemented at the Mariner spacecraft for missions between 1969 and 1977.

The Voyager 1 and Voyager 2 missions, which started in 1977, were designed to deliver color imaging amongst scientific information of Jupiter and Saturn. This resulted in increased coding requirements, and thus the spacecraft were supported by (optimally Viterbi-decoded) convolutional codes that could be concatenated with an outer Golay (24,12,8) code.

The Voyager 2 craft additionally supported an implementation of a Reed–Solomon code: the concatenated Reed–Solomon–Viterbi (RSV) code allowed for very powerful error correction, and enabled the spacecraft's extended journey to Uranus and Neptune. Both craft use V2 RSV coding due to ECC system upgrades after 1989.

The CCSDS currently recommends usage of error correction codes with performance similar to the Voyager 2 RSV code as a minimum. Concatenated codes are increasingly falling out of favor with space missions, and are replaced by more powerful codes such as Turbo codes or LDPC codes.

The different kinds of deep space and orbital missions that are conducted suggest that trying to find a "one size fits all" error correction system will be an ongoing problem for some time to come. For missions close to Earth the nature of the channel noise is different from that which a spacecraft on an interplanetary mission experiences. Additionally, as a spacecraft increases its distance from Earth, the problem of correcting for noise gets larger.

Satellite Broadcasting (DVB)

The demand for satellite transponder bandwidth continues to grow, fueled by the desire to deliver television (including new channels and High Definition TV) and IP data. Transponder availability and bandwidth constraints have limited this growth, because transponder capacity is determined by the selected modulation scheme and Forward error correction (FEC) rate.

Overview

- QPSK coupled with traditional Reed Solomon and Viterbi codes have been used for nearly 20 years for the delivery of digital satellite TV.

- Higher order modulation schemes such as 8PSK, 16QAM and 32QAM have enabled the satellite industry to increase transponder efficiency by several orders of magnitude.

- This increase in the information rate in a transponder comes at the expense of an increase in the carrier power to meet the threshold requirement for existing antennas.

- Tests conducted using the latest chipsets demonstrate that the performance achieved by using Turbo Codes may be even lower than the 0.8 dB figure assumed in early designs.

Data Storage

Error detection and correction codes are often used to improve the reliability of data storage media. A "parity track" was present on the first magnetic tape data storage in 1951. The "Optimal Rectangular Code" used in group coded recording tapes not only detects but also corrects single-bit errors. Some file formats, particularly archive formats, include a checksum (most often CRC32) to detect corruption and truncation and can employ redundancy and/or parity files to recover portions of corrupted data. Reed Solomon codes are used in compact discs to correct errors caused by scratches.

Modern hard drives use CRC codes to detect and Reed–Solomon codes to correct minor errors in sector reads, and to recover data from sectors that have "gone bad" and store that data in the spare sectors. RAID systems use a variety of error correction techniques to correct errors when a hard drive completely fails. Filesystems such as ZFS or Btrfs, as well as some RAID implementations, support data scrubbing and resilvering, which allows bad blocks to be detected and (hopefully) recovered before they are used. The recovered data may be re-written to exactly the same physical location, to spare blocks elsewhere on the same piece of hardware, or to replacement hardware.

Error-correcting Memory

DRAM memory may provide increased protection against soft errors by relying on error correcting codes. Such error-correcting memory, known as *ECC* or *EDAC-protected* memory, is particularly desirable for high fault-tolerant applications, such as servers, as well as deep-space applications due to increased radiation.

Error-correcting memory controllers traditionally use Hamming codes, although some use triple modular redundancy.

Interleaving allows distributing the effect of a single cosmic ray potentially upsetting multiple physically neighboring bits across multiple words by associating neighboring bits to different words. As long as a single event upset (SEU) does not exceed the error threshold (e.g., a single error) in any particular word between accesses, it can be corrected (e.g., by a single-bit error correcting code), and the illusion of an error-free memory system may be maintained.

In addition to hardware providing features required for ECC memory to operate, operating systems usually contain related reporting facilities that are used to provide notifications when soft errors are transparently recovered. An increasing rate of soft errors might indicate that a DIMM module needs replacing, and such feedback information would not be easily available without the related reporting capabilities. An example is the Linux kernel's *EDAC* subsystem (previously known as *bluesmoke*), which collects the data from error-checking-enabled components inside a computer system; beside collecting and reporting back the events related to ECC memory, it also supports other checksumming errors, including those detected on the PCI bus.

A few systems also support memory scrubbing.

Environmental interference and physical defects in the communication medium can cause random bit errors during data transmission. Error coding is a method of detecting and correcting these errors to ensure information is transferred intact from its source to its destination. Error coding is used for fault tolerant computing in computer memory, magnetic and optical data storage media, satellite and deep space communications, network communications, cellular telephone networks, and almost any other form of digital data communication. Error coding uses mathematical formulas to encode data bits at the source into longer bit words for transmission. The "code word" can then be decoded at the destination to retrieve the information. The extra bits in the code word provide *redundancy* that, according to the coding scheme used, will allow the destination to use the decoding process to determine if the communication medium introduced errors and in some cases correct them so that the data need not be retransmitted. Different error coding schemes are chosen depending on the types of errors expected, the communication medium's expected error rate, and whether or not data retransmission is possible. Faster processors and better communications technology make more complex coding schemes, with better error detecting and correcting capabilities, possible for smaller embedded systems, allowing for more robust communications. However, tradeoffs between bandwidth and coding overhead, coding complexity and allowable coding delay between transmissions, must be considered for each application.

Even if we know what type of errors can occur, we can't simple recognize them. We can do this simply by comparing this copy received with another copy of intended transmission. In this mechanism the source data block is send twice. The receiver compares them with the help of a comparator and if those two blocks differ, a request for re-transmission is made. To achieve forward error correction, three sets of the same data block are sent and majority decision selects the correct block. These methods are very inefficient and increase the traffic two or three times. Fortunately there are more efficient error detection and correction codes. There are two basic strategies for dealing with errors. One way is to include enough redundant information (extra bits are introduced into the data stream at the transmitter on a regular and logical basis) along with each block of data sent to enable the receiver to deduce what the transmitted character must have been. The other way is to include only enough redundancy to allow the receiver to deduce that error has occurred, but not which error has occurred and the receiver asks for a retransmission. The former strategy uses Error-Correcting Codes and latter uses Error-detecting Codes.

To understand how errors can be handled, it is necessary to look closely at what error really is. Normally, a frame consists of m-data bits (i.e., message bits) and r-redundant bits (or check bits). Let the total number of bits be n (m + r). An n-bit unit containing data and check-bits is often referred to as an n-bit codeword.

Given any two code-words, say 10010101 and 11010100, it is possible to determine how many corresponding bits differ, just EXCLUSIVE OR the two code-words, and count the number of 1's in the result. The number of bits position in which code words differ is called the Hamming distance. If two code words are a Hamming distance d-apart, it will require d single-bit errors to convert one code word to other. The error detecting and correcting properties depends on its Hamming distance.

- To detect d errors, you need a distance (d+1) code because with such a code there is no way that d-single bit errors can change a valid code word into another valid code word. Whenever receiver sees an invalid code word, it can tell that a transmission error has occurred.

- Similarly, to correct d errors, you need a distance 2d+1 code because that way the legal code words are so far apart that even with d changes, the original code-word is still closer than any other code-word, so it can be uniquely determined.

Types of Errors

These interferences can change the timing and shape of the signal. If the signal is carrying binary encoded data, such changes can alter the meaning of the data. These errors can be divided into two types: Single-bit error and Burst error.

Single-bit Error

The term single-bit error means that only one bit of given data unit (such as a byte, character, or data unit) is changed from 1 to 0 or from 0 to 1 as shown in figure.

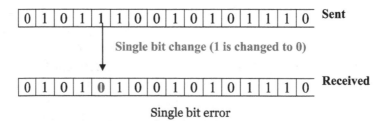

Single bit error

Single bit errors are least likely type of errors in serial data transmission. To see why, imagine a sender sends data at 10 Mbps. This means that each bit lasts only for 0.1 μs (micro-second). For a single bit error to occur noise must have duration of only 0.1 μs (micro-second), which is very rare. However, a single-bit error can happen if we are having a parallel data transmission. For example, if 16 wires are used to send all 16 bits of a word at the same time and one of the wires is noisy, one bit is corrupted in each word.

Burst Error

The term burst error means that two or more bits in the data unit have changed from 0 to 1 or vice-versa. Note that burst error doesn't necessary means that error occurs in consecutive bits. The length of the burst error is measured from the first corrupted bit to the last corrupted bit. Some bits in between may not be corrupted.

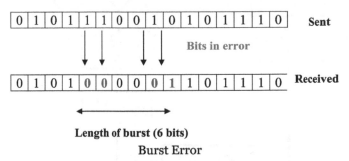

Length of burst (6 bits)

Burst Error

Burst errors are mostly likely to happen in serial transmission. The duration of the noise is normally longer than the duration of a single bit, which means that the noise affects data; it affects a set of bits as shown in figure. The number of bits affected depends on the data rate and duration of noise.

Error Detecting Codes

Basic approach used for error detection is the use of redundancy, where additional bits are added to facilitate detection and correction of errors. Popular techniques are:

- Simple Parity check
- Two-dimensional Parity check
- Checksum
- Cyclic redundancy check

Simple Parity Checking or One-dimension Parity Check

The most common and least expensive mechanism for error- detection is the simple parity check. In this technique, a redundant bit called parity bit, is appended to every data unit so that the number of 1s in the unit (including the parity becomes even).

Blocks of data from the source are subjected to a check bit or *Parity bit* generator form, where a parity of 1 is added to the block if it contains an odd number of 1's (ON bits) and 0 is added if it contains an even number of 1's. At the receiving end the parity bit is computed from the received data bits and compared with the received parity bit, as shown in figure. This scheme makes the total number of 1's even, that is why it is called *even parity checking*. Considering a 4-bit word, different combinations of the data words and the corresponding code words are given in table.

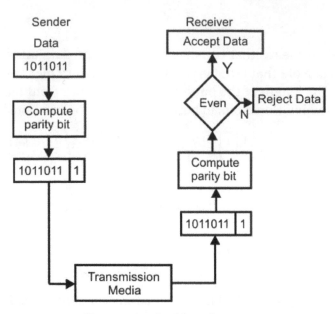

Even-parity checking scheme

Table Possible 4-bit data words and corresponding code words

Decimal value	Data Block	Parity bit	Code word
0	0000	0	00000
1	0001	1	00011
2	0010	1	00101
3	0011	0	00110
4	0100	1	01001
5	0101	0	01010
6	0110	0	01100
7	0111	1	01111
8	1000	1	10001
9	1001	0	10010
10	1010	0	10100
11	1011	1	10111
12	1100	0	11000
13	1101	1	11011
14	1110	1	11101
15	1111	0	11110

Note that for the sake of simplicity, we are discussing here the even-parity checking, where the number of 1's should be an even number. It is also possible to use *odd-parity* checking, where the number of 1's should be odd.

Performance

An observation of the table reveals that to move from one code word to another, at least two data bits should be changed. Hence these set of code words are said to have a minimum distance (*hamming distance*) of 2, which means that a receiver that has knowledge of the code word set can detect all single bit errors in each code word. However, if two errors occur in the code word, it becomes another valid member of the set and the decoder will see only another valid code word and know nothing of the error. Thus errors in more than one bit cannot be detected. In fact it can be shown that a single parity check code can detect only odd number of errors in a code word.

Two-dimension Parity Check

Performance can be improved by using two-dimensional parity check, which organizes the block of bits in the form of a table. Parity check bits are calculated for each row, which is equivalent to a simple parity check bit. Parity check bits are also calculated for all columns then both are sent along with the data. At the receiving end these are compared with the parity bits calculated on the received data. This is illustrated in figure.

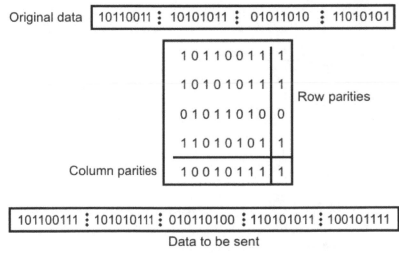

Two-dimension Parity Checking

Performance

Two- Dimension Parity Checking increases the likelihood of detecting burst errors. As we have shown in figure that a 2-D Parity check of n bits can detect a burst error of n bits. A burst error of more than n bits is also detected by 2-D Parity check with a high-probability. There is, however, one pattern of error that remains elusive. If two bits in one data unit are damaged and two bits in exactly same position in another data unit are also damaged, the 2-D Parity check checker will not detect an error. For example, if two data units: 11001100 and 10101100. If first and second from last bits in each of them is changed, making the data units as 01001110 and 00101110, the error cannot be detected by 2-D Parity check.

Checksum

In checksum error detection scheme, the data is divided into k segments each of m bits. In the sender's end the segments are added using 1's complement arithmetic to get the sum. The sum is complemented to get the checksum. The checksum segment is sent along with the data segments as shown in figure. At the receiver's end, all received segments are added using 1's complement arithmetic to get the sum. The sum is complemented. If the result is zero, the received data is accepted; otherwise discarded, as shown in figure.

Performance

The checksum detects all errors involving an odd number of bits. It also detects most errors involving even number of bits.

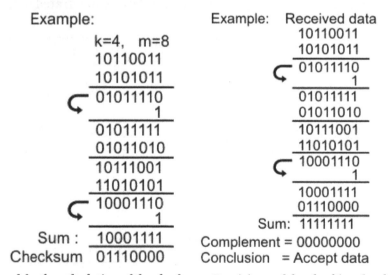

Sender's end for the calculation of the checksum, Receiving end for checking the checksum

Cyclic Redundancy Checks (CRC)

This Cyclic Redundancy Check is the most powerful and easy to implement technique. Unlike checksum scheme, which is based on addition, CRC is based on binary division. In CRC, a sequence of redundant bits, called cyclic redundancy check bits, are appended to the end of data unit so that the resulting data unit becomes exactly divisible by a second, predetermined binary number. At the destination, the incoming data unit is divided by the same number. If at this step there is no remainder, the data unit is assumed to be correct and is therefore accepted. A remainder indicates that the data unit has been damaged in transit and therefore must be rejected. The generalized technique can be explained as follows.

If a k bit message is to be transmitted, the transmitter generates an r-bit sequence, known as *Frame Check Sequence* (FCS) so that the $(k+r)$ bits are actually being transmitted. Now this r-bit FCS is generated by dividing the original number, appended by r zeros, by *a* predetermined number. This number, which is $(r+1)$ bit in length, can also be considered as the coefficients of a polynomial, called *Generator Polynomial*. The remainder of this division process generates the r-bit FCS. On receiving the packet, the receiver divides the $(k+r)$ bit frame by the same predetermined number and if it produces no remainder, it can be assumed that no error has occurred during the transmission. Operations at both the sender and receiver end are shown in figure.

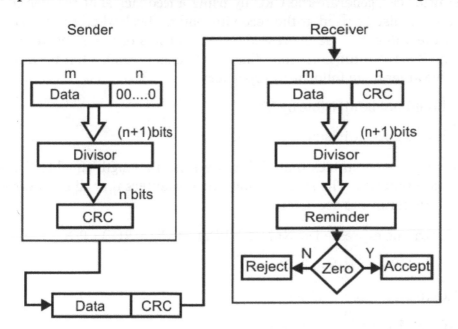

Basic scheme for Cyclic Redundancy Checking

This mathematical operation performed is illustrated in figure by dividing a sample 4-bit number by the coefficient of the generator polynomial x^3+x+1, which is 1011, using the modulo-2 arithmetic. Modulo-2 arithmetic is a binary addition process without any carry over, which is just the Exclusive-OR operation. Consider the case where k=1101. Hence we have to divide 1101000 (i.e. k appended by 3 zeros) by 1011, which produces the remainder r=001, so that the bit frame $(k+r)$ =1101001 is actually being transmitted through the communication channel. At the receiving end, if the received number, i.e., 1101001 is divided by the same generator polynomial 1011 to get the remainder as 000, it can be assumed that the data is free of errors.

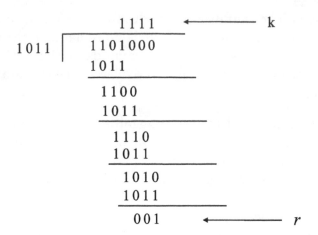

Cyclic Redundancy Checks (CRC)

The transmitter can generate the CRC by using a feedback shift register circuit. The same circuit can also be used at the receiving end to check whether any error has occurred. All the values can be expressed as polynomials of a dummy variable X. For example, for P = 11001 the corresponding polynomial is X^4+X^3+1. A polynomial is selected to have at least the following properties:

   o It should not be divisible by X.

   o It should not be divisible by (X+1).

The first condition guarantees that all burst errors of a length equal to the degree of polynomial are detected. The second condition guarantees that all burst errors affecting an odd number of bits are detected.

CRC process can be expressed as XnM(X)/P(X) = Q(X) + R(X) / P(X)

Commonly used divisor polynomials are:

   - CRC-16 = $X^{16} + X^{15} + X^2 + 1$

   - CRC-CCITT = $X^{16} + X^{12} + X^5 + 1$

   - CRC-32 = $X^{32} + X^{26} + X^{23} + X^{22} + X^{16} + X^{12} + X^{11} + X^{10} + X^8 + X^7 + X^5 + X^4 + X^2 + 1$

Performance

CRC is a very effective error detection technique. If the divisor is chosen according to the previously mentioned rules, its performance can be summarized as follows:

   - CRC can detect all single-bit errors

   - CRC can detect all double-bit errors (three 1's)

- CRC can detect any odd number of errors (X+1)

- CRC can detect all burst errors of less than the degree of the polynomial.

- CRC detects most of the larger burst errors with a high probability.

- For example CRC-12 detects 99.97% of errors with a length 12 or more.

Error Correcting Codes

The techniques that we have discussed so far can detect errors, but do not correct them. Error Correction can be handled in two ways.

o One is when an error is discovered; the receiver can have the sender retransmit the entire data unit. This is known as backward error correction.

o In the other, receiver can use an error-correcting code, which automatically corrects certain errors. This is known as forward error correction.

In theory it is possible to correct any number of errors atomically. Error-correcting codes are more sophisticated than error detecting codes and require more redundant bits. The number of bits required to correct multiple-bit or burst error is so high that in most of the cases it is inefficient to do so. For this reason, most error correction is limited to one, two or at the most three-bit errors.

Single-bit Error Correction

Concept of error-correction can be easily understood by examining the simplest case of single-bit errors. As we have already seen that a single-bit error can be detected by addition of a parity bit (VRC) with the data, which needed to be send. A single additional bit can detect error, but it's not sufficient enough to correct that error too. For correcting an error one has to know the exact position of error, i.e. exactly which bit is in error (to locate the invalid bits). For example, to correct a single-bit error in an ASCII character, the error correction must determine which one of the seven bits is in error. To this, we have to add some additional redundant bits.

To calculate the numbers of redundant bits (r) required to correct d data bits, let us find out the relationship between the two. So we have (d+r) as the total number of bits, which are to be transmitted; then r must be able to indicate at least d+r+1 different values. Of these, one value means no error, and remaining d+r values indicate error location of error in each of d+r locations. So, d+r+1 states must be distinguishable by r bits, and r bits can indicates 2^r states. Hence, 2^r must be greater than d+r+1.

$2^r >= d+r+1$

The value of r must be determined by putting in the value of d in the relation. For example, if d is 7, then the smallest value of r that satisfies the above relation is 4. So the total bits, which are to be transmitted is 11 bits (d+r = 7+4 =11).

Now let us examine how we can manipulate these bits to discover which bit is in error. A technique developed by R.W.Hamming provides a practical solution. The solution or coding scheme he developed is commonly known as Hamming Code. Hamming code can be applied to data units of any length and uses the relationship between the data bits and redundant bits as discussed.

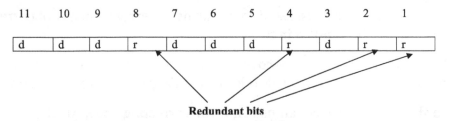

Redundant bits

Positions of redundancy bits in hamming code

Basic approach for error detection by using Hamming code is as follows:

- To each group of m information bits k parity bits are added to form (m+k) bit code as shown in figure.

- Location of each of the (m+k) digits is assigned a decimal value.

- The k parity bits are placed in positions 1, 2, ..., 2^{k-1} positions.–K parity checks are performed on selected digits of each codeword.

- At the receiving end the parity bits are recalculated. The decimal value of the k parity bits provides the bit-position in error, if any.

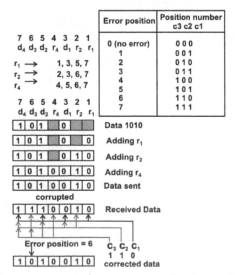

Use of Hamming code for error correction for a 4-bit data

Figure shows how hamming code is used for correction for 4-bit numbers $(d_4d_3d_2d_1)$ with the help of three redundant bits $(r_3r_2r_1)$. For the example data 1010, first r1 (0) is calculated considering the parity of the bit positions, 1, 3, 5 and 7. Then the parity bits r_2 is calculated considering bit positions 2, 3, 6 and 7. Finally, the parity bits r_4 is calculated considering bit positions 4, 5, 6 and 7 as shown. If any corruption occurs in any of the transmitted code 1010010, the bit position in error can be found out by calculating $r_3r_2r_1$ at the receiving end. For example, if the received code word is 1110010, the recalculated value of $r_3r_2r_1$ is 110, which indicates that bit position in error is 6, the decimal value of 110.

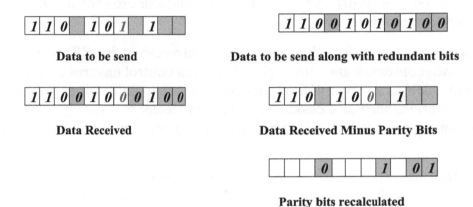

Calculations:

Parity recalculated (r8, r4, r2, r1) = 0101$_2$ = 5$_{10}$.

Hence, bit 5th is in error i.e. d5 is in error.

So, correct code-word which was transmitted is:

1	1	0		1	0	1		1		

Figure: Use of Hamming code for error correction for a 5-bit data

Flow Control and Error Control

As we have mentioned earlier, for reliable and efficient data communication a great deal of coordination is necessary between at least two machines. Some of these are necessary because of the following constraints:

- Both sender and receiver have limited speed

- Both sender and receiver have limited memory

It is necessary to satisfy the following requirements:

- A fast sender should not overwhelm a slow receiver, which must perform a certain amount of processing before passing the data on to the higher-level software.

- If error occur during transmission, it is necessary to devise mechanism to correct it

The most important functions of Data Link layer to satisfy the above requirements are error control and flow control. Collectively, these functions are known as data link control, as discussed in this lesson.

Flow Control is a technique so that transmitter and receiver with different speed characteristics can communicate with each other. Flow control ensures that a transmitting station, such as a server with higher processing capability, does not overwhelm a receiving station, such as a desktop system, with lesser processing capability. This is where there is an orderly flow of transmitted data between the source and the destination.

Error Control involves both error detection and error correction. It is necessary because errors are inevitable in data communication, in spite of the use of better equipment and reliable transmission media based on the current technology. In the preceding lesson we have already discussed how errors can be detected. In this lesson we shall discuss how error control is performed based on retransmission of the corrupted data. When an error is detected, the receiver can have the specified frame retransmitted by the sender. This process is commonly known as Automatic Repeat Request (ARQ). For example, Internet's Unreliable Delivery Model allows packets to be discarded if network resources are not available, and demands that ARQ protocols make provisions for retransmission.

In data communications, flow control is the process of managing the rate of data transmission between two nodes to prevent a fast sender from overwhelming a slow receiver. It provides a mechanism for the receiver to control the transmission speed, so that the receiving node is not overwhelmed with data from transmitting node. Flow control should be distinguished from congestion control, which is used for controlling the flow of data when congestion has actually occurred. Flow control mechanisms can be classified by whether or not the receiving node sends feedback to the sending node.

Flow control is important because it is possible for a sending computer to transmit information at a faster rate than the destination computer can receive and process it. This can happen if the receiving computers have a heavy traffic load in comparison to the sending computer, or if the receiving computer has less processing power than the sending computer.

Stop-and-wait

Stop-and-wait flow control is the simplest form of flow control. In this method, the receiver indicates its readiness to receive data for each frame, the message is broken into multiple frames. The sender waits for an ACK (acknowledgement) after every frame for specified time (called time out). It is sent to ensure that the receiver has received the frame correctly. It will then send the next frame only after the ACK has been received.

Operations

1. Sender: Transmits a single frame at a time.

2. Receiver: Transmits acknowledgement (ACK) as it receives a frame.

3. Sender receive ACK within time out.

4. Go to step 1.

If a frame or ACK is lost during transmission then it has to be transmitted again by sender. This re-transmission process is known as ARQ (automatic repeat request).

The problem with Stop-and wait is that only one frame can be transmitted at a time, and that often leads to inefficient transmission, because until the sender receives the ACK it cannot transmit any new packet. During this time both the sender and the channel are unutilised.

Pros and Cons of Stop and Wait

Pros

The only advantage of this method of flow control is its simplicity.

Cons

The sender needs to wait for the ACK after every frame it transmits. This is a source of inefficiency, and is particularly bad when the propagation delay is much longer than the transmission delay.

Stop and wait can also create inefficiencies when sending longer transmissions. When longer transmissions are sent there is more likely chance for error in this protocol. If the messages are short the errors are more likely to be detected early. More inefficiency is created when single messages are broken into separate frames because it makes the transmission longer.

Sliding Window

A method of flow control in which a receiver gives a transmitter permission to transmit data until a window is full. When the window is full, the transmitter must stop transmitting until the receiver advertises a larger window.

Sliding-window flow control is best utilized when the buffer size is limited and pre-established. During a typical communication between a sender and a receiver the receiver allocates buffer space for n frames (n is the buffer size in frames). The sender can send and the receiver can accept n frames without having to wait for an acknowledgement. A sequence number is assigned to frames in order to help keep track of those frames which did receive an acknowledgement. The receiver acknowledges a frame by sending an acknowledgement that includes the sequence number of the next frame expected. This acknowledgement announces that the receiver is ready to receive n frames, beginning with the number specified. Both the sender and receiver maintain what is called a window. The size of the window is less than or equal to the buffer size.

Sliding window flow control has a far better performance than stop-and-wait flow control. For example, in a wireless environment if data rates are low and noise level is very high, waiting for an acknowledgement for every packet that is transferred is not very feasible. Therefore, transferring data as a bulk would yield a better performance in terms of higher throughput.

Sliding window flow control is a point to point protocol assuming that no other entity tries to communicate until the current data transfer is complete. The window maintained by the sender indicates which frames he can send. The sender sends all the frames in the window and waits for an acknowledgement (as opposed to acknowledging after every frame). The sender then shifts the window to the corresponding sequence number, thus indicating that frames within the window starting from the current sequence number can be sent.

Go Back N

An automatic repeat request (ARQ) algorithm, used for error correction, in which a negative acknowledgement (NAK) causes retransmission of the word in error as well as the previous N–1 words. The value of N is usually chosen such that the time taken to transmit the N words is less than the round trip delay from transmitter to receiver and back again. Therefore, a buffer is not needed at the receiver.

The normalized propagation delay (a) $= \text{propagation time (Tp)}/\text{transmission time (Tt)}$, where Tp = Length (L) over propagation velocity (V) and Tt = bitrate (r) over Framerate (F). So that a $= \text{LF}/\text{Vr}$.

To get the utilization you must define a window size (N). If N is greater than or equal to 2a + 1 then the utilization is 1 (full utilization) for the transmission channel. If it is less than 2a + 1 then the equation $N/_{1+2a}$ must be used to compute utilization.

Selective Repeat

Selective Repeat is a connection oriented protocol in which both transmitter and receiver have a window of sequence numbers. The protocol has a maximum number of messages that can be sent without acknowledgement. If this window becomes full, the protocol is blocked until an acknowledgement is received for the earliest outstanding message. At this point the transmitter is clear to send more messages.

Comparison

This section is geared towards the idea of comparing Stop-and-wait, Sliding Window with the subsets of Go Back N and Selective Repeat.

Stop-and-wait

Error free: $\dfrac{1}{2a+1}$.

With errors: $\dfrac{1-P}{2a+1}$.

Selective Repeat

We define throughput T as the average number of blocks communicated per transmitted block. It is more convenient to calculate the average number of transmissions necessary to communicate a block, a quantity we denote by o, and then to determine T from the equation $T = \dfrac{1}{b}$.

Transmit Flow Control

Transmit flow control may occur:

- between data terminal equipment (DTE) and a switching center, via data circuit-terminating equipment (DCE), the opposite types interconnected straightforwardly,

- or between two devices of the same type (two DTEs, or two DCEs), interconnected by a crossover cable.

The transmission rate may be controlled because of network or DTE requirements. Transmit flow control can occur independently in the two directions of data transfer, thus permitting the transfer rates in one direction to be different from the transfer rates in the other direction. Transmit flow control can be

- either stop-and-wait,

- or use a sliding window.

Flow control can be performed

- either by control signal lines in a data communication interface.

- or by reserving in-band control characters to signal flow start and stop (such as the ASCII codes for XON/XOFF).

Hardware Flow Control

In common RS-232 there are pairs of control lines which are usually referred to as *hardware flow control*:

- RTS (Request To Send) and CTS (Clear To Send), used in RTS flow control

- DTR (Data Terminal Ready) and DSR (Data Set Ready), DTR flow control

Hardware flow control is typically handled by the DTE or "master end", as it is first raising or asserting its line to command the other side:

- In the case of RTS control flow, DTE sets its RTS, which signals the opposite end (the slave end such as a DCE) to begin monitoring its data input line. When ready for data, the slave end will raise its complementary line, CTS in this example, which signals the master to start sending data, and for the master to begin monitoring the slave's data output line. If either end needs to stop the data, it lowers its respective "data readyness" line.

- For PC-to-modem and similar links, in the case of DTR flow control, DTR/DSR are raised for the entire modem session (say a dialup internet call where DTR is raised to signal the modem to dial, and DSR is raised by the modem when the connection is complete), and RTS/CTS are raised for each block of data.

An example of hardware flow control is a Half-duplex radio modem to computer interface. In this case, the controlling software in the modem and computer may be written to give priority to incoming radio signals such that outgoing data from the computer is paused by lowering CTS if the modem detects a reception.

Polarity

- RS-232 level signals are inverted by the driver ICs, so line is TxD-, RxD-, CTS+, RTS+ (Clear to send when HI, Data 1 is a LO)

- for microprocessor pins the signals are TxD+, RxD+, CTS-, RTS- (Clear to send when LO, Data 1 is a HI)

Software Flow Control

Conversely, XON/XOFF is usually referred to as software flow control.

Open-loop Flow Control

The open-loop flow control mechanism is characterized by having no feedback between the receiver and the transmitter. This simple means of control is widely used. The allocation of resources must be a "prior reservation" or "hop-to-hop" type.

Open-loop flow control has inherent problems with maximizing the utilization of network resources. Resource allocation is made at connection setup using a CAC (Connection Admission Control) and this allocation is made using information that is already "old news" during the lifetime of the connection. Often there is an over-allocation of resources and reserved but unused capacities are wasted. Open-loop flow control is used by ATM in its CBR, VBR and UBR services.

Open-loop flow control incorporates two controls; the controller and a regulator. The regulator is able to alter the input variable in response to the signal from the controller. An open-loop system has no feedback or feed forward mechanism, so the input and output signals are not directly related and there is increased traffic variability. There is also a lower arrival rate in such system and a higher loss rate. In an open control system, the controllers can operate the regulators at regular intervals, but there is no assurance that the output variable can be maintained at the desired level. While it may be cheaper to use this model, the open-loop model can be unstable.

Closed-loop Flow Control

The closed-loop flow control mechanism is characterized by the ability of the network to report pending network congestion back to the transmitter. This information is then used by the transmitter in various ways to adapt its activity to existing network conditions. Closed-loop flow control is used by ABR (see traffic contract and congestion control). Transmit flow control described above is a form of closed-loop flow control.

This system incorporates all the basic control elements, such as, the sensor, transmitter, controller and the regulator. The sensor is used to capture a process variable. The process variable is sent to a transmitter which translates the variable to the controller. The controller examines the information with respect to a desired value and initiates a correction action if required. The controller then communicates to the regulator what action is needed to ensure that the output variable value is matching the desired value. Therefore, there is a high degree of assurance that the output variable can be maintained at the desired level. The closed-loop control system can be a feedback or a feed forward system:

A feedback closed-loop system has a feed-back mechanism that directly relates the input and output signals. The feed-back mechanism monitors the output variable and determines if additional correction is required. The output variable value that is fed backward is used to initiate that corrective action on a regulator. Most control loops in the industry are of the feedback type.

In a feed-forward closed loop system, the measured process variable is an input variable. The measured signal is then used in the same fashion as in a feedback system.

The closed-loop model produces lower loss rate and queuing delays, as well as it results in congestion-responsive traffic. The closed-loop model is always stable, as the number of active lows is bounded.

Error Control Techniques

When an error is detected in a message, the receiver sends a request to the transmitter to retransmit the ill-fated message or packet. The most popular retransmission scheme is known as Automatic-Repeat-Request (ARQ). Such schemes, where receiver asks transmitter to re-transmit if it detects an error, are known as reverse error correction techniques. There exist three popular ARQ techniques, as shown in figure.

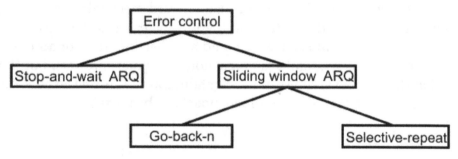

Error control techniques

Stop-and-Wait ARQ

In Stop-and-Wait ARQ, which is simplest among all protocols, the sender (say station A) transmits a frame and then waits till it receives positive acknowledgement (ACK) or negative acknowledgement (NACK) from the receiver (say station B). Station B sends an ACK if the frame is received correctly, otherwise it sends NACK. Station A sends a new frame after receiving ACK; otherwise it retransmits the old frame, if it receives a NACK. This is illustrated in figure.

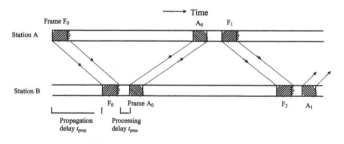

Stop-And-Wait ARQ technique

To tackle the problem of a lost or damaged frame, the sender is equipped with a timer. In case of a lost ACK, the sender transmits the old frame. In the figure, the second PDU of Data is lost during transmission. The sender is unaware of this loss, but starts a timer after sending each PDU. Normally an ACK PDU is received before the timer expires. In this case no ACK is received, and the timer counts down to zero and triggers retransmission of the same PDU by the sender. The sender always starts a timer following transmission, but in the second transmission receives an ACK PDU before the timer expires, finally indicating that the data has now been received by the remote node.

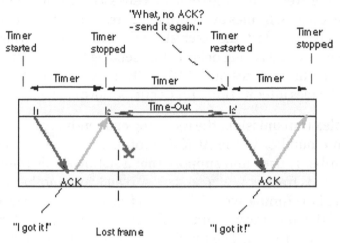

Retransmission due to lost frame

The receiver now can identify that it has received a duplicate frame from the label of the frame and it is discarded

To tackle the problem of damaged frames, say a frame that has been corrupted during the transmission due to noise, there is a concept of NACK frames, i.e. Negative Acknowledge frames. Receiver transmits a NACK frame to the sender if it founds the received frame to be corrupted. When a NACK is received by a transmitter before the time-out, the old frame is sent again as shown in figure.

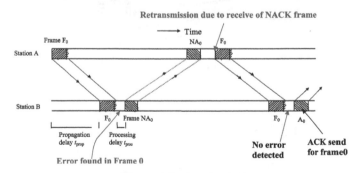

Retransmission due to damaged frame

The main advantage of stop-and-wait ARQ is its simplicity. It also requires minimum buffer size. However, it makes highly inefficient use of communication links, particularly when 'a' is large.

Go-back-N ARQ

The most popular ARQ protocol is the go-back-N ARQ, where the sender sends the frames continuously without waiting for acknowledgement. That is why it is also called as *continuous ARQ*. As the receiver receives the frames, it keeps on sending ACKs or a NACK, in case a frame is incorrectly received. When the sender receives a NACK, it retransmits the frame in error plus all the succeeding frames as shown in figure. Hence, the name of the protocol is go-back-N ARQ. If a frame is lost, the receiver sends NAK after receiving the next frame as shown in figure. In case there is long delay before sending the NAK, the sender will resend the lost frame after its timer times out. If the ACK frame sent by the receiver is lost, the sender resends the frames after its timer times out as shown in figure.

Assuming full-duplex transmission, the receiving end sends piggybacked acknowledgement by using some number in the ACK field of its data frame. Let us assume that a 3-bit sequence number is used and suppose that a station sends frame 0 and gets back an RR1, and then sends frames 1, 2, 3, 4, 5, 6, 7, 0 and gets another RR1.This might either mean that RR1 is a cumulative ACK or all 8 frames were damaged. This ambiguity can be overcome if the maximum window size is limited to 7, i.e. for a k-bit sequence number field it is limited to 2^k-1. The number N ($=2^k-1$) specifies how many frames can be sent without receiving acknowledgement.

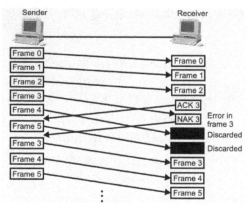

Frames in error in go–Back-N ARQ

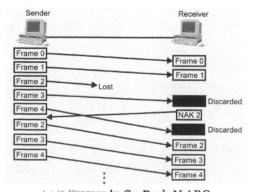

Lost Frames in Go-Back-N ARQ

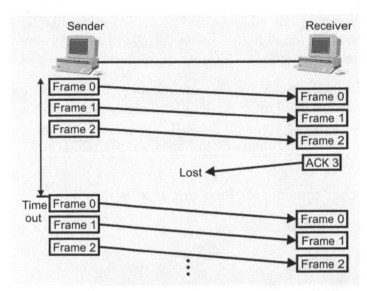

Lost ACK in Go-Back-N ARQ

If no acknowledgement is received after sending N frames, the sender takes the help of a timer. After the time-out, it resumes retransmission. The go-back-N protocol also takes care of damaged frames and damaged ACKs. This scheme is little more complex than the previous one but gives much higher throughput.

Assuming full-duplex transmission, the receiving end sends piggybacked acknowledgement by using some number in the ACK field of its data frame. Let us assume that a 3-bit sequence number is used and suppose that a station sends frame 0 and gets back an RR1, and then sends frames 1, 2, 3, 4, 5, 6, 7, 0 and gets another RR1.This might either mean that RR1 is a cumulative ACK or all 8 frames were damaged. This ambiguity can be overcome if the maximum window size is limited to 7, i.e. for a k-bit sequence number field it is limited to 2^k-1. The number N $(=2^k-1)$ specifies how many frames can be sent without receiving acknowledgement. If no acknowledgement is received after sending N frames, the sender takes the help of a timer. After the time-out, it resumes retransmission. The go-back-N protocol also takes care of damaged frames and damaged ACKs. This scheme is little more complex than the previous one but gives much higher throughput.

High-Level Data Link Control

HDLC is a bit-oriented protocol. It was developed by the International Organization for Standardization (ISO). It falls under the ISO standards ISO 3309 and ISO 4335. It specifies a packitization standard for serial links. It has found itself being used throughout the world. It has been so widely implemented because it supports both half-duplex and full-duplex communication lines, point-to-point (peer to peer) and multi-point networks, and switched or non-switched channels. HDLC supports several modes of operation, including a simple sliding-window mode for reliable delivery. Since Internet provides retransmission at higher levels (i.e., TCP), most Internet applications use HDLC's unreliable delivery mode, Unnumbered Information.

Other benefits of HDLC are that the control information is always in the same position, and specific bit patterns used for control differ dramatically from those in representing data, which reduces the chance of errors. It has also led to many subsets. Two subsets widely in use are Synchronous Data Link Control (SDLC) and Link Access Procedure-Balanced (LAP-B).

In this lesson we shall consider the following aspects of HDLC:

- Stations and Configurations

- Operational Modes

- Non-Operational Modes

- Frame Structure

- Commands and Responses

- HDLC Subsets (SDLC and LAPB)

HDLC Stations and Configurations

HDLC specifies the following three types of stations for data link control:

- Primary Station

- Secondary Station

- Combined Station

Primary Station

Within a network using HDLC as its data link protocol, if a configuration is used in which there is a primary station, it is used as the controlling station on the link. It has the responsibility of controlling all other stations on the link (usually secondary stations). A primary issues *commands* and secondary issues *responses*. Despite this important aspect of being on the link, the primary station is also responsible for the organization of data flow on the link. It also takes care of error recovery at the data link level (layer 2 of the OSI model).

Secondary Station

If the data link protocol being used is HDLC, and a primary station is present, a secondary station must also be present on the data link. The secondary station is under the control of the primary station. It has no ability, or direct responsibility for controlling the link. It is only activated when requested by the primary station. It only responds to the primary station. The secondary station's frames are called responses. It can only send response frames when requested by the primary station. A primary station maintains a separate logical link with each secondary station.

Combined Station

A combined station is a combination of a primary and secondary station. On the link, all combined stations are able to send and receive commands and responses without any permission from any other stations on the link. Each combined station is in full control of itself, and does not rely on any other stations on the link. No other stations can control any combined station. May issue both commands and responses.

HDLC also defines three types of configurations for the three types of stations. The word configuration refers to the relationship between the hardware devices on a link. Following are the three configurations defined by HDLC:

- Unbalanced Configuration

- Balanced Configuration

- Symmetrical Configuration

Unbalanced Configuration

The unbalanced configuration in an HDLC link consists of a primary station and one or more secondary stations. The unbalanced condition arises because one station controls the other stations. In an unbalanced configuration, any of the following can be used:

- Full-Duplex or Half-Duplex operation

- Point to Point or Multi-point networks

An example of an unbalanced configuration can be found below in figure

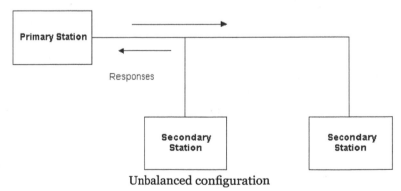

Unbalanced configuration

Balanced Configuration

The balanced configuration in an HDLC link consists of two or more combined stations. Each of the stations has equal and complimentary responsibility compared to each other. Balanced configurations can use only the following:

- Full - Duplex or Half - Duplex operation

- Point to Point networks

An example of a balanced configuration can be found below in figure.

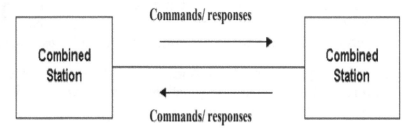

balanced configuration

Symmetrical Configuration

This third type of configuration is not widely in use today. It consists of two independent point-to-point, unbalanced station configurations as shown in figure. In this configuration, each station has a primary and secondary status. Each station is logically considered as two stations.

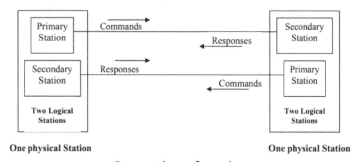

Symmetric configuration

HDLC Operational Modes

A mode in HDLC is the relationship between two devices involved in an exchange; the mode describes who controls the link. Exchanges over unbalanced configurations are always conducted in normal response mode. Exchanges over symmetric or balanced configurations can be set to specific mode using a frame design to deliver the command. HDLC offers three different modes of operation. These three modes of operations are:

- Normal Response Mode (NRM)

- Asynchronous Response Mode (ARM)

- Asynchronous Balanced Mode (ABM)

Normal Response Mode

This is the mode in which the primary station initiates transfers to the secondary station. The secondary station can only transmit a response when, and only when, it is instructed to do so by the primary station. In other words, the secondary station must receive explicit permission from the primary station to transfer a response. After receiving permission from the primary station, the secondary station initiates its transmission. This transmission from the secondary station to the primary station may be much more than just an acknowledgment of a frame. It may in fact be more than one information frame. Once the last frame is transmitted by the secondary station, it must wait once again from explicit permission to transfer anything, from the primary station. Normal Response Mode is only used within an unbalanced configuration.

Asynchronous Response Mode

In this mode, the primary station doesn't initiate transfers to the secondary station. In fact, the secondary station does not have to wait to receive explicit permission from the primary station to transfer any frames. The frames may be more than just acknowledgment frames. They may contain data, or control information regarding the status of the secondary station. This mode can reduce overhead on the link, as no frames need to be transferred in order to give the secondary station permission to initiate a transfer. However, some limitations do exist. Due to the fact that this mode is asynchronous, the secondary station must wait until it detects and idle channel before it can transfer any frames. This is when the ARM link is operating at half-duplex. If the ARM link is operating at full duplex, the secondary station can transmit at any time. In this mode, the primary station still retains responsibility for error recovery, link setup, and link disconnection.

Synchronous Balanced Mode

This mode is used in case of combined stations. There is no need for permission on the part of any station in this mode. This is because combined stations do not require any sort of instructions to perform any task on the link.

Normal Response Mode is used most frequently in multi-point lines, where the primary station controls the link. Asynchronous Response Mode is better for point-to-point links, as it reduces overhead. Asynchronous Balanced Mode is not used widely today. The "asynchronous" in both ARM and ABM does not refer to the format of the data on the link. It refers to the fact that any given station can transfer frames without explicit permission or instruction from any other station.

HDLC Non-Operational Modes

HDLC also defines three non-operational modes. These three non-operational modes are:

- Normal Disconnected Mode (NDM)

- Asynchronous Disconnected Mode (ADM)

- Initialization Mode (IM)

The two disconnected modes (NDM and ADM) differ from the operational modes in that the secondary station is logically disconnected from the link (note the secondary station is not physically disconnected from the link). The IM mode is different from the operations modes in that the secondary station's data link control program is in need of regeneration or it is in need of an exchange of parameters to be used in an operational mode.

HDLC Frame Structure

There are three different types of frames as shown in figure and the size of different fields are shown table.

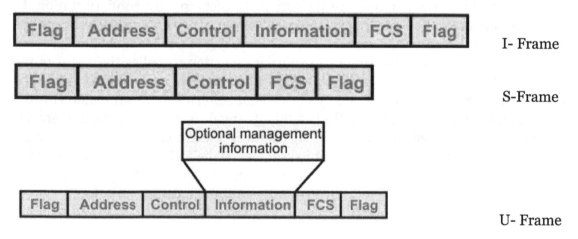

Different types of frames used in HDLC

Table: Size of different fields Field Name	Size(in bits)
Flag Field(F)	8 bits
Address Field(A)	8 bits
Control Field(C)	8 or 16 bits
Information Field(I) OR Data	Variable; Not used in some frames
Frame Check Sequence(FCS)	16 or 32 bits
Closing Flag Field(F)	8 bits

The Flag Field

Every frame on the link must begin and end with a flag sequence field (F). Stations attached to the data link must continually listen for a flag sequence. The flag sequence is an octet looking like 01111110. Flags are continuously transmitted on the link between frames to keep the link active. Two other bit sequences are used in HDLC as signals for the stations on the link. These two bit sequences are:

- Seven 1's, but less than 15 signal an abort signal. The stations on the link know there is a problem on the link.

- 15 or more 1's indicate that the channel is in an idle state.

The time between the transmissions of actual frames is called the interframe time fill. The interframe time fill is accomplished by transmitting continuous flags between frames. The flags may be in 8 bit multiples.

HDLC is a code-transparent protocol. It does not rely on a specific code for interpretation of line control. This means that if a bit at position N in an octet has a specific meaning, regardless of the other bits in the same octet. If an octet has a bit sequence of 01111110, but is not a flag field, HLDC uses a technique called bit-stuffing to differentiate this bit sequence from a flag field.

At the receiving end, the receiving station inspects the incoming frame. If it detects 5 consecutive 1's it looks at the next bit. If it is a 0, it pulls it out. If it is a 1, it looks at the 8th bit. If the 8th bit is a 0, it knows an abort or idle signal has been sent. It then proceeds to inspect the following bits to determine appropriate action. This is the manner in which HDLC achieves code-transparency. HDLC is not concerned with any specific bit code inside the data stream. It is only concerned with keeping flags unique.

The Address Field

The address field (A) identifies the primary or secondary stations involvement in the frame transmission or reception. Each station on the link has a unique address. In an unbalanced configuration, the A field in both commands and responses refer to the secondary station. In a balanced configuration, the command frame contains the destination station address and the response frame has the sending station's address.

The Control Field

HDLC uses the control field (C) to determine how to control the communications process. This field contains the commands, responses and sequences numbers used to maintain the data flow accountability of the link, defines the functions of the frame and initiates the logic to control the movement of traffic between sending and receiving stations. There three control field formats:

- Information Transfer Format: The frame is used to transmit end-user data between two devices.

- Supervisory Format: The control field performs control functions such as acknowledgment of frames, requests for re-transmission, and requests for temporary suspension of frames being transmitted. Its use depends on the operational mode being used.

- Unnumbered Format: This control field format is also used for control purposes. It is used to perform link initialization, link disconnection and other link control functions.

The Poll/Final Bit (P/F)

The 5th bit position in the control field is called the poll/final bit, or P/F bit. It can only be recognized when it is set to 1. If it is set to 0, it is ignored. The poll/final bit is used to provide dialogue between the primary station and secondary station. The primary station uses P=1 to acquire a status response from the secondary station. The P bit signifies a poll. The secondary station responds to the P bit by transmitting a data or status frame to the primary station with the P/F bit set to F=1. The F bit can also be used to signal the end of a transmission from the secondary station under Normal Response Mode.

The Information Field or Data Field

This field is not always present in a HDLC frame. It is only present when the Information Transfer Format is being used in the control field. The information field contains the actually data the sender is transmitting to the receiver in an I-Frame and network management information in U-Frame.

The Frame Check Sequence Field

This field contains a 16-bit, or 32-bit cyclic redundancy check bits.

HDLC Commands and Responses

The set of commands and responses in HDLC is summarized in table.

Information Transfer Format Command and Response (I-Frame)

The function of the information command and response is to transfer sequentially numbered frames, each containing an information field, across the data link.

Supervisory Format Command and Responses (S-Frame)

Supervisory (S) commands and responses are used to perform numbered supervisory functions such as acknowledgment, polling, temporary suspension of information transfer, or error recovery. Frames with the S format control field cannot contain an information field. A primary station may use the S format command frame with the P bit set to 1 to request a response from a secondary station regarding its status. Supervisory Format commands and responses are as follows:

- Receive Ready (RR) is used by the primary or secondary station to indicate that it is ready to receive an information frame and/or acknowledge previously received frames.

- Receive Not Ready (RNR) is used to indicate that the primary or secondary station is not ready to receive any information frames or acknowledgments.

- Reject (REJ) is used to request the retransmission of frames.

- Selective Reject (SREJ) is used by a station to request retransmission of specific frames. An SREJ must be transmitted for each erroneous frame; each frame is treated as a separate error. Only one SREJ can remain outstanding on the link at any one time.

TABLE: HDLC Commands and Responses **Information Transfer**	**Information Transfer**
Format Commands	**Format Responses**
I - Information	I - Information
Supervisory Format	**Supervisory Format**
Commands	**Responses**
RR - Receive ready	RR - Receive ready
RNR - Receive not ready	RNR - Receive not ready
REJ - Reject	REJ - Reject
SREJ - Selective reject	SREJ - Selective reject
Unnumbered Format	**Unnumbered Format**
Commands	**Commands**
SNRM - Set Normal Response Mode	UA - Unnumbered Acknowledgment
SARM - Set Asynchronous Response Mode	DM - Disconnected Mode
SABM - Set Asynchronous Balanced Mode	RIM - Request Initialization Mode
DISC - Disconnect	RD - Request Disconnect
SNRME - Set Normal Response Mode Extended	UI - Unnumbered Information
SARME - Set Asynchronous Response Mode Extended	XID - Exchange Identification
SABME - Set Asynchronous Balanced Mode Extended	FRMR - Frame Reject
SIM - Set Initialization Mode	TEST - Test

UP - Unnumbered Poll
UI - Unnumbered Information
XID - Exchange identification
RSET - Reset
TEST - Test

Unnumbered Format Commands and Responses (U-Frame)

The unnumbered format commands and responses are used to extend the number of data link control functions. The unnumbered format frames have 5 modifier bits, which allow for up to 32 additional commands and 32 additional response functions. Below, 13 command functions, and 8 response functions are described.

- Set Normal Response Mode (SNRM) places the secondary station into NRM. NRM does not allow the secondary station to send any unsolicited frames. Hence the primary station has control of the link.

- Set Asynchronous Response Mode (SARM) allows a secondary station to transmit frames without a poll from the primary station.

- Set Asynchronous Balanced Mode (SABM) sets the operational mode of the link to ABM.

- Disconnect (DISC) places the secondary station in to a disconnected mode.

- Set Normal Response Mode Extended (SNRME) increases the size of the control field to 2 octets instead of one in NRM. This is used for extended sequencing. The same applies for *SARME* and *SABME*.

- Set Initialization Mode (SIM) is used to cause the secondary station to initiate a station-specific procedure(s) to initialize its data link level control functions.

- Unnumbered Poll (UP) polls a station without regard to sequencing or acknowledgment.

- Unnumbered Information (UI) is used to send information to a secondary station.

- Exchange Identification (XID) is used to cause the secondary station to identify itself and provide the primary station identifications characteristics of itself.

- Reset (RSET) is used to reset the receive state variable in the addressed station.

- Test (TEST) is used to cause the addressed secondary station to respond with a TEST response at the first response opportunity. It performs a basic test of the data link control.

- Unnumbered Acknowledgment (UA) is used by the secondary station to acknowledge the receipt and acceptance of an *SNRM, SARM, SABM, SNRME, SARME, SABME, RSET, SIM,* or *DISC* commands.

- Disconnected Mode (DM) is transmitted from a secondary station to indicate it is in disconnected mode(non-operational mode.)

- Request Initialization Mode (RIM) is a request from a secondary station for initialization to a primary station. Once the secondary station sends *RIM*, it can only respond to *SIM, DSIC, TEST* or *XID* commands.

- Request Disconnect (RD) is sent by the secondary station to inform the primary station that it wishes to disconnect from the link and go into a non-operational mode(NDM or ADM).

- Frame Reject (FRMR) is used by the secondary station in an operation mode to report that a condition has occurred in transmission of a frame and retransmission of the frame will not correct the condition.

References

- Shannon, C.E. (1948), "A Mathematical Theory of Communication", Bell System Tech. Journal, p. 418, 27

- Gary Cutlack (25 August 2010). "Mysterious Russian 'Numbers Station' Changes Broadcast After 20 Years". Gizmodo. Retrieved 12 March 2012

- Huffman, William Cary; Pless, Vera S. (2003). Fundamentals of Error-Correcting Codes. Cambridge University Press. ISBN 978-0-521-78280-7

- "Using StrongArm SA-1110 in the On-Board Computer of Nanosatellite". Tsinghua Space Center, Tsinghua University, Beijing. Retrieved 2009-02-16

- Thompson, Thomas M. (1983), From Error-Correcting Codes through Sphere Packings to Simple Groups, The Carus Mathematical Monographs (#21), The Mathematical Association of America, p. vii, ISBN 0-88385-023-0

4

An Integrated Study of Internetworking

Internetworking is a method of inter-connecting various computer networks together. The most famous example of internetworking is Internet, which is incorporated using Internet protocol suite as the hardware differs in the combined networks. Internet Protocol (IP) delivers information from the source host to destination host using the IP address. The chapter closely examines the key concepts of internetworking to provide an extensive understanding of the subject.

Internetworking

Internetworking is the practice of connecting a computer network with other networks through the use of gateways that provide a common method of routing information packets between the networks. The resulting system of interconnected networks are called an *internetwork*, or simply an *internet*. Internetworking is a combination of the words *inter* ("between") and networking; not *internet-working* or *international-network*.

The most notable example of internetworking is the Internet, a network of networks based on many underlying hardware technologies, but unified by an internetworking protocol standard, the Internet Protocol Suite, often also referred to as TCP/IP.

The smallest amount of effort to create an internet (an internetwork, not *the* Internet), is to have two LANs of computers connected to each other via a router. Simply using either a switch or a hub to connect two local area networks together doesn't imply internetworking; it just expands the original LAN.

Interconnection of Networks

Internetworking started as a way to connect disparate types of networking technology, but it became widespread through the developing need to connect two or more local area networks via some sort of wide area network. The original term for an internetwork was catenet.

The definition of an internetwork today includes the connection of other types of computer networks such as personal area networks. The network elements used to connect individual networks in the ARPANET, the predecessor of the Internet, were originally called gateways, but the term has been deprecated in this context, because of possible confusion with functionally different devices. Today the interconnecting gateways are called routers.

Another type of interconnection of networks often occurs within enterprises at the Link Layer of the networking model, i.e. at the hardware-centric layer below the level of the TCP/IP logical interfaces. Such interconnection is accomplished with network bridges and network switches. This is sometimes incorrectly termed internetworking, but the resulting system is simply a larger, single subnetwork, and no internetworking protocol, such as Internet Protocol, is required to traverse these devices. However, a single computer network may be converted into an internetwork by dividing the network into segments and logically dividing the segment traffic with routers. The Internet Protocol is designed to provide an unreliable (not guaranteed) packet service across the network. The architecture avoids intermediate network elements maintaining any state of the network. Instead, this function is assigned to the endpoints of each communication session. To transfer data reliably, applications must utilize an appropriate Transport Layer protocol, such as Transmission Control Protocol (TCP), which provides a reliable stream. Some applications use a simpler, connection-less transport protocol, User Datagram Protocol (UDP), for tasks which do not require reliable delivery of data or that require real-time service, such as video streaming or voice chat.

Networking Models

Two architectural models are commonly used to describe the protocols and methods used in internetworking.

The Open System Interconnection (OSI) reference model was developed under the auspices of the International Organization for Standardization (ISO) and provides a rigorous description for layering protocol functions from the underlying hardware to the software interface concepts in user applications. Internetworking is implemented in the Network Layer (Layer 3) of the model.

The Internet Protocol Suite, also called the TCP/IP model of the Internet was not designed to conform to the OSI model and does not refer to it in any of the normative specifications in Requests for Comment and Internet standards. Despite similar appearance as a layered model, it uses a much less rigorous, loosely defined architecture that concerns itself only with the aspects of logical networking. It does not discuss hardware-specific low-level interfaces, and assumes availability of a Link Layer interface to the local network link to which the host is connected. Internetworking is facilitated by the protocols of its Internet Layer.

Internetworking Devices

Repeaters

A single Ethernet segment can have a maximum length of 500 meters with a maximum of 100 stations (in a cheapernet segment it is 185m). To extend the length of the network, a *repeater* may be used as shown in figure. Functionally, a repeater can be considered as two transceivers joined together and connected to two different segments of coaxial cable. The repeater passes the digital signal bit-by-bit in both directions between the two segments. As the signal passes through a repeater, it is amplified and regenerated at the other end. The repeater does not isolate one segment from the other, if there is a collision on one segment, it is regenerated on the other segment. Therefore, the two segments form a single LAN and it is transparent to rest of the system. Ethernet allows five segments to be used in cascade to have a maximum network span of 2.5 km. With reference of the ISO model, a repeater is considered as a *level-1 relay* as depicted in figure. It simply repeats, retimes and amplifies the bits it receives. The repeater is merely used to extend the span of a single LAN. Important features of a repeater are as follows:

- A repeater connects different segments of a LAN

- A repeater forwards every frame it receives

- A repeater is a regenerator, not an amplifier

- It can be used to create a single extended LAN

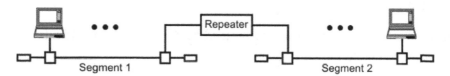

Repeater connecting two LAN segments

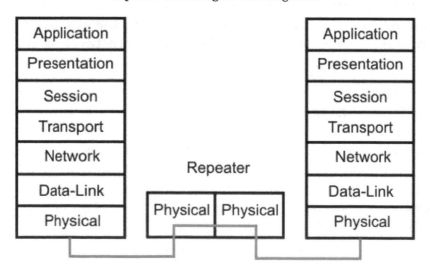

Operation of a repeater as a level-1 relay

Hubs

Hub is a generic term, but commonly refers to a multiport repeater. It can be used to create multiple levels of hierarchy of stations. The stations connect to the hub with

RJ-45 connector having maximum segment length is 100 meters. This type of intercon-nected set of stations is easy to maintain and diagnose. Figure shows how several hubs can be connected in a hierarchical manner to realize a single LAN of bigger size with a large number of nodes.

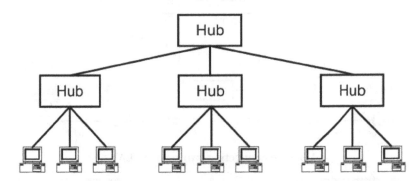

Hub as a multi-port repeater can be connected in a hierarchical manner to form a single LAN with many nodes

Bridges

The device that can be used to interconnect two separate LANs is known as a *bridge*. It is commonly used to connect two similar or dissimilar LANs as shown in figure. The bridge operates in layer 2, that is data-link layer and that is why it is called *level-2 relay* with reference to the OSI model. It links similar or dissimilar LANs, designed to store and forward frames, it is protocol independent and transparent to the end stations. The flow of information through a bridge is shown in figure. Use of bridges offer a number of advantages, such as higher reliability, performance, security, convenience and larger geographic coverage. But, it is desirable that the quality of service (QOS) offered by a bridge should match that of a single LAN. The parameters that define the QOS in-clude *availability, frame mishaps, transit delay, frame lifetime, undetected bit errors, frame size* and *priority*. Key features of a bridge are mentioned below:

- A bridge operates both in physical and data-link layer

- A bridge uses a table for filtering/routing

- A bridge does not change the physical (MAC) addresses in a frame

- Types of bridges:

  o Transparent Bridges

  o Source routing bridges

A bridge must contain addressing and routing capability. Two routing algorithms have been proposed for a bridged LAN environment. The first, produced as an extension of IEEE 802.1 and applicable to all IEEE 802 LANs, is known as *transparent bridge*.

And the other, developed for the IEEE 802.5 token rings, is based on *source routing approach*. It applies to many types of LAN including token ring, token bus and CSMA/CD bus.

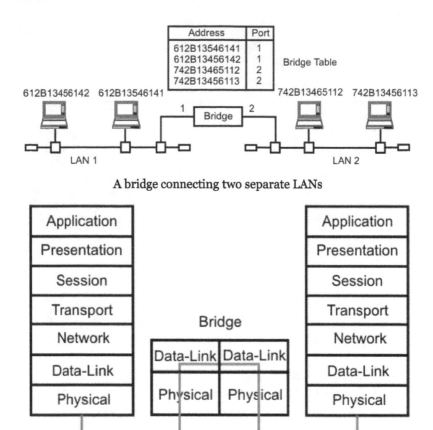

A bridge connecting two separate LANs

Information flow through a bridge

Transparent Bridges

The transparent bridge uses two processes known as bridge forwarding and bridge learning. If the destination address is present in the forwarding database already created, the packet is forwarded to the port number to which the destination host is attached. If it is not present, forwarding is done on all parts (flooding). This process is known as *bridge forwarding*. Moreover, as each frame arrives, its source address indicates where a particular host is situated, so that the bridge learns which way to forward frames to that address. This process is known as *bridge learning*. Key features of a transparent bridge are:

- The stations are unaware of the presence of a transparent bridge

- Reconfiguration of the bridge is not necessary; it can be added/removed without being noticed

- It performs two functions:
  - Forwarding of frames
  - Learning to create the forwarding table

Bridge Forwarding

Bridge forwarding operation is explained with the help of a flowchart in figure. Basic functions of the bridge forwarding are mentioned below:

- Discard the frame if source and destination addresses are same

- Forward the frame if the source and destination addresses are different and destination address is present in the table

- Use flooding if destination address is not present in the table

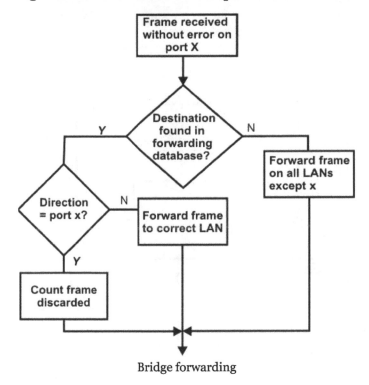

Bridge forwarding

Bridge Learning

At the time of installation of a transparent bridge, the database, in the form of a table, is empty. As a packet is encountered, the bridge checks its source address and build up a table by associating a source address with a port address to which it is connected. The flowchart of figure explains the learning process. The table building up operation is illustrated in figure.

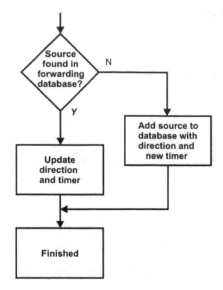

Bridge learning

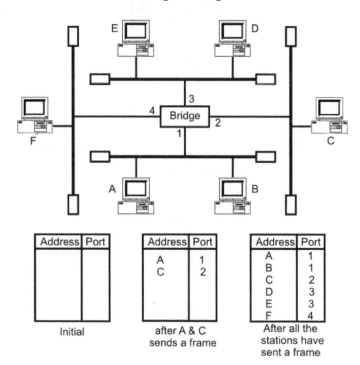

Address	Port

Initial

Address	Port
A	1
C	2

after A & C
sends a frame

Address	Port
A	1
B	1
C	2
D	3
E	3
F	4

After all the
stations have
sent a frame

Creation of a bridge-forwarding table

Loop Problem

Forwarding and learning processes work without any problem as long as there is no redundant bridge in the system. On the other hand, redundancy is desirable from the viewpoint of reliability, so that the function of a failed bridge is taken over by a redundant bridge. The existence of redundant bridges creates the so-called *loop problem* as illustrated with the help of figure. Assuming that after initialization tables in both the bridges are empty let us consider the following steps:

Step 1. Station-A sends a frame to Station-B. Both the bridges forward the frame to LAN Y and update the table with the source address of A.

Step 2. Now there are two copies of the frame on LAN-Y. The copy sent by Bridge-a is received by Bridge-b and vice versa. As both the bridges have no information about Station B, both will forward the frames to LAN-X.

Step 3. Again both the bridges will forward the frames to LAN-Y because of the lack of information of the Station B in their database and again Step-2 will be repeated, and so on.

So, the frame will continue to loop around the two LANs indefinitely.

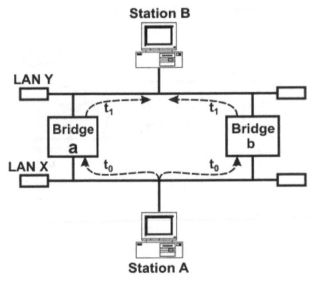

Loop problem in a network using bridges

Spanning Tree

As redundancy creates loop problem in the system, it is very undesirable. To prevent loop problem and proper working of the forwarding and learning processes, there must be only one path between any pair of bridges and LANs between any two segments in the entire bridged LAN. The IEEE specification requires that the bridges use a special topology. Such a topology is known as *spanning tree* (a graph where there is no loop) topology. The methodology for setting up a spanning tree is known as spanning tree algorithm, which creates a tree out of a graph. Without changing the physical topology, a logical topology is created that overlay on the physical one by using the following steps:

- Select a bridge as *Root-bridge,* which has the smallest ID.

- Select *Root ports* for all the bridges, except for the root bridge, which has least-cost path (say minimum number of hops) to the root bridge.

- Choose a *Designated bridge*, which has least-cost path to the Root-bridge, in each LAN.

- Select a port as *Designated port* that gives least-cost path from the Designated bridge to the Root bridge.

- Mark the designated port and the root ports as *Forwarding ports* and the remaining ones as *Blocking ports*.

The spanning tree of a network of bridges is shown in figure. The forwarding ports are shown as solid lines, whereas the blocked ports are shown as dotted lines.

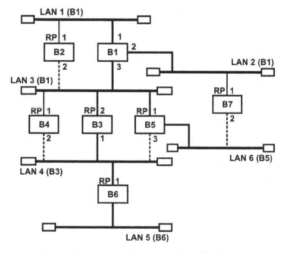

Spanning tree of a network of bridges

Source Routing Bridges

The second approach, known as *source routing,* where the routing operation is performed by the source host and the frame specifies which route the frame is to follow. A host can discover a route by sending a *discovery frame*, which spreads through the entire network using all possible paths to the destination. Each frame gradually gathers addresses as it goes. The destination responds to each frame and the source host chooses an appropriate route from these responses. For example, a route with minimum hop-count can be chosen. Whereas transparent bridges do not modify a frame, a source routing bridge adds a routing information field to the frame. Source routing approach provides a shortest path at the cost of the proliferation of discovery frames, which can put a serious extra burden on the network. Figure shows the frame format of a source routing bridge.

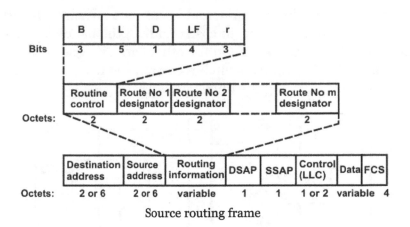

Source routing frame

Switches

A switch is essentially a fast bridge having additional sophistication that allows faster processing of frames. Some of important functionalities are:

- Ports are provided with buffer

- Switch maintains a directory: #address - port#

- Each frame is forwarded after examining the #address and forwarded to the proper port#

- Three possible forwarding approaches: Cut-through, Collision-free and Fully-buffered as briefly explained below.

Cut-through: A switch forwards a frame immediately after receiving the destination address. As a consequence, the switch forwards the frame without collision and error detection.

Collision-free: In this case, the switch forwards the frame after receiving 64 bytes, which allows detection of collision. However, error detection is not possible because switch is yet to receive the entire frame.

Fully buffered: In this case, the switch forwards the frame only after receiving the entire frame. So, the switch can detect both collision and error free frames are forwarded.

Comparison between a Switch and a Hub

Although a hub and a switch apparently look similar, they have significant differences. As shown in figure, both can be used to realize physical star topology, the hubs works like a logical bus, because the same signal is repeated on all the ports. On the other hand, a switch functions like a logical star with the possibility of the communication of separate signals between any pair of port lines. As a consequence, all the ports of a hub belong to the same collision domain, and in case of a switch each port operates on separate collision domain. Moreover, in case of a hub, the bandwidth is shared by all the stations connected to all the ports. On the other hand, in case of a switch, each port has dedicated bandwidth. Therefore, switches can be used to increase the bandwidth of a hub-based network by replacing the hubs by switches.

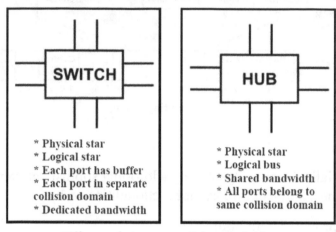

Difference between a switch and a bridge

Routers

A router is considered as a layer-3 relay that operates in the network layer, that is it acts on network layer frames. It can be used to link two dissimilar LANs. A router isolates LANs in to subnets to manage and control network traffic. However, unlike bridges it is not transparent to end stations. A schematic diagram of the router is shown on figure. A router has four basic components: Input ports, output ports, the routing processor and the switching fabric. The functions of the four components are briefly mentioned below.

- *Input port* performs physical and data-link layer functions of the router. As shown in figure, the ports are also provided with buffer to hold the packet before forwarding to the switching fabric.

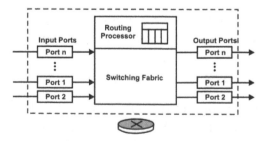

Schematic diagram of a router

- *Output ports*, as shown in figure, perform the same functions as the input ports, but in the reverse order.

- The *routing processor* performs the function of the network layer. The process involves table lookup.

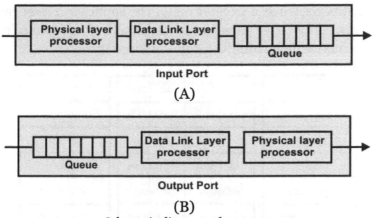

Input Port

(A)

Output Port

(B)

Schematic diagram of a router

- The *switching fabric*, shown in figure, moves the packet from the input queue to the output queue by using specialized mechanisms. The switching fabric is realized with the help of multistage interconnection networks.

- Communication of a frame through a router is shown in figure.

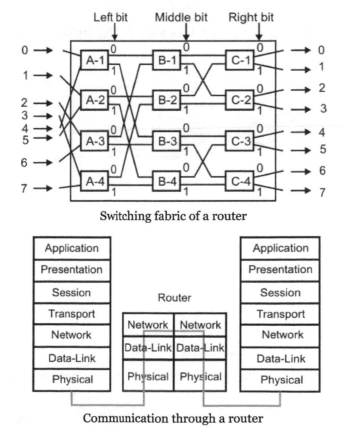

Switching fabric of a router

Communication through a router

Gateways

A gateway works above the network layer, such as application layer as shown in figure. As a consequence, it is known as a Layer-7 relay. The application level gateways can look into the content application layer packets such as email before forwarding it to the other side. This property has made it suitable for use in Firewalls.

Application	Application	Application	Application
Presentation	Presentation	Presentation	Presentation
Session	Session	Session	Session
Transport	Transport	Transport	Transport
Network	Network	Network	Network
Data-Link	Data-Link	Data-Link	Data-Link
Physical	Physical	Physical	Physical

Communication through a gateway

A Simple Internet

A simple internet comprising several LANs and WANs linked with the help of routers is shown in figure.

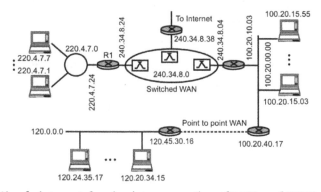

Simple internet showing interconnection of LANs and WANs

Internet Protocol

The Internet Protocol (IP) is the principal communications protocol in the Internet protocol suite for relaying datagrams across network boundaries. Its routing function enables internetworking, and essentially establishes the Internet.

IP has the task of delivering packets from the source host to the destination host solely based on the IP addresses in the packet headers. For this purpose, IP defines packet structures that encapsulate the data to be delivered. It also defines addressing methods that are used to label the datagram with source and destination information.

Historically, IP was the connectionless datagram service in the original *Transmission Control Program* introduced by Vint Cerf and Bob Kahn in 1974; the other being the connection-oriented Transmission Control Protocol (TCP). The Internet protocol suite is therefore often referred to as TCP/IP.

The first major version of IP, Internet Protocol Version 4 (IPv4), is the dominant protocol of the Internet. Its successor is Internet Protocol Version 6 (IPv6).

Function

The Internet Protocol is responsible for addressing hosts and for routing datagrams (packets) from a source host to a destination host across one or more IP networks. For this purpose, the Internet Protocol defines the format of packets and provides an addressing system that has two functions: Identifying hosts and providing a logical location service.

Datagram Construction

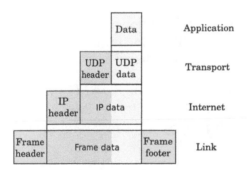

Sample encapsulation of application data from UDP to a Link protocol frame

Each datagram has two components: a header and a payload. The IP header is tagged with the source IP address, the destination IP address, and other meta-data needed to route and deliver the datagram. The payload is the data that is transported. This method of nesting the data payload in a packet with a header is called encapsulation.

IP Addressing and Routing

IP addressing entails the assignment of IP addresses and associated parameters to host interfaces. The address space is divided into networks and subnetworks, involving the designation of network or routing prefixes. IP routing is performed by all hosts, as well as routers, whose main function is to transport packets across network boundaries. Routers communicate with one another via specially designed routing protocols, either interior gateway protocols or exterior gateway protocols, as needed for the topology of the network.

IP routing is also common in local networks. For example, many Ethernet switches support IP multicast operations. These switches use IP addresses and Internet Group Management Protocol to control multicast routing but use MAC addresses for the actual routing.

Version History

The versions currently relevant are IPv4 and IPv6.

In May 1974, the Institute of Electrical and Electronic Engineers (IEEE) published a paper entitled "A Protocol for Packet Network Intercommunication". The paper's authors, Vint Cerf and Bob Kahn, described an internetworking protocol for sharing resources using packet switching among network nodes. A central control component of this model was the "Transmission Control Program" that incorporated both connection-oriented links and datagram services between hosts. The monolithic Transmission Control Program was later divided into a modular architecture consisting of the Transmission Control Protocol and User Datagram Protocol at the transport layer and the Internet Protocol at the network layer. The model became known as the *Department of Defense (DoD) Internet Model* and *Internet protocol suite*, and informally as *TCP/IP*.

IP versions 0 to 3 were experimental versions, used between 1977 and 1979. The following Internet Experiment Note (IEN) documents describe versions of the Internet Protocol prior to the modern version of IPv4:

- IEN 2 (*Comments on Internet Protocol and TCP*), dated August 1977 describes the need to separate the TCP and Internet Protocol functionalities (which were previously combined.) It proposes the first version of the IP header, using 0 for the version field.

- IEN 26 (*A Proposed New Internet Header Format*), dated February 1978 describes a version of the IP header that uses a 1-bit version field.

- IEN 28 (*Draft Internetwork Protocol Description Version 2*), dated February 1978 describes IPv2.

- IEN 41 (*Internetwork Protocol Specification Version 4*), dated June 1978 describes the first protocol to be called IPv4. The IP header is different from the modern IPv4 header.

- IEN 44 (*Latest Header Formats*), dated June 1978 describes another version of IPv4, also with a header different from the modern IPv4 header.

- IEN 54 (*Internetwork Protocol Specification Version 4*), dated September 1978 is the first description of IPv4 using the header that would be standardized in RFC 760.

The dominant internetworking protocol in the Internet Layer in use today is IPv4; the number 4 is the protocol version number carried in every IP datagram. IPv4 is described in RFC 791 (1981).

Version 5 was used by the Internet Stream Protocol, an experimental streaming protocol.

The successor to IPv4 is IPv6. Its most prominent difference from version 4 is the size of the addresses. While IPv4 uses 32 bits for addressing, yielding c. 4.3 billion (4.3×10^9) addresses, IPv6 uses 128-bit addresses providing ca. 340 undecillion, or 3.4×10^{38} addresses. Although adoption of IPv6 has been slow, as of June 2008, all United States government systems have demonstrated basic infrastructure support for IPv6. IPv6 was a result of several years of experimentation and dialog during which various protocol models were proposed, such as TP/IX (RFC 1475), PIP (RFC 1621) and TUBA (TCP and UDP with Bigger Addresses, RFC 1347).

The assignment of the new protocol as IPv6 was uncertain until due diligence revealed that IPv6 had not yet been used previously. Other protocol proposals named *IPv9* and *IPv8* briefly surfaced, but had no affiliation with any international standards body, and have had no support.

Reliability

The design of the Internet protocols is based on the end-to-end principle. The network infrastructure is considered inherently unreliable at any single network element or transmission medium and is dynamic in terms of availability of links and nodes. No central monitoring or performance measurement facility exists that tracks or maintains the state of the network. For the benefit of reducing network complexity, the intelligence in the network is purposely located in the end nodes.

As a consequence of this design, the Internet Protocol only provides best-effort delivery and its service is characterized as unreliable. In network architectural language, it is a connectionless protocol, in contrast to connection-oriented communication. Various error conditions may occur, such as data corruption, packet loss, duplication and out-of-order delivery. Because routing is dynamic, meaning every packet is treated independently, and because the network maintains no state based on the path of prior packets, different packets may be routed to the same destination via different paths, resulting in out-of-order sequencing at the receiver.

IPv4 provides safeguards to ensure that the IP packet header is error-free. A routing node calculates a checksum for a packet. If the checksum is bad, the routing node discards the packet. Although the Internet Control Message Protocol (ICMP) allows such notification, the routing node is not required to notify either end node of these errors. By contrast, in order to increase performance, and since current link layer technology is assumed to provide sufficient error detection, the IPv6 header has no checksum to protect it.

All error conditions in the network must be detected and compensated by the end nodes of a transmission. The upper layer protocols of the internet protocol suite are responsible for resolving reliability issues. For example, a host may buffer network data to ensure correct ordering before the data is delivered to an application.

Link capacity and capability

The dynamic nature of the Internet and the diversity of its components provide no guarantee that any particular path is actually capable of, or suitable for, performing the data transmission requested, even if the path is available and reliable. One of the technical constraints is the size of data packets allowed on a given link. An application must assure that it uses proper transmission characteristics. Some of this responsibility lies also in the upper layer protocols. Facilities exist to examine the maximum transmission unit (MTU) size of the local link and Path MTU Discovery can be used for the entire projected path to the destination. The IPv4 internetworking layer has the capability to automatically fragment the original datagram into smaller units for transmission. In this case, IP provides re-ordering of fragments delivered out of order.

The Transmission Control Protocol (TCP) is an example of a protocol that adjusts its segment size to be smaller than the MTU. The User Datagram Protocol (UDP) and the Internet Control Message Protocol (ICMP) disregard MTU size, thereby forcing IP to fragment oversized datagrams.

An IPv6 network does not perform fragmentation or reassembly, and as per the end-to-end principle, requires end stations and higher-layer protocols to avoid exceeding the network's MTU.

Security

During the design phase of the ARPANET and the early Internet, the security aspects and needs of a public, international network could not be adequately anticipated. Consequently, many Internet protocols exhibited vulnerabilities highlighted by network attacks and later security assessments. In 2008, a thorough security assessment and proposed mitigation of problems was published. The Internet Engineering Task Force (IETF) has been pursuing further studies.

Transmission Control Protocol

The Transmission Control Protocol (TCP) is one of the main protocols of the Internet protocol suite. It originated in the initial network implementation in which it complemented the Internet Protocol (IP). Therefore, the entire suite is commonly referred to as TCP/IP. TCP provides reliable, ordered, and error-checked delivery of a stream of octets between applications running on hosts communicating by an IP network. Major Internet applications such as the World Wide Web, email, remote administration, and file transfer rely on TCP. Applications that do not require reliable data stream service may use the User Datagram Protocol (UDP), which provides a connectionless datagram service that emphasizes reduced latency over reliability.

Historical Origin

During May 1974, the Institute of Electrical and Electronic Engineers (IEEE) published a paper titled *A Protocol for Packet Network Intercommunication*. The paper's authors, Vint Cerf and Bob Kahn, described an internetworking protocol for sharing resources using packet-switching among the nodes. A central control component of this model was the *Transmission Control Program* that incorporated both connection-oriented links and datagram services between hosts. The monolithic Transmission Control Program was later divided into a modular architecture consisting of the *Transmission Control Protocol* at the connection-oriented layer and the *Internet Protocol* at the internetworking (datagram) layer. The model became known informally as *TCP/IP*, although formally it was henceforth termed the *Internet Protocol Suite*.

Network Function

The Transmission Control Protocol provides a communication service at an intermediate level between an application program and the Internet Protocol. It provides host-to-host connectivity at the Transport Layer of the Internet model. An application does not need to know the particular mechanisms for sending data via a link to another host, such as the required packet fragmentation on the transmission medium. At the transport layer, the protocol handles all handshaking and transmission details and presents an abstraction of the network connection to the application.

At the lower levels of the protocol stack, due to network congestion, traffic load balancing, or other unpredictable network behaviour, IP packets may be lost, duplicated, or delivered out of order. TCP detects these problems, requests re-transmission of lost data, rearranges out-of-order data and even helps minimize network congestion to reduce the occurrence of the other problems. If the data still remains undelivered, the source is notified of this failure. Once the TCP receiver has reassembled the sequence of octets originally transmitted, it passes them to the receiving application. Thus, TCP abstracts the application's communication from the underlying networking details.

TCP is used extensively by many applications available by internet, including the World Wide Web (WWW), E-mail, File Transfer Protocol, Secure Shell, peer-to-peer file sharing, and streaming media applications.

TCP is optimized for accurate delivery rather than timely delivery and can incur relatively long delays (on the order of seconds) while waiting for out-of-order messages or re-transmissions of lost messages. Therefore, it is not particularly suitable for real-time applications such as Voice over IP. For such applications, protocols like the Real-time Transport Protocol (RTP) operating over the User Datagram Protocol (UDP) are usually recommended instead.

TCP is a reliable stream delivery service which guarantees that all bytes received will be identical with bytes sent and in the correct order. Since packet transfer by many networks is not reliable, a technique known as 'positive acknowledgement with re-transmission' is used to guarantee reliability. This fundamental technique requires the receiver to respond with an acknowledgement message as it receives the data. The sender keeps a record of each packet it sends and maintains a timer from when the packet was sent. The sender re-transmits a packet if the timer expires before receiving the message acknowledgement. The timer is needed in case a packet gets lost or corrupted.

While IP handles actual delivery of the data, TCP keeps track of 'segments' - the individual units of data transmission that a message is divided into for efficient routing through the network. For example, when an HTML file is sent from a web server, the TCP software layer of that server divides the sequence of file octets into segments and forwards them individually to the IP software layer (Internet Layer). The Internet Layer encapsulates each TCP segment into an IP packet by adding a header that includes (among other data) the destination IP address. When the client program on the destination computer receives them, the TCP layer (Transport Layer) re-assembles the individual segments and ensures they are correctly ordered and error-free as it streams them to an application.

TCP Segment Structure

Transmission Control Protocol accepts data from a data stream, divides it into chunks, and adds a TCP header creating a TCP segment. The TCP segment is then encapsulated into an Internet Protocol (IP) datagram, and exchanged with peers.

The term *TCP packet* appears in both informal and formal usage, whereas in more precise terminology *segment* refers to the TCP protocol data unit (PDU), *datagram* to the IP PDU, and *frame* to the data link layer PDU:

Processes transmit data by calling on the TCP and passing buffers of data as arguments. The TCP packages the data from these buffers into segments and calls on the internet module [e.g. IP] to transmit each segment to the destination TCP.

A TCP segment consists of a segment *header* and a *data* section. The TCP header contains 10 mandatory fields, and an optional extension field (*Options*, pink background in table).

The data section follows the header. Its contents are the payload data carried for the application. The length of the data section is not specified in the TCP segment header. It can be calculated by subtracting the combined length of the TCP header and the encapsulating IP header from the total IP datagram length (specified in the IP header).

TCP Header

Offsets		0								1								2								3							
Octet	Bit	0	1	2	3	4	5	6	7	8	9	10	11	12	13	14	15	16	17	18	19	20	21	22	23	24	25	26	27	28	29	30	31
0	0	Source port																Destination port															
4	32	Sequence number																															
8	64	Acknowledgment number (if ACK set)																															
12	96	Data offset				Reserved 0 0 0			N S	C W R	E C E	U R G	A C K	P S H	R S T	S Y N	F I N	Window Size															
16	128	Checksum																Urgent pointer (if URG set)															
20 ...	160 ...	Options (if *data offset* > 5. Padded at the end with "o" bytes if necessary.) ...																															

Source port (16 bits)

Identifies the sending port

Destination port (16 bits)

Identifies the receiving port

Sequence number (32 bits)

Has a dual role:

- If the SYN flag is set (1), then this is the initial sequence number. The sequence number of the actual first data byte and the acknowledged number in the corresponding ACK are then this sequence number plus 1.

- If the SYN flag is clear (0), then this is the accumulated sequence number of the first data byte of this segment for the current session.

Acknowledgment number (32 bits)

If the ACK flag is set then the value of this field is the next sequence number that the sender is expecting. This acknowledges receipt of all prior bytes (if any). The first ACK sent by each end acknowledges the other end's initial sequence number itself, but no data.

Data offset (4 bits)

Specifies the size of the TCP header in 32-bit words. The minimum size header is 5 words and the maximum is 15 words thus giving the minimum size of 20 bytes and maximum of 60 bytes, allowing for up to 40 bytes of options in the header. This field gets its name from the fact that it is also the offset from the start of the TCP segment to the actual data.

Reserved (3 bits)

For future use and should be set to zero

Flags (9 bits) (aka Control bits)

Contains 9 1-bit flags

- NS (1 bit): ECN-nonce concealment protection.

- CWR (1 bit): Congestion Window Reduced (CWR) flag is set by the sending host to indicate that it received a TCP segment with the ECE flag set and had responded in congestion control mechanism (added to header by RFC 3168).

- ECE (1 bit): ECN-Echo has a dual role, depending on the value of the SYN flag. It indicates:

- If the SYN flag is set (1), that the TCP peer is ECN capable.

- If the SYN flag is clear (0), that a packet with Congestion Experienced flag set (ECN=11) in IP header received during normal transmission (added to header by RFC 3168). This serves as an indication of network congestion (or impending congestion) to the TCP sender.

- URG (1 bit): indicates that the Urgent pointer field is significant

- ACK (1 bit): indicates that the Acknowledgment field is significant. All packets after the initial SYN packet sent by the client should have this flag set.

- PSH (1 bit): Push function. Asks to push the buffered data to the receiving application.

- RST (1 bit): Reset the connection

- SYN (1 bit): Synchronize sequence numbers. Only the first packet sent from each end should have this flag set. Some other flags and fields change meaning based on this flag, and some are only valid for when it is set, and others when it is clear.

- FIN (1 bit): Last package from sender.

Window size (16 bits)

The size of the *receive window*, which specifies the number of window size units (by default, bytes) (beyond the segment identified by the sequence number in the acknowledgment field) that the sender of this segment is currently willing to receive

Checksum (16 bits)

The 16-bit checksum field is used for error-checking of the header and data

Urgent pointer (16 bits)

if the URG flag is set, then this 16-bit field is an offset from the sequence number indicating the last urgent data byte

Options (Variable 0–320 bits, divisible by 32)

The length of this field is determined by the data offset field. Options have up to three fields: Option-Kind (1 byte), Option-Length (1 byte), Option-Data (variable). The Option-Kind field indicates the type of option, and is the only field that is not optional. Depending on what kind of option we are dealing with, the next two fields may be set: the Option-Length field indicates the total length of the option, and the Option-Data field contains the value of the option, if applicable. For example, an Option-Kind byte of 0x01 indicates that this is a No-Op option used only for padding, and does not have an Option-Length or Option-Data byte following it. An Option-Kind byte of 0 is the End Of Options option, and is also only one byte. An Option-Kind byte of 0x02 indicates that this is the Maximum Segment Size option, and will be followed by a byte specifying the length of the MSS field (should be 0x04). This length is the total length of the given options field, including Option-Kind and Option-Length bytes. So while the MSS value is typically expressed in two bytes, the length of the field will be 4 bytes (+2 bytes of kind and length). In short, an MSS option field with a value of 0x05B4 will show up as (0x02 0x04 0x05B4) in the TCP options section.

Some options may only be sent when SYN is set; they are indicated below as [SYN]. Option-Kind and standard lengths given as (Option-Kind,Option-Length).

- o (8 bits): End of options list

- 1 (8 bits): No operation (NOP, Padding) This may be used to align option fields on 32-bit boundaries for better performance.

- 2,4,*SS* (32 bits): Maximum segment size

- 3,3,*S* (24 bits): Window scale

- 4,2 (16 bits): Selective Acknowledgement permitted.

- 5,*N*,*BBBB*,*EEEE*,... (variable bits, *N* is either 10, 18, 26, or 34)- Selective AC-Knowledgement (SACK) These first two bytes are followed by a list of 1–4 blocks being selectively acknowledged, specified as 32-bit begin/end pointers.

- 8,10,*TTTT*,*EEEE* (80 bits)- Timestamp and echo of previous timestamp (*see TCP timestamps for details*)

(The remaining options are historical, obsolete, experimental, not yet standardized, or unassigned)

Padding

The TCP header padding is used to ensure that the TCP header ends and data begins on a 32 bit boundary. The padding is composed of zeros.

Protocol Operation

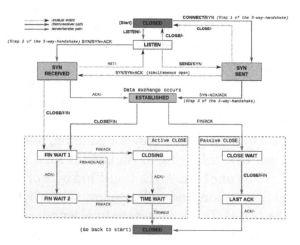

A Simplified TCP State Diagram.

TCP protocol operations may be divided into three phases. Connections must be properly established in a multi-step handshake process (*connection establishment*) before entering the *data transfer* phase. After data transmission is completed, the *connection termination* closes established virtual circuits and releases all allocated resources.

A TCP connection is managed by an operating system through a programming interface that represents the local end-point for communications, the *Internet socket*. During the lifetime of a TCP connection the local end-point undergoes a series of state changes:

Listen

(server) represents waiting for a connection request from any remote TCP and port.

Syn-Sent

(client) represents waiting for a matching connection request after having sent a connection request.

Syn-Received

(server) represents waiting for a confirming connection request acknowledgment after having both received and sent a connection request.

Established

(both server and client) represents an open connection, data received can be delivered to the user. The normal state for the data transfer phase of the connection.

Fin-Wait-1

(both server and client) represents waiting for a connection termination request from the remote TCP, or an acknowledgment of the connection termination request previously sent.

Fin-Wait-2

(both server and client) represents waiting for a connection termination request from the remote TCP.

Close-Wait

(both server and client) represents waiting for a connection termination request from the local user.

Closing

(both server and client) represents waiting for a connection termination request acknowledgment from the remote TCP.

Last-Ack

(both server and client) represents waiting for an acknowledgment of the connection termination request previously sent to the remote TCP (which includes an acknowledgment of its connection termination request).

Time-Wait

(either server or client) represents waiting for enough time to pass to be sure the remote TCP received the acknowledgment of its connection termination request. [According to RFC 793 a connection can stay in TIME-WAIT for a maximum of four minutes known as two MSL (maximum segment lifetime).]

Closed

(both server and client) represents no connection state at all.

Connection Establishment

To establish a connection, TCP uses a three-way handshake. Before a client attempts to connect with a server, the server must first bind to and listen at a port to open it up for connections: this is called a passive open. Once the passive open is established, a client may initiate an active open. To establish a connection, the three-way (or 3-step) handshake occurs:

1. SYN: The active open is performed by the client sending a SYN to the server. The client sets the segment's sequence number to a random value A.

2. SYN-ACK: In response, the server replies with a SYN-ACK. The acknowledgment number is set to one more than the received sequence number i.e. A+1, and the sequence number that the server chooses for the packet is another random number, B.

3. ACK: Finally, the client sends an ACK back to the server. The sequence number is set to the received acknowledgement value i.e. A+1, and the acknowledgement number is set to one more than the received sequence number i.e. B+1.

At this point, both the client and server have received an acknowledgment of the connection. The steps 1, 2 establish the connection parameter (sequence number) for one direction and it is acknowledged. The steps 2, 3 establish the connection parameter (sequence number) for the other direction and it is acknowledged. With these, a full-duplex communication is established.

Connection Termination

The connection termination phase uses a four-way handshake, with each side of the connection terminating independently. When an endpoint wishes to stop its half of the connection, it transmits a FIN packet, which the other end acknowledges with an ACK. Therefore, a typical tear-down requires a pair of FIN and ACK segments from each TCP endpoint. After the side that sent the first FIN has responded with the final ACK, it waits for a timeout before finally closing the connection, during which time the local port is unavailable for new connections; this prevents confusion due to delayed packets being delivered during subsequent connections.

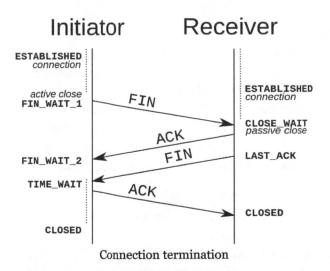

Connection termination

A connection can be "half-open", in which case one side has terminated its end, but the other has not. The side that has terminated can no longer send any data into the connection, but the other side can. The terminating side should continue reading the data until the other side terminates as well.

It is also possible to terminate the connection by a 3-way handshake, when host A sends a FIN and host B replies with a FIN & ACK (merely combines 2 steps into one) and host A replies with an ACK.

Some host TCP stacks may implement a half-duplex close sequence, as Linux or HP-UX do. If such a host actively closes a connection but still has not read all the incoming data the stack already received from the link, this host sends a RST instead of a FIN (Section 4.2.2.13 in RFC 1122). This allows a TCP application to be sure the remote application has read all the data the former sent—waiting the FIN from the remote side, when it actively closes the connection. But the remote TCP stack cannot distinguish between a *Connection Aborting RST* and *Data Loss RST*. Both cause the remote stack to lose all the data received.

Some application protocols using the TCP open/close handshaking for the application protocol open/close handshaking may find the RST problem on active close. As an example:

s = connect(remote);

send(s, data);

close(s);

For a program flow like above, a TCP/IP stack like that described above does not guarantee that all the data arrives to the other application if unread data has arrived at this end.

Resource Usage

Most implementations allocate an entry in a table that maps a session to a running operating system process. Because TCP packets do not include a session identifier, both endpoints identify the session using the client's address and port. Whenever a packet is received, the TCP implementation must perform a lookup on this table to find the destination process. Each entry in the table is known as a Transmission Control Block or TCB. It contains information about the endpoints (IP and port), status of the connection, running data about the packets that are being exchanged and buffers for sending and receiving data.

The number of sessions in the server side is limited only by memory and can grow as new connections arrive, but the client must allocate a random port before sending the first SYN to the server. This port remains allocated during the whole conversation, and effectively limits the number of outgoing connections from each of the client's IP addresses. If an application fails to properly close unrequired connections, a client can run out of resources and become unable to establish new TCP connections, even from other applications.

Both endpoints must also allocate space for unacknowledged packets and received (but unread) data.

Data Transfer

There are a few key features that set TCP apart from User Datagram Protocol:

- Ordered data transfer: the destination host rearranges according to sequence number

- Retransmission of lost packets: any cumulative stream not acknowledged is retransmitted

- Error-free data transfer

- Flow control: limits the rate a sender transfers data to guarantee reliable delivery. The receiver continually hints the sender on how much data can be received (controlled by the sliding window). When the receiving host's buffer fills, the next acknowledgment contains a 0 in the window size, to stop transfer and allow the data in the buffer to be processed.

- Congestion control

Reliable Transmission

TCP uses a *sequence number* to identify each byte of data. The sequence number identifies the order of the bytes sent from each computer so that the data can be reconstructed in order, regardless of any packet reordering, or packet loss that may occur during transmission. The sequence number of the first byte is chosen by the transmitter for the first packet, which is flagged SYN. This number can be arbitrary, and should in fact be unpredictable to defend against TCP sequence prediction attacks.

Acknowledgements (Acks) are sent with a sequence number by the receiver of data to tell the sender that data has been received to the specified byte. Acks do not imply that the data has been delivered to the application. They merely signify that it is now the receiver's responsibility to deliver the data.

Reliability is achieved by the sender detecting lost data and retransmitting it. TCP uses two primary techniques to identify loss. Retransmission timeout (abbreviated as RTO) and duplicate cumulative acknowledgements (DupAcks).

Dupack Based Retransmission

If a single packet (say packet 100) in a stream is lost, then the receiver cannot acknowledge packets above 100 because it uses cumulative acks. Hence the receiver acknowledges packet 100 again on the receipt of another data packet. This duplicate acknowledgement is used as a signal for packet loss. That is, if the sender receives three duplicate acknowledgements, it retransmits the last unacknowledged packet. A threshold of three is used because the network may reorder packets causing duplicate acknowledgements. This threshold has been demonstrated to avoid spurious retransmissions due to reordering. Sometimes selective acknowledgements (SACKs) are used to give more explicit feedback on which packets have been received. This greatly improves TCP's ability to retransmit the right packets.

Timeout Based Retransmission

Whenever a packet is sent, the sender sets a timer that is a conservative estimate of when that packet will be acked. If the sender does not receive an ack by then, it transmits that packet again. The timer is reset every time the sender receives an acknowledgement. This means that the retransmit timer fires only when the sender has received no acknowledgement for a long time. Typically the timer value is set to smoothed $RTT + \max(G, 4 \times RTT \text{ variation})$ where G is the clock granularity. Further, in case a retransmit timer has fired and still no acknowledgement is received, the next timer is set to twice the previous value (up to a certain threshold). Among other things, this helps defend against a man-in-the-middle denial of service attack that tries to fool the sender into making so many retransmissions that the receiver is overwhelmed.

If the sender infers that data has been lost in the network using one of the two techniques described above, it retransmits the data.

Error Detection

Sequence numbers allow receivers to discard duplicate packets and properly sequence reordered packets. Acknowledgments allow senders to determine when to retransmit lost packets.

To assure correctness a checksum field is included; see checksum computation section for details on checksumming. The TCP checksum is a weak check by modern standards. Data Link Layers with high bit error rates may require additional link error correction/detection capabilities. The weak checksum is partially compensated for by the common use of a CRC or better integrity check at layer 2, below both TCP and IP, such as is used in PPP or the Ethernet frame. However, this does not mean that the 16-bit TCP checksum is redundant: remarkably, introduction of errors in packets between CRC-protected hops is common, but the end-to-end 16-bit TCP checksum catches most of these simple errors. This is the end-to-end principle at work.

Flow Control

TCP uses an end-to-end flow control protocol to avoid having the sender send data too fast for the TCP receiver to receive and process it reliably. Having a mechanism for flow control is essential in an environment where machines of diverse network speeds communicate. For example, if a PC sends data to a smartphone that is slowly processing received data, the smartphone must regulate the data flow so as not to be overwhelmed.

TCP uses a sliding window flow control protocol. In each TCP segment, the receiver specifies in the *receive window* field the amount of additionally received data (in bytes) that it is willing to buffer for the connection. The sending host can send only up to that amount of data before it must wait for an acknowledgment and window update from the receiving host.

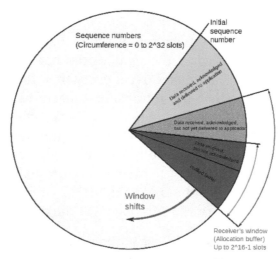

TCP sequence numbers and receive windows behave very much like a clock. The receive window shifts each time the receiver receives and acknowledges a new segment of data. Once it runs out of sequence numbers, the sequence number loops back to 0.

When a receiver advertises a window size of 0, the sender stops sending data and starts the *persist timer*. The persist timer is used to protect TCP from a deadlock situation that could arise if a subsequent window size update from the receiver is lost, and the sender cannot send more data until receiving a new window size update from the receiver. When the persist timer expires, the TCP sender attempts recovery by sending a small packet so that the receiver responds by sending another acknowledgement containing the new window size.

If a receiver is processing incoming data in small increments, it may repeatedly advertise a small receive window. This is referred to as the silly window syndrome, since it is inefficient to send only a few bytes of data in a TCP segment, given the relatively large overhead of the TCP header.

Congestion Control

The final main aspect of TCP is congestion control. TCP uses a number of mechanisms to achieve high performance and avoid congestion collapse, where network performance can fall by several orders of magnitude. These mechanisms control the rate of data entering the network, keeping the data flow below a rate that would trigger collapse. They also yield an approximately max-min fair allocation between flows.

Acknowledgments for data sent, or lack of acknowledgments, are used by senders to infer network conditions between the TCP sender and receiver. Coupled with timers, TCP senders and receivers can alter the behavior of the flow of data. This is more generally referred to as congestion control and/or network congestion avoidance.

Modern implementations of TCP contain four intertwined algorithms: slow-start, congestion avoidance, fast retransmit, and fast recovery (RFC 5681).

In addition, senders employ a *retransmission timeout* (RTO) that is based on the estimated round-trip time (or RTT) between the sender and receiver, as well as the variance in this round trip time. The behavior of this timer is specified in RFC 6298. There are subtleties in the estimation of RTT. For example, senders must be careful when calculating RTT samples for retransmitted packets; typically they use Karn's Algorithm or TCP timestamps. These individual RTT samples are then averaged over time to create a Smoothed Round Trip Time (SRTT) using Jacobson's algorithm. This SRTT value is what is finally used as the round-trip time estimate.

Enhancing TCP to reliably handle loss, minimize errors, manage congestion and go fast in very high-speed environments are ongoing areas of research and standards development. As a result, there are a number of TCP congestion avoidance algorithm variations.

Maximum Segment Size

The maximum segment size (MSS) is the largest amount of data, specified in bytes, that TCP is willing to receive in a single segment. For best performance, the MSS should be set small enough to avoid IP fragmentation, which can lead to packet loss and excessive retransmissions. To try to accomplish this, typically the MSS is announced by each side using the MSS option when the TCP connection is established, in which case it is derived from the maximum transmission unit (MTU) size of the data link layer of the networks to which the sender and receiver are directly attached. Furthermore, TCP senders can use path MTU discovery to infer the minimum MTU along the network path between the sender and receiver, and use this to dynamically adjust the MSS to avoid IP fragmentation within the network.

MSS announcement is also often called "MSS negotiation". Strictly speaking, the MSS is not "negotiated" between the originator and the receiver, because that would imply that both originator and receiver will negotiate and agree upon a single, unified MSS that applies to all communication in both directions of the connection. In fact, two completely independent values of MSS are permitted for the two directions of data flow in a TCP connection. This situation may arise, for example, if one of the devices participating in a connection has an extremely limited amount of memory reserved (perhaps even smaller than the overall discovered Path MTU) for processing incoming TCP segments.

Selective Acknowledgments

Relying purely on the cumulative acknowledgment scheme employed by the original TCP protocol can lead to inefficiencies when packets are lost. For example, suppose 10,000 bytes are sent in 10 different TCP packets, and the first packet is lost during transmission. In a pure cumulative acknowledgment protocol, the receiver cannot say that it received bytes 1,000 to 9,999 successfully, but failed to receive the first packet, containing bytes 0 to 999. Thus the sender may then have to resend all 10,000 bytes.

To alleviate this issue TCP employs the *selective acknowledgment (SACK)* option, defined in RFC 2018, which allows the receiver to acknowledge discontinuous blocks of packets which were received correctly, in addition to the sequence number of the last contiguous byte received successively, as in the basic TCP acknowledgment. The acknowledgement can specify a number of *SACK blocks*, where each SACK block is conveyed by the starting and ending sequence numbers of a contiguous range that the receiver correctly received. In the example above, the receiver would send SACK with sequence numbers 1000 and 9999. The sender would accordingly retransmit only the first packet (bytes 0 to 999).

A TCP sender can interpret an out-of-order packet delivery as a lost packet. If it does so, the TCP sender will retransmit the packet previous to the out-of-order packet and slow its data delivery rate for that connection. The duplicate-SACK option, an extension to the SACK option that was defined in RFC 2883, solves this problem. The TCP receiver sends a D-ACK to indicate that no packets were lost, and the TCP sender can then reinstate the higher transmission-rate.

The SACK option is not mandatory, and comes into operation only if both parties support it. This is negotiated when a connection is established. SACK uses the optional part of the

TCP header. The use of SACK has become widespread—all popular TCP stacks support it. Selective acknowledgment is also used in Stream Control Transmission Protocol (SCTP).

Window Scaling

For more efficient use of high-bandwidth networks, a larger TCP window size may be used. The TCP window size field controls the flow of data and its value is limited to between 2 and 65,535 bytes.

Since the size field cannot be expanded, a scaling factor is used. The TCP window scale option, as defined in RFC 1323, is an option used to increase the maximum window size from 65,535 bytes to 1 gigabyte. Scaling up to larger window sizes is a part of what is necessary for TCP tuning.

The window scale option is used only during the TCP 3-way handshake. The window scale value represents the number of bits to left-shift the 16-bit window size field. The window scale value can be set from 0 (no shift) to 14 for each direction independently. Both sides must send the option in their SYN segments to enable window scaling in either direction.

Some routers and packet firewalls rewrite the window scaling factor during a transmission. This causes sending and receiving sides to assume different TCP window sizes. The result is non-stable traffic that may be very slow. The problem is visible on some sites behind a defective router.

TCP Timestamps

TCP timestamps, defined in RFC 1323, can help TCP determine in which order packets were sent. TCP timestamps are not normally aligned to the system clock and start at some random value. Many operating systems will increment the timestamp for every elapsed millisecond; however the RFC only states that the ticks should be proportional.

There are two timestamp fields:

a 4-byte sender timestamp value (my timestamp)

a 4-byte echo reply timestamp value (the most recent timestamp received from you).

TCP timestamps are used in an algorithm known as *Protection Against Wrapped Sequence* numbers, or *PAWS* PAWS is used when the receive window crosses the sequence number wraparound boundary. In the case where a packet was potentially retransmitted it answers the question: "Is this sequence number in the first 4 GB or the second?" And the timestamp is used to break the tie.

Also, the Eifel detection algorithm (RFC 3522) uses TCP timestamps to determine if retransmissions are occurring because packets are lost or simply out of order.

Out-of-band Data

It is possible to interrupt or abort the queued stream instead of waiting for the stream to finish. This is done by specifying the data as *urgent*. This tells the receiving program to process it immediately, along with the rest of the urgent data. When finished, TCP informs the application and resumes back to the stream queue. An example is when TCP is used for a remote login session, the user can send a keyboard sequence that interrupts or aborts the program at the other end. These signals are most often needed when a program on the remote machine fails to operate correctly. The signals must be sent without waiting for the program to finish its current transfer.

TCP OOB data was not designed for the modern Internet. The *urgent* pointer only alters the processing on the remote host and doesn't expedite any processing on the network itself. When it gets to the remote host there are two slightly different interpretations of the protocol, which means only single bytes of OOB data are reliable. This is assuming it is reliable at all as it is one of the least commonly used protocol elements and tends to be poorly implemented.

Forcing Data Delivery

Normally, TCP waits for 200 ms for a full packet of data to send (Nagle's Algorithm tries to group small messages into a single packet). This wait creates small, but potentially serious delays if repeated constantly during a file transfer. For example, a typical send block would be 4 KB, a typical MSS is 1460, so 2 packets go out on a 10 Mbit/s ethernet taking ~1.2 ms each followed by a third carrying the remaining 1176 after a 197 ms pause because TCP is waiting for a full buffer.

In the case of telnet, each user keystroke is echoed back by the server before the user can see it on the screen. This delay would become very annoying.

Setting the socket option TCP_NODELAY overrides the default 200 ms send delay. Application programs use this socket option to force output to be sent after writing a character or line of characters.

The RFC defines the PSH push bit as "a message to the receiving TCP stack to send this data immediately up to the receiving application". There is no way to indicate or control it in user space using Berkeley sockets and it is controlled by protocol stack only.

Vulnerabilities

TCP may be attacked in a variety of ways. The results of a thorough security assessment of TCP, along with possible mitigations for the identified issues, were published in 2009, and is currently being pursued within the IETF.

Denial of Service

By using a spoofed IP address and repeatedly sending purposely assembled SYN packets, followed by many ACK packets, attackers can cause the server to consume large amounts of resources keeping track of the bogus connections. This is known as a SYN flood attack. Proposed solutions to this problem include SYN cookies and cryptographic puzzles, though SYN cookies come with their own set of vulnerabilities. Sockstress is a similar attack, that might be mitigated with system resource management. An advanced DoS attack involving the exploitation of the TCP Persist Timer was analyzed in Phrack #66.

Connection Hijacking

An attacker who is able to eavesdrop a TCP session and redirect packets can hijack a TCP connection. To do so, the attacker learns the sequence number from the ongoing communication and forges a false segment that looks like the next segment in the stream. Such a simple hijack can result in one packet being erroneously accepted at one end. When the receiving host acknowledges the extra segment to the other side of the connection, synchronization is lost. Hijacking might be combined with Address Resolution Protocol (ARP) or routing attacks that allow taking control of the packet flow, so as to get permanent control of the hijacked TCP connection.

Impersonating a different IP address was not difficult prior to RFC 1948, when the initial *sequence number* was easily guessable. That allowed an attacker to blindly send a sequence of packets that the receiver would believe to come from a different IP address, without the need to deploy ARP or routing attacks: it is enough to ensure that the legitimate host of the impersonated IP address is down, or bring it to that condition using denial-of-service attacks. This is why the initial sequence number is now chosen at random.

TCP Veto

An attacker who can eavesdrop and predict the size of the next packet to be sent can cause the receiver to accept a malicious payload without disrupting the existing connection. The attacker injects a malicious packet with the sequence number and a payload size of the next expected packet. When the legitimate packet is ultimately received, it is found to have the same sequence number and length as a packet already received and is silently dropped as a normal duplicate packet—the legitimate packet is "vetoed" by the malicious packet. Unlike in connection hijacking, the connection is never desynchronized and communication continues as normal after the malicious payload is accepted. TCP veto gives the attacker less control over the communication, but makes the attack particularly resistant to detection. The large increase in network traffic from the ACK storm is avoided. The only evidence to the receiver that something is amiss is a single duplicate packet, a normal occurrence in an IP network. The sender of the vetoed packet never sees any evidence of an attack.

Another vulnerability is TCP reset attack.

TCP ports

TCP and UDP use port numbers to identify sending and receiving application endpoints on a host, often called Internet sockets. Each side of a TCP connection has an associated 16-bit unsigned port number (0-65535) reserved by the sending or receiving application. Arriving TCP packets are identified as belonging to a specific TCP connection by its sockets, that is, the combination of source host address, source port, destination host address, and destination port. This means that a server computer can provide several clients with several services simultaneously, as long as a client takes care of initiating any simultaneous connections to one destination port from different source ports.

Port numbers are categorized into three basic categories: well-known, registered, and dynamic/private. The well-known ports are assigned by the Internet Assigned Numbers Authority (IANA) and are typically used by system-level or root processes. Well-known applications running as servers and passively listening for connections typically use these ports. Some examples include: FTP (20 and 21), SSH (22), TELNET (23), SMTP (25), HTTP over SSL/TLS (443), and HTTP (80). Registered ports are typically used by end user applications as ephemeral source ports when contacting servers, but they can also identify named services that have been registered by a third party. Dynamic/private ports can also be used by end user applications, but are less commonly so. Dynamic/private ports do not contain any meaning outside of any particular TCP connection.

Network Address Translation (NAT), typically uses dynamic port numbers, on the ("Internet-facing") public side, to disambiguate the flow of traffic that is passing between a public network and a private subnetwork, thereby allowing many IP addresses (and their ports) on the subnet to be serviced by a single public-facing address.

Development

TCP is a complex protocol. However, while significant enhancements have been made and proposed over the years, its most basic operation has not changed significantly since its first specification RFC 675 in 1974, and the v4 specification RFC 793, published in September 1981. RFC 1122, Host Requirements for Internet Hosts, clarified a number of TCP protocol implementation requirements. A list of the 8 required specifications and over 20 strongly encouraged enhancements is available in RFC 7414. Among this list is RFC 2581, TCP Congestion Control, one of the most important TCP-related RFCs in recent years, describes updated algorithms that avoid undue congestion. In 2001, RFC 3168 was written to describe Explicit Congestion Notification (ECN), a congestion avoidance signaling mechanism.

The original TCP congestion avoidance algorithm was known as "TCP Tahoe", but many alternative algorithms have since been proposed (including TCP Reno, TCP Vegas, FAST TCP, TCP New Reno, and TCP Hybla).

TCP Interactive (iTCP) is a research effort into TCP extensions that allows applications to subscribe to TCP events and register handler components that can launch applications for various purposes, including application-assisted congestion control.

Multipath TCP (MPTCP) is an ongoing effort within the IETF that aims at allowing a TCP connection to use multiple paths to maximize resource usage and increase redundancy. The redundancy offered by Multipath TCP in the context of wireless networks enables the simultaneous utilization of different networks, which brings higher throughput and better handover capabilities. Multipath TCP also brings performance benefits in datacenter environments. The reference implementation of Multipath TCP is being developed in the Linux kernel. Multipath TCP is used to support the Siri voice recognition application on iPhones, iPads and Macs

TCP Cookie Transactions (TCPCT) is an extension proposed in December 2009 to secure servers against denial-of-service attacks. Unlike SYN cookies, TCPCT does not conflict with other TCP extensions such as window scaling. TCPCT was designed due to necessities of DNSSEC, where servers have to handle large numbers of short-lived TCP connections.

tcpcrypt is an extension proposed in July 2010 to provide transport-level encryption directly in TCP itself. It is designed to work transparently and not require any configuration. Unlike TLS (SSL), tcpcrypt itself does not provide authentication, but provides simple primitives down to the application to do that. As of 2010, the first tcpcrypt IETF draft has been published and implementations exist for several major platforms.

TCP Fast Open is an extension to speed up the opening of successive TCP connections between two endpoints. It works by skipping the three-way handshake using a cryptographic "cookie". It is similar to an earlier proposal called T/TCP, which was not widely adopted due to security issues. As of July 2012, it is an IETF Internet draft.

Proposed in May 2013, Proportional Rate Reduction (PRR) is a TCP extension developed by Google engineers. PRR ensures that the TCP window size after recovery is as close to the Slow-start threshold as possible. The algorithm is designed to improve the speed of recovery and is the default congestion control algorithm in Linux 3.2+ kernels.

TCP Over Wireless Networks

TCP was originally designed for wired networks. Packet loss is considered to be the result of network congestion and the congestion window size is reduced dramatically as a precaution. However, wireless links are known to experience sporadic and usually temporary losses due to fading, shadowing, hand off, interference, and other radio effects, that are not strictly congestion. After the (erroneous) back-off of the congestion window size, due to wireless packet loss, there may be a congestion avoidance phase with a conservative decrease in window size. This causes the radio link to be underutilized. Extensive research on combating these harmful effects has been conducted. Suggested solutions can be categorized as end-to-end solutions, which require modifications at the client or server, link layer solutions, such as Radio Link Protocol (RLP) in cellular networks, or proxy-based solutions which require some changes in the network without modifying end nodes.

A number of alternative congestion control algorithms, such as Vegas, Westwood, Veno, and Santa Cruz, have been proposed to help solve the wireless problem.

Hardware Implementations

One way to overcome the processing power requirements of TCP is to build hardware implementations of it, widely known as TCP offload engines (TOE). The main problem of TOEs is that they are hard to integrate into computing systems, requiring extensive changes in the operating system of the computer or device. One company to develop such a device was Alacritech.

Debugging

A packet sniffer, which intercepts TCP traffic on a network link, can be useful in debugging networks, network stacks, and applications that use TCP by showing the user what packets are passing through a link. Some networking stacks support the SO_DEBUG socket option, which can be enabled on the socket using setsockopt. That option dumps all the packets, TCP states, and events on that socket, which is helpful in debugging. Netstat is another utility that can be used for debugging.

Alternatives

For many applications TCP is not appropriate. One problem (at least with normal implementations) is that the application cannot access the packets coming after a lost packet until the retransmitted copy of the lost packet is received. This causes problems for real-time applications such as streaming media, real-time multiplayer games and voice over IP (VoIP) where it is generally more useful to get most of the data in a timely fashion than it is to get all of the data in order.

For historical and performance reasons, most storage area networks (SANs) use Fibre Channel Protocol (FCP) over Fibre Channel connections.

Also, for embedded systems, network booting, and servers that serve simple requests from huge numbers of clients (e.g. DNS servers) the complexity of TCP can be a problem. Finally, some tricks such as transmitting data between two hosts that are both behind NAT (using STUN or similar systems) are far simpler without a relatively complex protocol like TCP in the way.

Generally, where TCP is unsuitable, the User Datagram Protocol (UDP) is used. This provides the application multiplexing and checksums that TCP does, but does not handle streams or retransmission, giving the application developer the ability to code them in a way suitable for the situation, or to replace them with other methods like forward error correction or interpolation.

Stream Control Transmission Protocol (SCTP) is another protocol that provides reliable stream oriented services similar to TCP. It is newer and considerably more complex than TCP, and has not yet seen widespread deployment. However, it is especially designed to be used in situations where reliability and near-real-time considerations are important.

Venturi Transport Protocol (VTP) is a patented proprietary protocol that is designed to replace TCP transparently to overcome perceived inefficiencies related to wireless data transport.

TCP also has issues in high-bandwidth environments. The TCP congestion avoidance algorithm works very well for ad-hoc environments where the data sender is not known in advance. If the environment is predictable, a timing based protocol such as Asynchronous Transfer Mode (ATM) can avoid TCP's retransmits overhead.

UDP-based Data Transfer Protocol (UDT) has better efficiency and fairness than TCP in networks that have high bandwidth-delay product.

Multipurpose Transaction Protocol (MTP/IP) is patented proprietary software that is designed to adaptively achieve high throughput and transaction performance in a wide variety of network conditions, particularly those where TCP is perceived to be inefficient.

Checksum Computation

TCP Checksum for IPv4

When TCP runs over IPv4, the method used to compute the checksum is defined in RFC 793:

The checksum field is the 16 bit one's complement of the one's complement sum of all 16-bit words in the header and text. If a segment contains an odd number of header and text octets to be checksummed, the last octet is padded on the right with zeros to form a 16-bit word for checksum purposes. The pad is not transmitted as part of the segment. While computing the checksum, the checksum field itself is replaced with zeros.

In other words, after appropriate padding, all 16-bit words are added using one's complement arithmetic. The sum is then bitwise complemented and inserted as the checksum field. A pseudo-header that mimics the IPv4 packet header used in the checksum computation is shown in the table below.

TCP pseudo-header for checksum computation (IPv4)				
Bit offset	0–3	4–7	8–15	16–31
0	Source address			
32	Destination address			
64	Zeros		Protocol	TCP length
96	Source port			Destination port
128	Sequence number			
160	Acknowledgement number			
192	Data offset	Reserved	Flags	Window
224	Checksum			Urgent pointer
256	Options (optional)			
256/288+	Data			

The source and destination addresses are those of the IPv4 header. The protocol value is 6 for TCP (cf. List of IP protocol numbers). The TCP length field is the length of the TCP header and data (measured in octets).

TCP Checksum for IPv6

When TCP runs over IPv6, the method used to compute the checksum is changed, as per RFC 2460:

Any transport or other upper-layer protocol that includes the addresses from the IP header in its checksum computation must be modified for use over IPv6, to include the 128-bit IPv6 addresses instead of 32-bit IPv4 addresses.

A pseudo-header that mimics the IPv6 header for computation of the checksum is shown below.

TCP pseudo-header for checksum computation (IPv6)				
Bit offset	0–7	8–15	16–23	24–31
0	Source address			
32				
64				
96				
128	Destination address			
160				
192				
224				
256	TCP length			
288	Zeros			Next header

320	Source port		Destination port
352	Sequence number		
384	Acknowledgement number		
416	Data offset	Re-served	Flags	Window
448	Checksum		Urgent pointer
480	Options (optional)		
480/512+	Data		

- Source address: the one in the IPv6 header

- Destination address: the final destination; if the IPv6 packet doesn't contain a Routing header, TCP uses the destination address in the IPv6 header, otherwise, at the originating node, it uses the address in the last element of the Routing header, and, at the receiving node, it uses the destination address in the IPv6 header.

- TCP length: the length of the TCP header and data

- Next Header: the protocol value for TCP

Checksum Offload

Many TCP/IP software stack implementations provide options to use hardware assistance to automatically compute the checksum in the network adapter prior to transmission onto the network or upon reception from the network for validation. This may relieve the OS from using precious CPU cycles calculating the checksum. Hence, overall network performance is increased.

This feature may cause packet analyzers that are unaware or uncertain about the use of checksum offload to report invalid checksums in outbound packets that have not yet reached the network adapter. This will only occur for packets that are intercepted before being being transmitted by the network adapter; all packets transmitted by the network adaptor on the wire will have valid checksums. This issue can also occur when monitoring packets being transmitted between virtual machines on the same host, where a virtual device driver may omit the checksum calculation (as an optimization), knowing that the checksum will be calculated later by the VM host kernel or its physical hardware.

IP Addressing

Every host and router on the internet is provided with a unique standard form of network address, which encodes its network number and host number. The combination is unique; no two nodes have the same IP addresses. The IP addresses are 32-bit long having the formats shown in Figure. The three main address formats are assigned with network addresses (net id) and host address (host id) fields of different sizes. The class A format allows up to 126 networks with 16 million hosts each. Class B allows up to 16,382 networks with up to 64 K hosts each. Class C allows 2 million networks with up to 254 hosts each. The Class D is used for multicasting in which a datagram is directed to multiple hosts. Addresses beginning with 11110 are reserved for future use. Network addresses are usually written in dotted decimal notation, such as 126.12.15.220, where each byte is written in decimal number corresponding to the binary value. Figure illustrates how the dotted decimal representation is obtained for a particular IP address in binary form. Range of IP addresses for different classes is given in figure. Some IP addresses, which are used in special situations such as the same host, a host the same network, broadcast on the same network, broadcast on a distant network, or loopback are given in figure. This approach of representing IP addresses in terms of classes is known as *classful addressing*. In mid 90's another approach known as *classlees addressing* has been proposed, which may supersede the existing classful addressing approach in future.

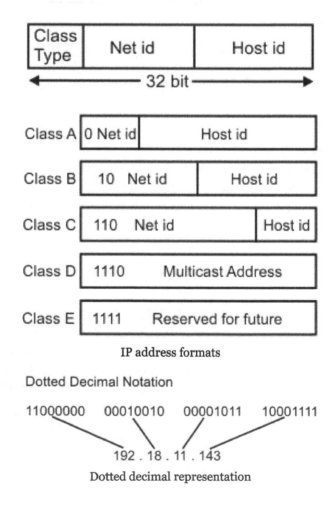

IP address formats

Dotted Decimal Notation

Dotted decimal representation

Range of Host Addresses

Class A	1.0.0.0	to 127.255.255.255
Class B	128.0.0.0	to 191.255.255.255
Class C	192.0.0.0	to 233.255.255.255
Class D	244.0.0.0	to 239.255.255.255
Class E	240.0.0.0	to 247.255.255.255

Dotted decimal notation of the IP addresses

00000000	00000000	00000000	00000000	This host
0000 00000 00	hostid			A host on this network
11111111	11111111	11111111	11111111	Broadcast on this network
netid	1111..............................1111			Broadcast on a distant network
127	Anything			Loopback

Special IP addresses

Subnetting

To filter packets for a particular network, a router uses a concept known as *masking*, which filters out the net id part (by ANDing with all 1's) by removing the host id part (by ANDing with all 0's). The net id part is then compared with the network address as shown in figure. All the hosts in a network must have the same network number. This property of IP addressing causes problem as the network grows. To overcome this problem, a concept known as *subnets* is used, which splits a network into several parts for internal use, but still acts like a single network to the outside world. To facilitate routing, a concept known as *subnet mask* is used. As shown in figure, a part of hostid is used as subnet address with a corresponding subnet mask. Subnetting reduces router table space by creating a three-level hierarchy; net id, subnet id followed by hosted.

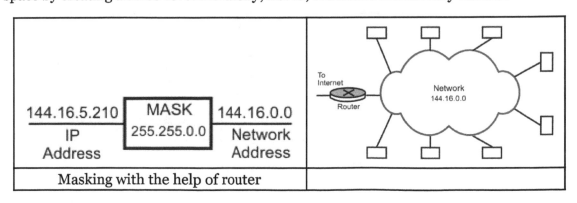

Masking with the help of router

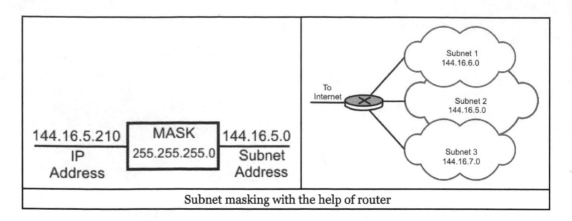

Subnet masking with the help of router

Network Address Translation (NAT)

With the increasing number of internet users requiring an unique IP address for each host, there is an acute shortage of IP addresses (until everybody moves to IPV6). The *Network Address Translation* (NAT) approach is a quick interim solution to this problem. NAT allows a large set of IP addresses to be used in an internal (private) network and a handful of addresses to be used for the external internet. The internet authorities has set aside three sets of addresses to be used as private addresses as shown in table. It may be noted that these addresses can be reused within different internal networks simultaneously, which in effect has helped to increase the lifespan of the IPV4. However, to make use of the concept, it is necessary to have a router to perform the operation of address translation between the private network and the internet. As shown in figure, the NAT router maintains a table with a pair of entries for private and internet address. The source address of all outgoing packets passing through the NAT router gets replaced by an internet address based on table look up. Similarly, the destination address of all incoming packets passing through the NAT router gets replaced by the corresponding private address, as shown in the figure. The NAT can use a pool of internet addresses to have internet access by a limited number of stations of the private network at a time.

Table: Addresses for Private Network

Range of addresses	Total number
10.0.0.0 to 10.255.255.255	2^{24}
172.16.0.0 to 172.31.255.255	2^{20}
192.168.0.0 to 192.168.255.255	2^{16}

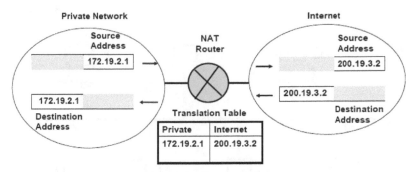

NAT Address translation

Address Resolution Protocol (ARP)

It may be noted that the knowledge of hosts' IP address is not sufficient for sending packets, because *data link hardware does not understand internet addresses*. For example, in an Ethernet network, the Ethernet controller card can send and receive using 48-bit Ethernet addresses. The 32-bit IP addresses are unknown to these cards. This requires a mapping of the IP addresses to the corresponding Ethernet addresses. This mapping is accomplished by using a technique known as *Address Resolution Protocol (ARP)*.

One possible approach is to have a *configuration file* somewhere in the system that maps IP addresses onto the Ethernet addresses. Although this approach is straightforward, maintaining an up-too-date table has a high overhead on the system. Another elegant approach is to broadcast packet onto the Ethernet asking "*who owns the destination IP address?*". The destination node responds with its Ethernet address after hearing the request. This protocol of asking the question and getting the reply is called ARP (Addressing Resolution Protocol), which is widely used. ARP is a dynamic mapping approach for finding a physical address for a known IP address. It involves following two basic steps as shown in figure.

- An ARP request is broadcast to all stations in the network

- An ARP reply is an unicast to the host requesting the mapping

(A)

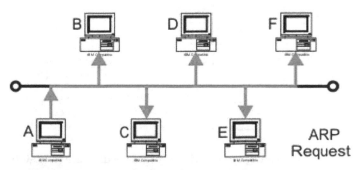

(a) ARP request with a broadcast to all the stations and

(B)

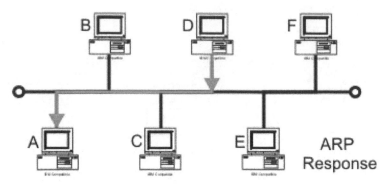

(b) ARP response is a unicast only to the requesting host

Various optimizations are commonly used to improve the efficiency of the ARP proto-col. One possible approach is to use cache memory to hold the recently acquired frame containing the physical address. As a consequence, no broadcasting is necessary in near future. Figure shows how an ARP packet is encapsulated into the data field of a MAC frame.

Reverse ARP (RARP)

The TCP/IP protocols include another related protocol known as reverse ARP, which can be used by a computer such as a diskless host to find out its own IP address. It in-volves the following steps:

- Diskless host A broadcasts a RARP request specifying itself as the target

- RARP server responds with the reply directly to host A

- Host A preserves the IP address in its main memory for future use until it re-boots

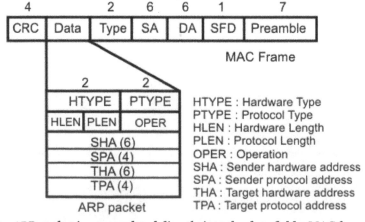

ARP packet

An ARP packet is encapsulated directly into the data field a MAC frame

IP Datagram

As we have mentioned earlier, IP is an unreliable and connectionless *best-effort* delivery service protocol. By best effort we mean that there is no error and flow control. However, IP performs error detection and discards a packet, if it is corrupted. To achieve reliability, it is necessary to combine it with a reliable protocol such as TCP. Packets in IP layer are called *datagrams*. The IP header provides information about various functions the IP performs. The IP header format is shown in figure. The 20 to 60 octets of header has a number of fields to provide:

- Source and destination IP addresses

- Non transparent fragmentation

- Error checking

- Priority

- Security

- Source routing option

- Route Recording option

- Stream identification

- Time stamping

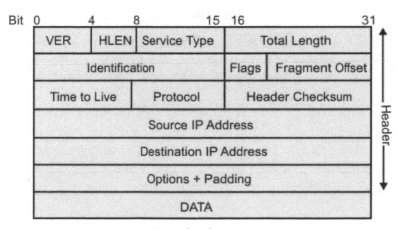

IP packet format

A brief description of each of the fields are given below:

- VER (4 bits): Version of the IP protocol in use (typically 4).

- HLEN (4 bits): Length of the header, expressed as the number of 32-bit words. Minimum size is 5, and maximum 15.

- Total Length (16 bits): Length in bytes of the datagram, including headers. Maximum datagram size is (2^{16}) 65536 bytes.

- Service Type (8 bits): Allows packet to be assigned a priority. Router can use this field to route packets. Not universally used.

- Time to Live (8 bits): Prevents a packet from traveling forever in a loop. Senders sets a value, that is decremented at each hop. If it reaches zero, packet is discarded.

- Protocol: Defines the higher level protocol that uses the service of the IP layer

- Source IP address (32 bits): Internet address of the sender.

- Destination IP address (32 bits): Internet address of the destination.

- Identification, Flags, Fragment Offset: Used for handling fragmentation.

- Options (variable width): Can be used to provide more functionality to the IP datagram

- Header Checksum (16 bits):

  o Covers only the IP header.

  o Steps:

  o Header treated as a sequence of 16-bit integers

  o The integers are all added using ones complement arithmetic

  o Ones complement of the final sum is taken as the checksum

  o Datagram is discarded in case of mismatch in checksum values

Multiplexing and Demultiplexing

IP datagram can encapsulate data from several higher-level protocols such as TCP, UDP, ICMP, etc. The Protocol field in the datagram specifies the final destination protocol to which IP datagram to be delivered. When the datagram arrives at the destination, the information in this field is used to perform demultiplex the operation. The multiplexing and demultiplexing operations are shown in figure.

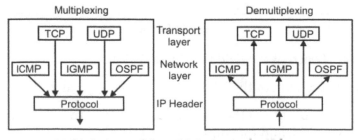

Multiplexing and demultiplexing in the IP layer

Fragmentation and Reassembly

Each network imposes a limit on maximum size, known as *maximum transfer unit* (MTU) of a packet because of various reasons. One approach is to prevent the problem to occur in the first place, i.e. send packets smaller than the MTU. Second approach is to deal with the problem using fragmentation. When a gateway connects two networks that have different maximum and or minimum packet sizes, it is necessary to allow the gateway to break packets up into fragments, sending each one as an internet packet. The technique is known as *fragmentation*. The following fields of an IP datagram are related to fragmentation:

- Identification: A16-bit field identifies a datagram originating from the source host.

- Flags: There are 3 bits, the first bit is reserved, the second bit is *do not fragment* bit, and the last bit *is more fragment* bit.

- Fragmentation offset: This 13-bit field shows the relative position of the segment with respect to the complete datagram measured in units of 8 bytes.

Figure shows a fragmentation example, where a packet is fragmented into packets of 1600 bytes. So, the offset of the second fragmented packet is 1600/8 = 200 and the offset of the third fragmented packet is 400 and so on.

The reverse process, known as *reassembly*, which puts the fragments together, is a more difficult task. There are two opposing strategies for performing the re-assembly. In the first case, the fragmentation in one network is made transparent to any subsequent networks. This requires that packets to be reassembled before sending it to subsequent networks as shown in figure. This strategy is used in ATM. As re-assembly requires sufficient buffer space for storage of all the fragments, this approach has large storage overhead. To overcome this problem in the second strategy, re-assembly is done only at the ultimate destination. This approach does not require large buffer but additional fields are to be added to each packet for independent addressing and to indicate the fragment number as shown in figure.

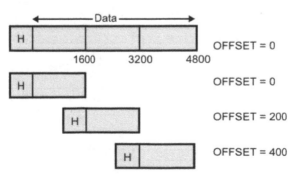

Fragmentation example

(A)

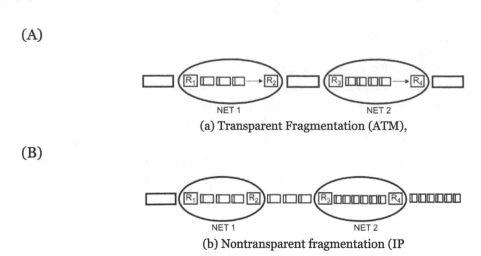

NET 1   NET 2

(a) Transparent Fragmentation (ATM),

(B)

NET 1   NET 2

(b) Nontransparent fragmentation (IP

ICMP

To make efficient use of the network resources, IP was designed to provide unreliable and connectionless best-effort datagram delivery service. As a consequence, IP has no error-control mechanism and also lacks mechanism for host and management queries. A companion protocol known as *Internet Control Message Protocol* (ICMP), has been designed to compensate these two deficiencies. ICMP messages can be broadly divided into two broad categories: error reporting messages and query messages as follows.

- Error reporting Messages: Destination unreachable, Time exceeded, Source quench, Parameter problems, Redirect

- Query: Echo request and reply, Timestamp request and reply, Address mask request and reply

The frame formats of these query and messages are shown in figure.

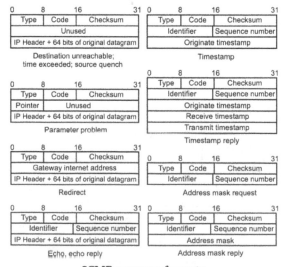

ICMP message formats

IPV6

The network layer that is present in use in commonly referred to as IPv4. Although IPv4 is well designed and has helped the internet to grow rapidly, it has some deficiencies, These deficiencies has made it unsuitable for the fast growing internet. To overcome these deficiencies, Internet Protocol, Version 6 protocol has been proposed and it has evolved into a standard. Important features of IPv6 are highlighted below:

- IPv6 uses 128-bit address instead of 32-bit address to provide larger address space

- Uses more flexible header format, which simplifies and speeds up the routing process

- Basic header followed by extended header

- Resource Allocation options, which was not present in IPv4

- Provision of new/future protocol options

- Support for security with the help of encryption and authentication

- Support for fragmentation at source

Transport Level Protocol

So far we have discussed the delivery of data in the following two ways:

- Node-to-node delivery: At the data-link level, delivery of frames take place between two nodes connected by a point-to-point link or a LAN, by using the data-link layers address, say MAC address.

- Host-to-host delivery: At the network level, delivery of datagrams can take place between two hosts by using IP address.

From user's point of view, the TCP/IP-based internet can be considered as a set of application programs that use the internet to carry out useful communication tasks. Most popular internet applications include Electronic mail, File transfer, and Remote login. IP allows transfer of IP datagrams among a number of stations or hosts, where the datagram is routed through the internet based on the IP address of the destination. But, in this case, several application programs (processes) simultaneously running on a source host has to communicate with the corresponding processes running on a remote destination host through the internet. This requires an additional mechanism called *process-to-process delivery*, which is implemented with the help of a transport-level protocol. The transport level protocol will require an additional address, known as *port number*, to select a particular process among multiple processes running on the destination host. So, there is a requirement of the following third type of delivery system.

- Process-to-process delivery: At the transport level, communication can take place between processes or application programs by using port addresses

Basic communication mechanism is shown in figure. The additional mechanism needed to facilitate multiple application programs in different stations to communicate with each other simultaneously can be provided by a transport level protocol such as UDP or TCP, which are discussed in this lesson.

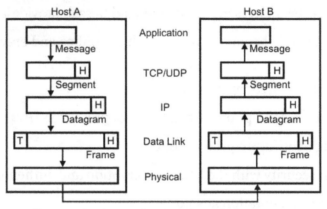

Communication mechanism through the internet

User Datagram protocol (UDP)

UDP is responsible for differentiating among multiple source and destination processes within one host. Multiplexing and demultiplexing operations are performed using the port mechanism as depicted in figure.

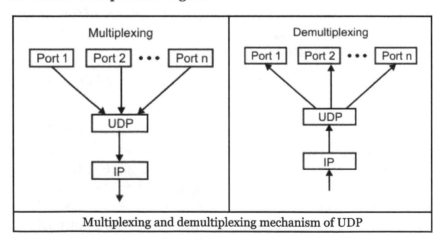

Multiplexing and demultiplexing mechanism of UDP

Port Numbers

Transport layer address is specified with the help a 16-bit Port number in the range of 0 and 65535. Internet Assigned Number Authority (IANA) has divided the addresses in three ranges:

- Well-known ports: The ports in the range from 0 to 1023 are assigned and controlled by IANA. These port numbers are commonly used as universal port numbers in the servers for the convenience of many clients the servers serve. Some commonly used well-known ports used with UDP is given in table.

- Registered ports: Registered ports in the range from 1024 to 49151 are not assigned or controlled by IANA. However, they can only be registered with IANA to avoid duplication.

- Dynamic ports: Dynamic ports (49152 to 65535) are neither controlled by IANA nor need to be registered. They can be defined at the client site and chosen randomly by the transport layer software.

Table Well-known ports used by UDP

Port	Protocol	Description
7	Echo	Echoes a received datagram back to the sender
9	Discard	Discards any datagram that is received
11	Users	Active users
13	Daytime	Returns the date and the time
17	Quote	Returns a quote of the day
19	Chargen	Returns a string of characters
53	Nameserver	Domain Name Service
67	Bootpc	Server port to download bootstrap information
68	Bootpc	Client port to download bootstrap information
69	TFTP	Trivial File Transfer Protocol
111	RPC	Remote Procedure Call
123	NTP	Network Time Protocol
161	SNMP	Simple Network Management Protocol
162	SNMP	Simple Network Management Protocol (trap)

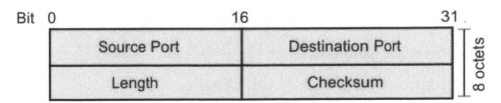

UDP Datagram Format

UDP Datagram

The UDP datagram format is shown in figure. A brief description of different fields of the datagram are given below:

- Source port (16 bits): It defines the port number of the application program in the host of the sender

- Destination port (16 bits): It defines the port number of the application program in the host of the receiver

- Length: It provides a count of octets in the UDP datagram, minimum length = 8

- Checksum: It is optional, 0 in case it is not in use

Characteristics of the UDP

Key characteristics of UDP are given below:

- UDP provides an unreliable connectionless delivery service using IP to transport messages between two processes

- UDP messages can be lost, duplicated, delayed and can be delivered out of order

- UDP is a thin protocol, which does not add significantly to the functionality of IP

- It cannot provide reliable stream transport service

The above limitations can be overcome by using connection-oriented transport layer protocol known as *Transmission Control Protocol* (TCP), which is presented in the following section.

Transmission Control Protocol (TCP)

TCP provides a connection-oriented, full-duplex, reliable, streamed delivery service using IP to transport messages between two processes.

Reliability is ensured by:

- Connection-oriented service

- Flow control using sliding window protocol

- Error detection using checksum

- Error control using go-back-N ARQ technique

- Congestion avoidance algorithms; multiplicative decrease and slow-start

TCP Datagram

The TCP datagram format is shown in figure. A brief explanation of the functions of different fields are given below:

- Source port (16 bits): It defines the port number of the application program in the host of the sender

- Destination port (16 bits): It defines the port number of the application program in the host of the receiver

- Sequence number (32 bits): It conveys the receiving host which octet in this sequence comprises the first byte in the segment

- Acknowledgement number (32 bits): This specifies the sequence number of the next octet that receiver expects to receive

- HLEN (4 bits): This field specifies the number of 32-bit words present in the TCP header

- Control flag bits (6 bits): URG: Urgent pointer

- ACK: Indicates whether acknowledge field is valid

- PSH: Push the data without buffering

- RST: Resent the connection

- SYN: Synchronize sequence numbers during connection establishment

- FIN: Terminate the connection

- Window (16 bits): Specifies the size of window

- Checksum (16 bits): Checksum used for error detection.

- User pointer (16 bits): Used only when URG flag is valid

- Options: Optional 40 bytes of information

The well-known ports used by TCP are given in table and the three types of addresses used in TCP/IP are shown in figure. TCP establishes a virtual path between the source and destination processes before any data communication by using two procedures, connection establishment to start reliably and connection termination to terminate gracefully, as discussed in the following subsection.

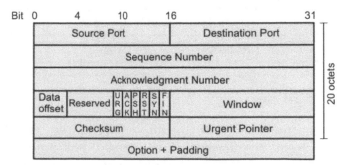

The TCP datagram format

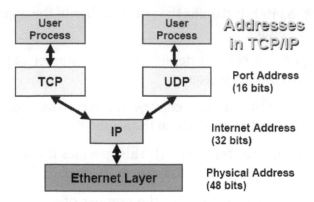

Three types of addresses used in TCP/IP

Table Well-known ports used by TCP

Port	Protocol	Description
7	Echo	Echoes a received datagram back to the sender
9	Discard	Discards any datagram that is received
11	Users	Active users
13	Daytime	Returns the date and the time
17	Quote	Returns a quote of the day
19	Chargen	Returns a string of characters
20	FTP, Data	File Transfer Protocol (data connections)
21	FTP, Control	File Transfer Protocol (control connection)
23	TELNET	Terminal Network
25	SMTP	Simple Mail Transfer Protocol
53	DNS	Domain Name Server
67	BOOTP	BOOTP Protocol
79	Finger	Finger
80	HTTP	Hypertext Transfer Protocol
111	RPC	Remote Procedure Call

Connection-oriented Service

TCP performs data communication in full-duplex mode, that is both the sender and receiver processes can send segments simultaneously. For connection establishment in full-duplex mode, a four-way protocol can be used. However, the second and third steps can be combined to form a three-way handshaking protocol with the following three steps as shown in figure.

Step 1: The client sends SYN segment, which includes, source and destination port numbers, and an *initialization sequence number* (ISN), which is essentially the byte number to be sent from the client to the server.

Step 2: The server sends a segment, which is a two-in-one segment. It acknowledges the receipt of the previous segment and it also acts as initialization segment for the server.

Step3: The sends an ACK segment, which acknowledges the receipt of the second segment

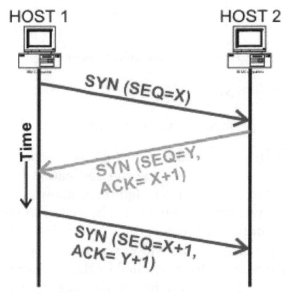

Protocol for connection establishment

X, Y = Initialization Sequence Numbers

Similarly for connection termination, a four-way handshaking protocol is necessary for termination of connection in both directions as shown in figure. The four steps are as follows:

Step 1: The client sends a FIN segment to the server.

Step 2: The server sends an ACK segment indicating the receipt of the FIN segment and the segment also acts as initialization segment for the server.

Step3: The server can still continue to send data and when the data transfer is complete it sends a FIN segment to the client.

Step4: The client sends an ACK segment, which acknowledges the receipt of the FIN segment sent by the server.

Both the connections are terminated after this four-way handshake protocol.

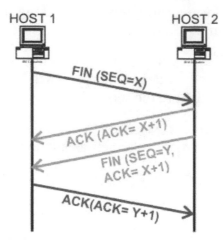

Protocol for connection termination

Reliable Communication

To ensure reliability, TCP performs flow control, error control and congestion control.

Flow control: TCP uses byte-oriented sliding window protocol, which allows efficient transmission of data and at the same time the destination host is not overwhelmed with data. The flow control operation is in figure. As shown in the figure, the receiver has a buffer size of 8 Kbytes. After receiving 4 K bytes, the window size is reduced to 4 Kbytes. After receiving another 3 K bytes, the window size reduces to 1 K bytes. After the buffer gets empty by 4 K bytes, the widow size increases to 7 K bytes. So it may be noted that the window size is totally controlled by the receiver window size, which can be increased or decreased dynamically by the destination. The destination host can send acknowledgement any time.

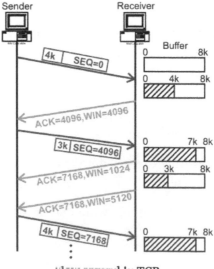

Flow control in TCP

Error Control: Error control in TCP includes mechanism for detecting corrupted segments with the help of checksum field. Acknowledgement method is used to confirm the receipt of uncorrupted data. If the acknowledgement is not received before the time-out, it is assumed that the data or the acknowledgement has been corrupted or lost. It may

be noted that there is no negative acknowledgement in TCP. To keep track of lost or discarded segments and to perform the operations smoothly, the following four timers are used by TCP:

- Retransmission; it is dynamically decided by the round trip delay time.

- Persistence; this is used to deal with window size advertisement.

- Keep-alive; commonly used in situations where there is long idle connection between two processes

- Time-waited; it is used during connection terminations

Congestion control: To avoid congestion, the sender process uses two strategies known as slow-start and additive increase, and the send one is known as multiplicative decrease as shown in figure. To start with, the congestion widow size is set to the maximum segment size and for each segment that is acknowledged, the size of the congestion window size is increased by maximum segment size until it reaches one-half of the allowable window size. Ironically, this is known as *slow-start*, although the rate of increase is exponential as shown in the figure. After reaching the threshold, the window size is increased by one segment for each acknowledgement. This continues till there is no time-out. When a time-out occurs, the threshold is set to one-half of the last congestion window size

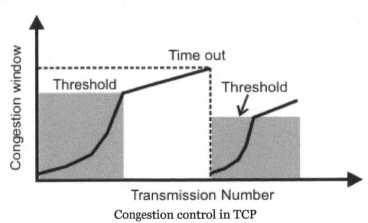

Congestion control in TCP

Client-Server Paradigm and its Applications

The way the application programs communicate with each other is based on client-server model as shown in figure. This provides the foundation on which distributed algorithms are developed. A client process formulates a request, sends it to the server and then waits for response. A server process awaits a request at a well-known port that has been reserved for the service and sends responses. Two identifiers, namely IP address and the port number, are necessary for process-to-process communication. The combination of the two is called a *socket address*. A pair of socket addresses; one of the client and the other of the server, are necessary for the transport-layer protocol. This allows multiplexing and demultiplexing by the transport layer as we have already discussed. There are several applications such as Doman Name System, Telnet, FTP, Email and SNMP, based on client-server paradigm are briefly discussed in the following subsections.

Domain Name System

Although IP addresses are convenient and compact way for identifying machines and are fundamental in TCP/IP, it is unsuitable for human user. Meaningful high-level symbolic names are more convenient for humans. Application software permits users to use symbolic names, but the underlying network protocols require addresses. This requires the use of names with proper syntax with efficient translation mechanism. A concept known as *Domain Name System* (DNS) was invented for this purpose. DNS is a naming scheme that uses a hierarchical, domain-based naming scheme on a distributed database system. The basic approach is to divide the internet into several hundred top-level domains, which come in two flavors - *generic* and *countries*. Nearly all organizations in USA, are under generic name, where each domain is partitioned into subdomains, and these are further partitioned, and so on, as represented in the form of a tree as shown in figure. The leaves of the tree represent domains that contain no subdomains, represent single hosts, or a company or contains a thousand of hosts. Naming follows organizational boundaries, not physical networks. The hierarchical naming system, which is used by DNS has many advantages over flat addressing scheme used earlier. Key features of the two approaches are highlighted below:

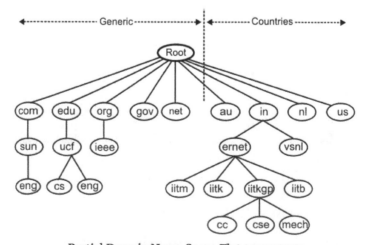

Partial Domain Name Space Flat namespace

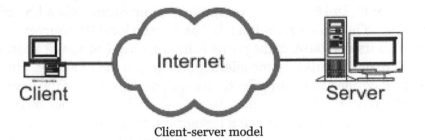

Client-server model

- Each machine is given a unique (by NIC) name

- Special file is used to keep name-address mapping

- All hosts must know the current mapping for all other hosts with which they want to communicate

- Large mapping file, if communication with a large number of machines is required

Not a good scheme for communicating to arbitrary machines over large networks such as Internet

Hierarchical Namespace

- Break complete namespace into domains

- Domains broken up recursively into one or more subdomains, each of which is basically a domain again

- Further division to create any level of hierarchy – Namespace Tree

- Delegate task of name allocation/resolution of parts of the tree to distributed name servers

Name-address Resolution

Although the names used by the DNS is very convenient to humans, it cannot be used for communication through the internet. This requires mapping a name to an address known as *Name-address Resolution*. The mapping of the name to the address can be done using a *name server*, where a look-up table is maintained. A single name server could contain the entire DNS database and respond to all queries about it. However, the server would be very much overloaded and when it would fail, the entire Internet would be crippled. To avoid this problem, the entire name space is divided into non-overlapping zones. Each zone contains some part of the tree and also contains *name servers* holding the authorization information about the zone. In practice, a zone will have a primary name server and one or more secondary name servers, which get their information from the primary name servers. This is how smaller databases are maintained in a distributed manner as shown in figure.

To map a name onto an IP address, an application program calls a library procedure known as *resolver*. The resolver sends a UDP packet to a local DNS server, which searches for the name in its database. If the name is found, it returns the IP address to the resolver, which in turn informs it to the client. After having the IP address, the client then establishes a TCP connection with a destination node. However, if the local DNS server does not have the requested information, it seeks the help from other servers and finally reports back. This is known as *recursive resolution*, as shown in figure. The client may not ask for a recursive answer and in that case the mapping can be done iteratively. If a server is an authority for the name, the reply is sent. Otherwise, it sends the IP address of another server that is likely to resolve the query. The client sends query to the second server and so on. This process is known as iterative resolution.

To avoid another search when a query is received for a name that is not in its domain, the information is stored in the cash memory of the server. This mechanism is known as *caching*. This improves the efficiency of resolution. However, the mapping is not stored in the cache memory indefinitely. A *time-to-live* TTL) counter is associated with each mapping and when the time expires, the mapping is purged.

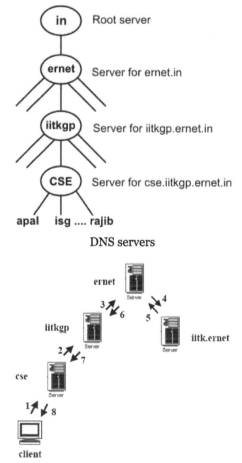

Recursive resolution performed in ARP protocol

Electronic Mail

Electronic mail is among the most widely available application services. Each user, who intends to participate in email communication, is assigned a mailbox, where out-going and incoming messages are buffered, allowing the transfer to take place in the background. The message contains a header that specifies the sender, recipients, and subject, followed by a body that contains message. The TCP/IP protocol that supports electronic mail on the internet is called *Simple Mail Transfer Protocol* (SMTP), which supports the following:

- Sending a message to one or more recipients

- Sending messages that include text, voice, video, or graphics

A software package, known as *User Agent*, is used to compose, read, reply or forward emails and handle mailboxes. The email address consists of two parts divided by a @ character. The first part is the local name that identifies mailbox and the second part is a domain name.

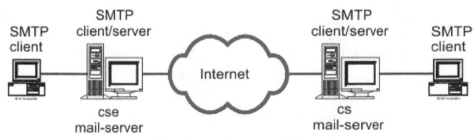

Simple Mail Transfer Protocol (SMTP)

Telnet

Telnet is a simple remote terminal protocol that provides a remote log-on capability, which enables a user to log on to a remote computer and behaves as if it is directly connected to it. The following three basic services are offered by TELNET:

- It defines a network virtual terminal that provides a standard interface to remote systems

- It includes a mechanism that allows the client and server to negotiate options from a standard set

- It treats both ends symmetrically

File Transfer Protocol (FTP)

File Transfer Protocol (FTP) is a TCP/IP client-server application for transfer files between two remote machines through internet. A TCP connection is set up before file transfer and it persists throughout the session. It is possible to send more than one file before disconnecting the link. A control connection is established first with a remote host before any file can be transferred. Two connections required are shown in figure. Users view FTP as an interactive system.

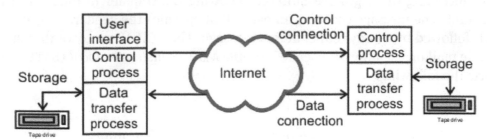

File Transfer Protocol (FTP)

Simple Network Management Protocol (SNMP)

Network managers use network management software that help them to locate, diagnose and rectify problems. Simple Network Management Protocol (SMTP) provides a systematic way for managing network resources. It uses transport layer protocol for communication. It allows them to monitor switches, routers and hosts. There are four components of the protocol:

- Management of systems

- Management of nodes; hosts, routers, switches

- Management of Information Base; specifies data items a host or a router must keep and the operations allowed on each (eight categories)

- Management of Protocol; specifies communication between network management client program a manager invokes and a network management server running on a host or router

References

- Goldwasser, S.; Micali, S.; Rackoff, C. (1989). "The Knowledge Complexity of Interactive Proof Systems". SIAM Journal on Computing. 18 (1): 186–208. doi:10.1137/0218012

- "Cryptology (definition)". Merriam-Webster's Collegiate Dictionary (11th ed.). Merriam-Webster. Retrieved 26 March 2015

- Comer, Douglas E. (2006). Internetworking with TCP/IP:Principles, Protocols, and Architecture. 1 (5th ed.). Prentice Hall. ISBN 0-13-187671-6

- Blaze, Matt; Diffie, Whitefield; Rivest, Ronald L.; Schneier, Bruce; Shimomura, Tsutomu; Thompson, Eric; Wiener, Michael (January 1996). "Minimal key lengths for symmetric ciphers to provide adequate commercial security". Fortify. Retrieved 26 March 2015

- Coppersmith, D. (May 1994). "The Data Encryption Standard (DES) and its strength against attacks" (PDF). IBM Journal of Research and Development. 38 (3): 243–250. doi:10.1147/ rd.383.0243. Retrieved 26 March 2015

- Richard W. Stevens (2006). November 2011 TCP/IP Illustrated. Vol. 1, The protocols Check |url= value (help). Addison-Wesley. pp. Chapter 20. ISBN 978-0-201-63346-7

- Gont, Fernando (November 2008). "On the implementation of TCP urgent data". 73rd IETF meeting. Retrieved 2009-01-04

- Biham, E.; Shamir, A. (1991). "Differential cryptanalysis of DES-like cryptosystems" (PDF). Journal of Cryptology. Springer-Verlag. 4 (1): 3–72. doi:10.1007/bf00630563. Retrieved 26 March 2015

5

Understanding Network Security

Network security refers to the measures taken to ensure protection and prevention against activities such as misuse, unauthorized access, etc. A network may be private or public and the access to it is granted depending on its type. However, there is a possibility that a third-party may try to access private information. This intrusion is prevented with the use of cryptography, which is the study as well as the practice to create a secure communication. All the diverse principles of network security have been carefully analyzed in this chapter.

Network Security

Network security consists of the policies and practices adopted to prevent and monitor unauthorized access, misuse, modification, or denial of a computer network and network-accessible resources. Network security involves the authorization of access to data in a network, which is controlled by the network administrator. Users choose or are assigned an ID and password or other authenticating information that allows them access to information and programs within their authority. Network security covers a variety of computer networks, both public and private, that are used in everyday jobs; conducting transactions and communications among businesses, government agencies and individuals. Networks can be private, such as within a company, and others which might be open to public access. Network security is involved in organizations, enterprises, and other types of institutions. It does as its title explains: It secures the network, as well as protecting and overseeing operations being done. The most common and simple way of protecting a network resource is by assigning it a unique name and a corresponding password.

Network Security Concept

Network security starts with authenticating, commonly with a username and a password. Since this requires just one detail authenticating the user name—i.e., the password—this is sometimes termed one-factor authentication. With two-factor authentication, something the user 'has' is also used (e.g., a security token or 'dongle', an ATM card, or a mobile phone); and with three-factor authentication, something the user 'is' is also used (e.g., a fingerprint or retinal scan).

Once authenticated, a firewall enforces access policies such as what services are allowed to be accessed by the network users. Though effective to prevent unauthorized access, this component may fail to check potentially harmful content such as computer worms or Trojans being transmitted over the network. Anti-virus software or an intrusion pre-vention system (IPS) help detect and inhibit the action of such malware. An anoma-ly-based intrusion detection system may also monitor the network like wireshark traffic and may be logged for audit purposes and for later high-level analysis. Newer systems combining unsupervised machine learning with full network traffic analysis can detect active network attackers from malicious insiders or targeted external attackers that have compromised a user machine or account.

Communication between two hosts using a network may be encrypted to maintain privacy.

Honeypots, essentially decoy network-accessible resources, may be deployed in a net-work as surveillance and early-warning tools, as the honeypots are not normally ac-cessed for legitimate purposes. Techniques used by the attackers that attempt to com-promise these decoy resources are studied during and after an attack to keep an eye on new exploitation techniques. Such analysis may be used to further tighten security of the actual network being protected by the honeypot. A honeypot can also direct an attacker's attention away from legitimate servers. A honeypot encourages attackers to spend their time and energy on the decoy server while distracting their attention from the data on the real server. Similar to a honeypot, a honeynet is a network set up with intentional vulnerabilities. Its purpose is also to invite attacks so that the attacker's methods can be studied and that information can be used to increase network security. A honeynet typically contains one or more honeypots.

Security Managements

Security management for networks is different for all kinds of situations. A home or small office may only require basic security while large businesses may require high-maintenance and advanced software and hardware to prevent malicious attacks from hacking and spamming.

Types of Attacks

Networks are subject to attacks from malicious sources. Attacks can be from two cat-egories: "Passive" when a network intruder intercepts data traveling through the net-work, and "Active" in which an intruder initiates commands to disrupt the network's normal operation or to conduct reconnaissance and lateral movement to find and gain access to assets available via the network.

Types of attacks include:

- Passive

  o Network

- Wiretapping

- Port scanner
- Idle scan
- Encryption
- Traffic Analisys
- Active:
- Virus
- Eavesdropping
- Data Modification
  - Denial-of-service attack
  - DNS spoofing
  - Man in the middle
  - ARP poisoning
  - VLAN hopping
  - Smurf attack
  - Buffer overflow
  - Heap overflow
  - Format string attack
  - SQL injection
  - Phishing
  - Cross-site scripting
  - CSRF
  - Cyber-attack

Cryptography

Cryptography or cryptology is the practice and study of techniques for secure communication in the presence of third parties called adversaries. More generally, cryptography is about constructing and analyzing protocols that prevent third parties or the public from reading private messages; various aspects in information security such as data confidentiality, data integrity, authentication, and non-repudiation are central to modern cryptography. Modern cryptography exists at the intersection of the disciplines of mathematics, computer science, and electrical engineering. Applications of cryptography include military communications, electronic commerce, ATM cards, and computer passwords.

Cryptography prior to the modern age was effectively synonymous with *encryption*, the conversion of information from a readable state to apparent nonsense. The originator of an encrypted message (Alice) shared the decoding technique needed to recover the original information only with intended recipients (Bob), thereby precluding unwanted persons (Eve) from doing the same. The cryptography literature often uses Alice ("A") for the sender, Bob ("B") for the intended recipient, and Eve ("eavesdropper") for the adversary. Since the development of rotor cipher machines in World War I and the advent of computers in World War II, the methods used to carry out cryptology have become increasingly complex and its application more widespread.

Modern cryptography is heavily based on mathematical theory and computer science practice; cryptographic algorithms are designed around computational hardness assumptions, making such algorithms hard to break in practice by any adversary. It is theoretically possible to break such a system, but it is infeasible to do so by any known practical means. These schemes are therefore termed computationally secure; theoretical advances, e.g., improvements in integer factorization algorithms, and faster computing technology require these solutions to be continually adapted. There exist information-theoretically secure schemes that provably cannot be broken even with unlimited computing power—an example is the one-time pad but these schemes are more difficult to implement than the best theoretically breakable but computationally secure mechanisms.

The growth of cryptographic technology has raised a number of legal issues in the information age. Cryptography's potential for use as a tool for espionage and sedition has led many governments to classify it as a weapon and to limit or even prohibit its use and export. In some jurisdictions where the use of cryptography is legal, laws permit investigators to compel the disclosure of encryption keys for documents relevant to an investigation. Cryptography also plays a major role in digital rights management and copyright infringement of digital media.

Terminology

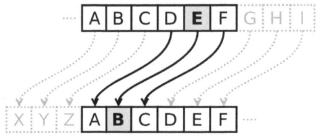

Alphabet shift ciphers are believed to have been used by Julius Caesar over 2,000 years ago. This is an example with k=3. In other words, the letters in the alphabet are shifted three in one direction to encrypt and three in the other direction to decrypt.

Until modern times, cryptography referred almost exclusively to *encryption*, which is the process of converting ordinary information (called plaintext) into unintelligible text (called ciphertext). Decryption is the reverse, in other words, moving from the unintelligible ciphertext back to plaintext. A *cipher* (or *cypher*) is a pair of algorithms that create the encryption and the reversing decryption. The detailed operation of a cipher is controlled both by the algorithm and in each instance by a "key". The key is a secret (ideally known only to the communicants), usually a short string of characters, which is needed to decrypt the ciphertext. Formally, a "cryptosystem" is the ordered list of elements of finite possible plaintexts, finite possible cyphertexts, finite possible keys, and the encryption and decryption algorithms which correspond to each key. Keys are important both formally and in actual practice, as ciphers without variable keys can be trivially broken with only the knowledge of the cipher used and are therefore useless (or even counter-productive) for most purposes. Historically, ciphers were often used directly for encryption or decryption without additional procedures such as authentication or integrity checks. There are two kinds of cryptosystems: symmetric and asymmetric. In symmetric systems the same key (the secret key) is used to encrypt and decrypt a message. Data manipulation in symmetric systems is faster than asymmetric systems as they generally use shorter key lengths. Asymmetric systems use a public key to encrypt a message and a private key to decrypt it. Use of asymmetric systems enhances the security of communication. Examples of asymmetric systems include RSA (Rivest-Shamir-Adleman), and ECC (Elliptic Curve Cryptography). Symmetric models include the commonly used AES (Advanced Encryption Standard) which replaced the older DES (Data Encryption Standard).

In colloquial use, the term "code" is often used to mean any method of encryption or concealment of meaning. However, in cryptography, *code* has a more specific meaning. It means the replacement of a unit of plaintext (i.e., a meaningful word or phrase) with a code word (for example, "wallaby" replaces "attack at dawn").

Cryptanalysis is the term used for the study of methods for obtaining the meaning of encrypted information without access to the key normally required to do so; i.e., it is the study of how to crack encryption algorithms or their implementations.

Some use the terms *cryptography* and *cryptology* interchangeably in English, while others (including US military practice generally) use *cryptography* to refer specifically to the use and practice of cryptographic techniques and *cryptology* to refer to the combined study of cryptography and cryptanalysis. English is more flexible than several other languages in which *cryptology* (done by cryptologists) is always used in the second sense above. RFC 2828 advises that steganography is sometimes included in cryptology.

The study of characteristics of languages that have some application in cryptography or cryptology (e.g. frequency data, letter combinations, universal patterns, etc.) is called cryptolinguistics.

History of Cryptography and Cryptanalysis

Before the modern era, cryptography focused on message confidentiality (i.e., encryption) conversion of messages from a comprehensible form into an incomprehensible one and back again at the other end, rendering it unreadable by interceptors or eavesdroppers without secret knowledge (namely the key needed for decryption of that message). Encryption attempted to ensure secrecy in communications, such as those of spies, military leaders, and diplomats. In recent decades, the field has expanded beyond confidentiality concerns to include techniques for message integrity checking, sender/receiver identity authentication, digital signatures, interactive proofs and secure computation, among others.

Classic Cryptography

Reconstructed ancient Greek *scytale*, an early cipher device

The main classical cipher types are transposition ciphers, which rearrange the order of letters in a message (e.g., 'hello world' becomes 'ehlol owrdl' in a trivially simple rearrangement scheme), and substitution ciphers, which systematically replace letters or groups of letters with other letters or groups of letters (e.g., 'fly at once' becomes 'gmz bu podf' by replacing each letter with the one following it in the Latin alphabet). Simple versions of either have never offered much confidentiality from enterprising opponents. An early substitution cipher was the Caesar cipher, in which each letter in the plaintext was replaced by a letter some fixed number of positions further down the alphabet. Suetonius reports that Julius Caesar used it with a shift of three to communicate with his generals. Atbash is an example of an early Hebrew cipher. The earliest known use of cryptography is some carved ciphertext on stone in Egypt (ca 1900 BCE), but this may have been done for the amusement of literate observers rather than as a way of concealing information.

The Greeks of Classical times are said to have known of ciphers (e.g., the scytale transposition cipher claimed to have been used by the Spartan military). Steganography (i.e., hiding even the existence of a message so as to keep it confidential) was also first developed in ancient times. An early example, from Herodotus, was a message tattooed on a slave's shaved head and concealed under the regrown hair. More modern examples of steganography include the use of invisible ink, microdots, and digital watermarks to conceal information.

In India, the 2000-year-old Kamasutra of Vātsyāyana speaks of two different kinds of ciphers called Kautiliyam and Mulavediya. In the Kautiliyam, the cipher letter substitutions are based on phonetic relations, such as vowels becoming consonants. In the Mulavediya, the cipher alphabet consists of pairing letters and using the reciprocal ones.

In Sassanid Persia, there were two secret scripts, according to the Muslim author Ibn al-Nadim: the *šāh-dabīrīya* (literally "King's script") which was used for official correspondence, and the *rāz-saharīya* which was used to communicate secret messages with other countries.

First page of a book by Al-Kindi which discusses encryption of messages

Ciphertexts produced by a classical cipher (and some modern ciphers) will reveal statistical information about the plaintext, and that information can often be used to break the cipher. After the discovery of frequency analysis, perhaps by the Arab mathematician and polymath Al-Kindi (also known as *Alkindus*) in the 9th century, nearly all such ciphers could be broken by an informed attacker. Such classical ciphers still enjoy popularity today, though mostly as puzzles. Al-Kindi wrote a book on cryptography entitled *Risalah fi Istikhraj al-Mu'amma* (*Manuscript for the Deciphering Cryptographic Messages*), which described the first known use of frequency analysis cryptanalysis techniques.

16th-century book-shaped French cipher machine, with arms of Henri II of France

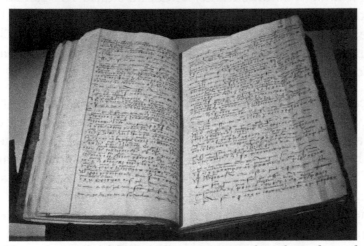

Enciphered letter from Gabriel de Luetz d'Aramon, French Ambassador to the Ottoman
Empire, after 1546, with partial decipherment

Language letter frequencies may offer little help for some extended historical encryption techniques such as homophonic cipher that tend to flatten the frequency distribution. For those ciphers, language letter group (or n-gram) frequencies may provide an attack.

Essentially all ciphers remained vulnerable to cryptanalysis using the frequency analysis technique until the development of the polyalphabetic cipher, most clearly by Leon Battista Alberti around the year 1467, though there is some indication that it was already known to Al-Kindi. Alberti's innovation was to use different ciphers (i.e., substitution alphabets) for various parts of a message (perhaps for each successive plaintext letter at the limit). He also invented what was probably the first automatic cipher device, a wheel which implemented a partial realization of his invention. In the polyalphabetic Vigenère cipher, encryption uses a *key word*, which controls letter substitution depending on which letter of the key word is used. In the mid-19th century Charles

Babbage showed that the Vigenère cipher was vulnerable to Kasiski examination, but this was first published about ten years later by Friedrich Kasiski.

Although frequency analysis can be a powerful and general technique against many ciphers, encryption has still often been effective in practice, as many a would-be cryptanalyst was unaware of the technique. Breaking a message without using frequency analysis essentially required knowledge of the cipher used and perhaps of the key involved, thus making espionage, bribery, burglary, defection, etc., more attractive approaches to the cryptanalytically uninformed. It was finally explicitly recognized in the 19th century that secrecy of a cipher's algorithm is not a sensible nor practical safeguard of message security; in fact, it was further realized that any adequate cryptographic scheme (including ciphers) should remain secure even if the adversary fully understands the cipher algorithm itself. Security of the key used should alone be sufficient for a good cipher to maintain confidentiality under an attack. This fundamental principle was first explicitly stated in 1883 by Auguste Kerckhoffs and is generally called Kerckhoffs's Principle; alternatively and more bluntly, it was restated by Claude Shannon, the inventor of information theory and the fundamentals of theoretical cryptography, as *Shannon's Maxim*—'the enemy knows the system'.

Different physical devices and aids have been used to assist with ciphers. One of the earliest may have been the scytale of ancient Greece, a rod supposedly used by the Spartans as an aid for a transposition cipher. In medieval times, other aids were invented such as the cipher grille, which was also used for a kind of steganography. With the invention of polyalphabetic ciphers came more sophisticated aids such as Alberti's own cipher disk, Johannes Trithemius' tabula recta scheme, and Thomas Jefferson's wheel cypher (not publicly known, and reinvented independently by Bazeries around 1900). Many mechanical encryption/decryption devices were invented early in the 20th century, and several patented, among them rotor machines—famously including the Enigma machine used by the German government and military from the late 1920s and during World War II. The ciphers implemented by better quality examples of these machine designs brought about a substantial increase in cryptanalytic difficulty after WWI.

Computer Era

Cryptanalysis of the new mechanical devices proved to be both difficult and laborious. In the United Kingdom, cryptanalytic efforts at Bletchley Park during WWII spurred the development of more efficient means for carrying out repetitious tasks. This culminated in the development of the Colossus, the world's first fully electronic, digital, programmable computer, which assisted in the decryption of ciphers generated by the German Army's Lorenz SZ40/42 machine.

Just as the development of digital computers and electronics helped in cryptanalysis, it made possible much more complex ciphers. Furthermore, computers allowed for the encryption of any kind of data representable in any binary format, unlike classical ciphers which only encrypted written language texts; this was new and significant. Computer use has thus supplanted linguistic cryptography, both for cipher design and cryptanalysis. Many computer ciphers can be characterized by their operation on binary bit sequences (sometimes in groups or blocks), unlike classical and mechanical schemes, which generally manipulate traditional characters (i.e., letters and digits) directly. However, computers have also assisted cryptanalysis, which has compensated to some extent for increased cipher complexity. Nonetheless, good modern ciphers have stayed ahead of cryptanalysis; it is typically the case that use of a quality cipher is very efficient (i.e., fast and requiring few resources, such as memory or CPU capability), while breaking it requires an effort many orders of magnitude larger, and vastly larger than that required for any classical cipher, making cryptanalysis so inefficient and impractical as to be effectively impossible.

Extensive open academic research into cryptography is relatively recent; it began only in the mid-1970s. In recent times, IBM personnel designed the algorithm that became the Federal (i.e., US) Data Encryption Standard; Whitfield Diffie and Martin Hellman published their key agreement algorithm; and the RSA algorithm was published in Martin Gardner's *Scientific American* column. Since then, cryptography has become a widely used tool in communications, computer networks, and computer security generally. Some modern cryptographic techniques can only keep their keys secret if certain mathematical problems are intractable, such as the integer factorization or the discrete logarithm problems, so there are deep connections with abstract mathematics. There are very few cryptosystems that are proven to be unconditionally secure. The one-time pad is one. There are a few important ones that are proven secure under certain unproven assumptions. For example, the infeasibility of factoring extremely large integers is the basis for believing that RSA is secure, and some other systems, but even there, the proof is usually lost due to practical considerations. There are systems similar to RSA, such as one by Michael O. Rabin that is provably secure provided factoring $n = pq$ is impossible, but the more practical system RSA has never been proved secure in this sense. The discrete logarithm problem is the basis for believing some other cryptosystems are secure, and again, there are related, less practical systems that are provably secure relative to the discrete log problem.

As well as being aware of cryptographic history, cryptographic algorithm and system designers must also sensibly consider probable future developments while working on their designs. For instance, continuous improvements in computer processing power have increased the scope of brute-force attacks, so when specifying key lengths, the required key lengths are similarly advancing. The potential effects of quantum computing are already being considered by some cryptographic system designers; the announced imminence of small implementations of these machines may be making the need for this preemptive caution rather more than merely speculative.

Essentially, prior to the early 20th century, cryptography was chiefly concerned with linguistic and lexicographic patterns. Since then the emphasis has shifted, and cryptography now makes extensive use of mathematics, including aspects of information theory, computational complexity, statistics, combinatorics, abstract algebra, number theory, and finite mathematics generally. Cryptography is also a branch of engineering, but an unusual one since it deals with active, intelligent, and malevolent opposition; other kinds of engineering (e.g., civil or chemical engineering) deal only with neutral natural forces. There is also active research examining the relationship between cryptographic problems and quantum physics.

Modern Cryptography

The modern field of cryptography can be divided into several areas of study. The chief ones are discussed here.

Symmetric-key Cryptography

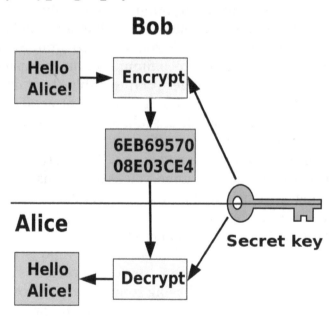

Symmetric-key cryptography, where a single key is used for encryption and decryption

Symmetric-key cryptography refers to encryption methods in which both the sender and receiver share the same key (or, less commonly, in which their keys are different, but related in an easily computable way). This was the only kind of encryption publicly known until June 1976.

Symmetric key ciphers are implemented as either block ciphers or stream ciphers. A block cipher enciphers input in blocks of plaintext as opposed to individual characters, the input form used by a stream cipher.

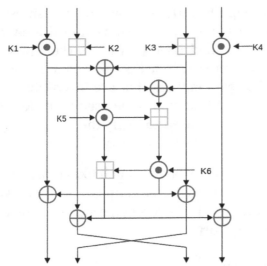

One round (out of 8.5) of the IDEA cipher, used in some versions of PGP for high-speed encryption of, for instance, e-mail

The Data Encryption Standard (DES) and the Advanced Encryption Standard (AES) are block cipher designs that have been designated cryptography standards by the US government (though DES's designation was finally withdrawn after the AES was adopted). Despite its deprecation as an official standard, DES (especially its still-approved and much more secure triple-DES variant) remains quite popular; it is used across a wide range of applications, from ATM encryption to e-mail privacy and secure remote access. Many other block ciphers have been designed and released, with considerable variation in quality. Many have been thoroughly broken, such as FEAL.

Stream ciphers, in contrast to the 'block' type, create an arbitrarily long stream of key material, which is combined with the plaintext bit-by-bit or character-by-character, somewhat like the one-time pad. In a stream cipher, the output stream is created based on a hidden internal state that changes as the cipher operates. That internal state is initially set up using the secret key material. RC4 is a widely used stream cipher. Block ciphers can be used as stream ciphers.

Cryptographic hash functions are a third type of cryptographic algorithm. They take a message of any length as input, and output a short, fixed length hash, which can be used in (for example) a digital signature. For good hash functions, an attacker cannot find two messages that produce the same hash. MD4 is a long-used hash function that is now broken; MD5, a strengthened variant of MD4, is also widely used but broken in practice. The US National Security Agency developed the Secure Hash Algorithm series of MD5-like hash functions: SHA-0 was a flawed algorithm that the agency withdrew; SHA-1 is widely deployed and more secure than MD5, but cryptanalysts have identified attacks against it; the SHA-2 family improves on SHA-1, but it isn't yet widely deployed; and the US standards authority thought it "prudent" from a security perspective to develop a new standard to "significantly improve the robustness of NIST's overall hash algorithm toolkit." Thus, a hash function design competition was meant to select a new U.S. national standard, to be called SHA-3, by 2012. The competition ended on October 2, 2012 when the NIST announced that Keccak would be the new SHA-3 hash algorithm. Unlike block and stream ciphers that are invertible, cryptographic hash functions produce a hashed output that cannot be used to retrieve the original input data. Cryptographic hash functions are used to verify the authenticity of data retrieved from an untrusted source or to add a layer of security.

Message authentication codes (MACs) are much like cryptographic hash functions, except that a secret key can be used to authenticate the hash value upon receipt; this additional complication blocks an attack scheme against bare digest algorithms, and so has been thought worth the effort.

Public-key Cryptography

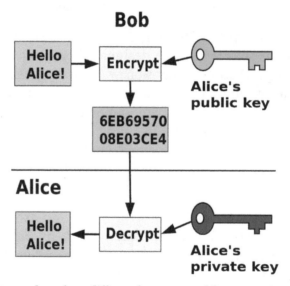

Public-key cryptography, where different keys are used for encryption and decryption

Symmetric-key cryptosystems use the same key for encryption and decryption of a message, though a message or group of messages may have a different key than others. A significant disadvantage of symmetric ciphers is the key management necessary to use them securely. Each distinct pair of communicating parties must, ideally, share a different key, and perhaps each ciphertext exchanged as well. The number of keys required increases as the square of the number of network members, which very quickly requires complex key management schemes to keep them all consistent and secret. The difficulty of securely establishing a secret key between two communicating parties, when a secure channel does not already exist between them, also presents a chicken-and-egg problem which is a considerable practical obstacle for cryptography users in the real world.

Whitfield Diffie and Martin Hellman, authors of the first published
paper on public-key cryptography

In a groundbreaking 1976 paper, Whitfield Diffie and Martin Hellman proposed the notion of *public-key* (also, more generally, called *asymmetric key*) cryptography in which two different but mathematically related keys are used—a *public* key and a *private* key. A public key system is so constructed that calculation of one key (the 'private key') is computationally infeasible from the other (the 'public key'), even though they are necessarily related. Instead, both keys are generated secretly, as an interrelated pair. The historian David Kahn described public-key cryptography as "the most revolutionary new concept in the field since polyalphabetic substitution emerged in the Renaissance".

In public-key cryptosystems, the public key may be freely distributed, while its paired private key must remain secret. In a public-key encryption system, the *public key* is used for encryption, while the *private* or *secret key* is used for decryption. While Diffie and Hellman could not find such a system, they showed that public-key cryptography was indeed possible by presenting the Diffie–Hellman key exchange protocol, a solution that is now widely used in secure communications to allow two parties to secretly agree on a shared encryption key.

Diffie and Hellman's publication sparked widespread academic efforts in finding a practical public-key encryption system. This race was finally won in 1978 by Ronald Rivest, Adi Shamir, and Len Adleman, whose solution has since become known as the RSA algorithm.

The Diffie–Hellman and RSA algorithms, in addition to being the first publicly known examples of high quality public-key algorithms, have been among the most widely used. Others include the Cramer–Shoup cryptosystem, ElGamal encryption, and various elliptic curve techniques.

To much surprise, a document published in 1997 by the Government Communications Headquarters (GCHQ), a British intelligence organization, revealed that cryptographers at GCHQ had anticipated several academic developments. Reportedly, around 1970, James H. Ellis had conceived the principles of asymmetric key cryptography. In

1973, Clifford Cocks invented a solution that essentially resembles the RSA algorithm. And in 1974, Malcolm J. Williamson is claimed to have developed the Diffie–Hellman key exchange.

Public-key cryptography can also be used for implementing digital signature schemes. A digital signature is reminiscent of an ordinary signature; they both have the characteristic of being easy for a user to produce, but difficult for anyone else to forge. Digital signatures can also be permanently tied to the content of the message being signed; they cannot then be 'moved' from one document to another, for any attempt will be detectable. In digital signature schemes, there are two algorithms: one for *signing*, in which a secret key is used to process the message (or a hash of the message, or both), and one for *verification,* in which the matching public key is used with the message to check the validity of the signature. RSA and DSA are two of the most popular digital signature schemes. Digital signatures are central to the operation of public key infrastructures and many network security schemes (e.g., SSL/TLS, many VPNs, etc.).

Public-key algorithms are most often based on the computational complexity of "hard" problems, often from number theory. For example, the hardness of RSA is related to the integer factorization problem, while Diffie–Hellman and DSA are related to the discrete logarithm problem. More recently, elliptic curve cryptography has developed, a system in which security is based on number theoretic problems involving elliptic curves. Because of the difficulty of the underlying problems, most public-key algorithms involve operations such as modular multiplication and exponentiation, which are much more computationally expensive than the techniques used in most block ciphers, especially with typical key sizes. As a result, public-key cryptosystems are commonly hybrid cryptosystems, in which a fast high-quality symmetric-key encryption algorithm is used for the message itself, while the relevant symmetric key is sent with the message, but encrypted using a public-key algorithm. Similarly, hybrid signature schemes are often used, in which a cryptographic hash function is computed, and only the resulting hash is digitally signed.

Cryptanalysis

The goal of cryptanalysis is to find some weakness or insecurity in a cryptographic scheme, thus permitting its subversion or evasion.

It is a common misconception that every encryption method can be broken. In connection with his WWII work at Bell Labs, Claude Shannon proved that the one-time pad cipher is unbreakable, provided the key material is truly random, never reused, kept secret from all possible attackers, and of equal or greater length than the message. Most ciphers, apart from the one-time pad, can be broken with enough computational effort by brute force attack, but the amount of effort needed may be exponentially dependent on the key size, as compared to the effort needed to make use of the cipher. In such cases, effective security could be achieved if it is proven that the effort required (i.e., "work factor", in Shannon's terms) is beyond the ability of any adversary. This means it must be shown that no efficient method (as opposed to the time-consuming brute force method) can be found to break the cipher. Since no such proof has been found to date, the one-time-pad remains the only theoretically unbreakable cipher.

Variants of the Enigma machine, used by Germany's military and civil authorities from the late 1920s through World War II, implemented a complex electro-mechanical polyalphabetic cipher. Breaking and reading of the Enigma cipher at Poland's Cipher Bureau, for 7 years before the war, and subsequent decryption at Bletchley Park, was important to Allied victory.

There are a wide variety of cryptanalytic attacks, and they can be classified in any of several ways. A common distinction turns on what Eve (an attacker) knows and what capabilities are available. In a ciphertext-only attack, Eve has access only to the ciphertext (good modern cryptosystems are usually effectively immune to ciphertext-only attacks). In a known-plaintext attack, Eve has access to a ciphertext and its corresponding plaintext (or to many such pairs). In a chosen-plaintext attack, Eve may choose a plaintext and learn its corresponding ciphertext (perhaps many times); an example is gardening, used by the British during WWII. In a chosen-ciphertext attack, Eve may be able to *choose* ciphertexts and learn their corresponding plaintexts. Finally in a man-in-the-middle attack Eve gets in between Alice (the sender) and Bob (the recipient), accesses and modifies the traffic and then forwards it to the recipient. Also important, often overwhelmingly so, are mistakes (generally in the design or use of one of the protocols involved).

Poznań monument (center) to Polish cryptologists whose breaking of Germany's Enigma machine ciphers, beginning in 1932, altered the course of World War II

Cryptanalysis of symmetric-key ciphers typically involves looking for attacks against the block ciphers or stream ciphers that are more efficient than any attack that could be against a perfect cipher. For example, a simple brute force attack against DES requires one known plaintext and 2^{55} decryptions, trying approximately half of the possible keys, to reach a point at which chances are better than even that the key sought will have been found. But this may not be enough assurance; a linear cryptanalysis attack against DES requires 2^{43} known plaintexts and approximately 2^{43} DES operations. This is a considerable improvement on brute force attacks.

Public-key algorithms are based on the computational difficulty of various problems. The most famous of these is integer factorization (e.g., the RSA algorithm is based on a problem related to integer factoring), but the discrete logarithm problem is also important. Much public-key cryptanalysis concerns numerical algorithms for solving these computational problems, or some of them, efficiently (i.e., in a practical time). For instance, the best known algorithms for solving the elliptic curve-based version of discrete logarithm are much more time-consuming than the best known algorithms for factoring, at least for problems of more or less equivalent size. Thus, other things being equal, to achieve an equivalent strength of attack resistance, factoring-based encryption techniques must use larger keys than elliptic curve techniques. For this reason, public-key cryptosystems based on elliptic curves have become popular since their invention in the mid-1990s.

While pure cryptanalysis uses weaknesses in the algorithms themselves, other attacks on cryptosystems are based on actual use of the algorithms in real devices, and are called *side-channel attacks*. If a cryptanalyst has access to, for example, the amount of time the device took to encrypt a number of plaintexts or report an error in a password or PIN character, he may be able to use a timing attack to break a cipher that is otherwise resistant to analysis. An attacker might also study the pattern and length of messages to derive valuable information; this is known as traffic analysis and can be quite useful to an alert adversary. Poor administration of a cryptosystem, such as permitting too short keys, will make any system vulnerable, regardless of other virtues. And, of course, social engineering, and other attacks against the personnel who work with cryptosystems or the messages they handle (e.g., bribery, extortion, blackmail, espionage, torture, ...) may be the most productive attacks of all.

Cryptographic Primitives

Much of the theoretical work in cryptography concerns cryptographic *primitives*—algorithms with basic cryptographic properties—and their relationship to other cryptographic problems. More complicated cryptographic tools are then built from these basic primitives. These primitives provide fundamental properties, which are used to develop more complex tools called *cryptosystems* or *cryptographic protocols*, which guarantee one or more high-level security properties. Note however, that the distinction between cryptographic *primitives* and cryptosystems, is quite arbitrary; for example, the RSA algorithm is sometimes considered a cryptosystem, and sometimes a primitive. Typical examples of cryptographic primitives include pseudorandom functions, one-way functions, etc.

Cryptosystems

One or more cryptographic primitives are often used to develop a more complex algorithm, called a cryptographic system, or *cryptosystem*. Cryptosystems (e.g., El-Gamal encryption) are designed to provide particular functionality (e.g., public key encryption) while guaranteeing certain security properties (e.g., chosen-plaintext attack (CPA) security in the random oracle model). Cryptosystems use the properties of the underlying cryptographic primitives to support the system's security properties. Of course, as the distinction between primitives and cryptosystems is somewhat arbitrary, a sophisticated cryptosystem can be derived from a combination of several more primitive cryptosystems. In many cases, the cryptosystem's structure involves back and forth communication among two or more parties in space (e.g., between the sender of a secure message and its receiver) or across time (e.g., cryptographically protected backup data). Such cryptosystems are sometimes called *cryptographic protocols*.

Some widely known cryptosystems include RSA encryption, Schnorr signature, El-Gamal encryption, PGP, etc. More complex cryptosystems include electronic cash systems, signcryption systems, etc. Some more 'theoretical' cryptosystems include interactive proof systems, (like zero-knowledge proofs), systems for secret sharing, etc.

Until recently, most security properties of most cryptosystems were demonstrated using empirical techniques or using ad hoc reasoning. Recently, there has been considerable effort to develop formal techniques for establishing the security of cryptosystems; this has been generally called *provable security*. The general idea of provable security is to give arguments about the computational difficulty needed to compromise some security aspect of the cryptosystem (i.e., to any adversary).

The study of how best to implement and integrate cryptography in software applications is itself a distinct field.

Legal Issues

Prohibitions

Cryptography has long been of interest to intelligence gathering and law enforcement agencies. Secret communications may be criminal or even treasonous. Because of its facilitation of privacy, and the diminution of privacy attendant on its prohibition, cryptography is also of considerable interest to civil rights supporters. Accordingly, there has been a history of controversial legal issues surrounding cryptography, especially since the advent of inexpensive computers has made widespread access to high quality cryptography possible.

In some countries, even the domestic use of cryptography is, or has been, restricted. Until 1999, France significantly restricted the use of cryptography domestically, though it has since relaxed many of these rules. In China and Iran, a license is still required to use cryptography. Many countries have tight restrictions on the use of cryptography. Among the more restrictive are laws in Belarus, Kazakhstan, Mongolia, Pakistan, Singapore, Tunisia, and Vietnam.

In the United States, cryptography is legal for domestic use, but there has been much conflict over legal issues related to cryptography. One particularly important issue has been the export of cryptography and cryptographic software and hardware. Probably because of the importance of cryptanalysis in World War II and an expectation that cryptography would continue to be important for national security, many Western governments have, at some point, strictly regulated export of cryptography. After World War II, it was illegal in the US to sell or distribute encryption technology overseas; in fact, encryption was designated as auxiliary military equipment and put on the United States Munitions List. Until the development of the personal computer, asymmetric key algorithms (i.e., public key techniques), and the Internet, this was not especially problematic. However, as the Internet grew and computers became more widely available, high-quality encryption techniques became well known around the globe.

Export Controls

In the 1990s, there were several challenges to US export regulation of cryptography. After the source code for Philip Zimmermann's Pretty Good Privacy (PGP) encryption program found its way onto the Internet in June 1991, a complaint by RSA Security (then called RSA Data Security, Inc.) resulted in a lengthy criminal investigation of Zimmermann by the US Customs Service and the FBI, though no charges were ever filed. Daniel J. Bernstein, then a graduate student at UC Berkeley, brought a lawsuit against the US government challenging some aspects of the restrictions based on free speech grounds. The 1995 case Bernstein v. United States ultimately resulted in a 1999 decision that printed source code for cryptographic algorithms and systems was protected as free speech by the United States Constitution.

In 1996, thirty-nine countries signed the Wassenaar Arrangement, an arms control treaty that deals with the export of arms and "dual-use" technologies such as cryptography. The treaty stipulated that the use of cryptography with short key-lengths (56-bit for symmetric encryption, 512-bit for RSA) would no longer be export-controlled. Cryptography exports from the US became less strictly regulated as a consequence of a major relaxation in 2000; there are no longer very many restrictions on key sizes in US-exported mass-market software. Since this relaxation in US export restrictions, and because most personal computers connected to the Internet include US-sourced web browsers such as Firefox or Internet Explorer, almost every Internet user worldwide has potential access to quality cryptography via their browsers (e.g., via Transport Layer Security). The Mozilla Thunderbird and Microsoft Outlook E-mail client programs similarly can transmit and receive emails via TLS, and can send and receive email encrypted with S/MIME. Many Internet users don't realize that their basic application software contains such extensive cryptosystems. These browsers and email programs are so ubiquitous that even governments whose intent is to regulate civilian use of cryptography generally don't find it practical to do much to control distribution or use of cryptography of this quality, so even when such laws are in force, actual enforcement is often effectively impossible.

NSA Involvement

NSA headquarters in Fort Meade, Maryland

Another contentious issue connected to cryptography in the United States is the influence of the National Security Agency on cipher development and policy. The NSA was involved with the design of DES during its development at IBM and its consideration by the National Bureau of Standards as a possible Federal Standard for cryptography. DES was designed to be resistant to differential cryptanalysis, a powerful and general cryptanalytic technique known to the NSA and IBM, that became publicly known only when it was rediscovered in the late 1980s. According to Steven Levy, IBM discovered differential cryptanalysis, but kept the technique secret at the NSA's request. The technique became publicly known only when Biham and Shamir re-discovered and announced it some years later. The entire affair illustrates the difficulty of determining what resources and knowledge an attacker might actually have.

Another instance of the NSA's involvement was the 1993 Clipper chip affair, an encryption microchip intended to be part of the Capstone cryptography-control initiative. Clipper was widely criticized by cryptographers for two reasons. The cipher algorithm (called Skipjack) was then classified (declassified in 1998, long after the Clipper initiative lapsed). The classified cipher caused concerns that the NSA had deliberately made the cipher weak in order to assist its intelligence efforts. The whole initiative was also criticized based on its violation of Kerckhoffs's Principle, as the scheme included a special escrow key held by the government for use by law enforcement, for example in wiretaps.

Digital Rights Management

Cryptography is central to digital rights management (DRM), a group of techniques for technologically controlling use of copyrighted material, being widely implemented and deployed at the behest of some copyright holders. In 1998, U.S. President Bill Clinton signed the Digital Millennium Copyright Act (DMCA), which criminalized all production, dissemination, and use of certain cryptanalytic techniques and technology (now known or later discovered); specifically, those that could be used to circumvent DRM technological schemes. This had a noticeable impact on the cryptography research community since an argument can be made that *any* cryptanalytic research violated, or might violate, the DMCA. Similar statutes have since been enacted in several countries and regions, including the implementation in the EU Copyright Directive. Similar restrictions are called for by treaties signed by World Intellectual Property Organization member-states.

The United States Department of Justice and FBI have not enforced the DMCA as rigorously as had been feared by some, but the law, nonetheless, remains a controversial one. Niels Ferguson, a well-respected cryptography researcher, has publicly stated that he will not release some of his research into an Intel security design for fear of prosecution under the DMCA. Cryptanalyst Bruce Schneier has argued that the DMCA encourages vendor lock-in, while inhibiting actual measures toward cyber-security. Both Alan Cox (longtime Linux kernel developer) and Edward Felten (and some of his students at Princeton) have encountered problems related to the Act. Dmitry Sklyarov was arrested during a visit to the US from Russia, and jailed for five months pending trial for alleged violations of the DMCA arising from work he had done in Russia, where the work was legal. In 2007, the cryptographic keys responsible for Blu-ray and HD DVD content scrambling were discovered and released onto the Internet. In both cases, the MPAA sent out numerous DMCA takedown notices, and there was a massive Internet backlash triggered by the perceived impact of such notices on fair use and free speech.

Forced Disclosure of Encryption Keys

In the United Kingdom, the Regulation of Investigatory Powers Act gives UK police the powers to force suspects to decrypt files or hand over passwords that protect encryption keys. Failure to comply is an offense in its own right, punishable on conviction by a two-year jail sentence or up to five years in cases involving national security. Successful prosecutions have occurred under the Act; the first, in 2009, resulted in a term of 13 months' imprisonment. Similar forced disclosure laws in Australia, Finland, France, and India compel individual suspects under investigation to hand over encryption keys or passwords during a criminal investigation.

In the United States, the federal criminal case of United States v. Fricosu addressed whether a search warrant can compel a person to reveal an encryption passphrase or password. The Electronic Frontier Foundation (EFF) argued that this is a violation of the protection from self-incrimination given by the Fifth Amendment. In 2012, the court ruled that under the All Writs Act, the defendant was required to produce an un-encrypted hard drive for the court.

In many jurisdictions, the legal status of forced disclosure remains unclear.

The 2016 FBI–Apple encryption dispute concerns the ability of courts in the United States to compel manufacturers' assistance in unlocking cell phones whose contents are cryptographically protected.

As a potential counter-measure to forced disclosure some cryptographic software supports plausible deniability, where the encrypted data is indistinguishable from unused random data (for example such as that of a drive which has been securely wiped).

Symmetric Key Cryptography

The cipher, an algorithm that is used for converting the plaintext to ciphertex, operates on a key, which is essentially a specially generated number (value). To decrypt a secret message (ciphertext) to get back the original message (plaintext), a decrypt algorithm uses a decrypt key. In symmetric key cryptography, same key is shared, i.e. the same key is used in both encryption and decryption as shown in figure. The algorithm used to decrypt is just the inverse of the algorithm used for encryption. For example, if addition and division is used for encryption, multiplication and subtraction are to be used for decryption.

Symmetric key cryptography algorithms are simple requiring lesser execution time. As a consequence, these are commonly used for long messages. However, these algorithms suffer from the following limitations:

- Requirement of large number of unique keys. For example for n users the number of keys required is n(n-1)/2.

- Distribution of keys among the users in a secured manner is difficult.

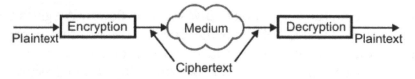

A simple symmetric key cryptography model

Monoalphabetic Substitution

One simple example of symmetric key cryptography is the *Monoalphabetic substitution*. In this case, the relationship between a character in the plaintext and a character in the ciphertext is always one-to-one. An example Monoalphabetic substitution is the Caesar cipher. As shown in figure, in this approach a character in the ciphertext is substituted by another character shifted by three places, e.g. A is substituted by D. Key feature of this approach is that it is very simple but the code can be attacked very easily.

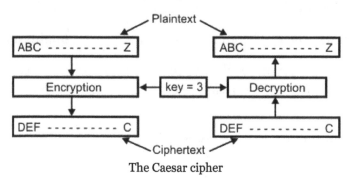

The Caesar cipher

Polyalphabetic Substitution

This is an improvement over the Caesar cipher. Here the relationship between a character in the plaintext and a character in the ciphertext is always one-to-many.

Example 8.1: Example of polyalphabetic substitution is the Vigenere cipher. In this case, a particular character is substituted by different characters in the ciphertext depending on its position in the plaintext. Figure explains the polyalphabetic substitution. Here the top row shows different characters in the plaintext and the characters in different bottom rows show the characters by which a particular character is to be replaced depending upon its position in different rows from row-0 to row-25.

- Key feature of this approach is that it is more complex and the code is harder to attack successfully.

Polyalphabetric substitution

Transpositional Cipher

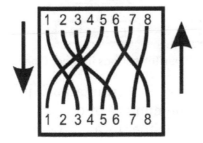

Operation of a transpositional cipher

The transpositional cipher, the characters remain unchanged but their positions are changed to create the ciphertext. Figure illustrates how five lines of a text get modified using transpositional cipher. The characters are arranged in two-dimensional matrix and columns are interchanged according to a key is shown in the middle portion of the diagram. The key defines which columns are to be swapped. As per the key shown in the figure, character of column is to be swapped to column 3, character of column 2 is to be swapped to column 6, and so on. Decryption can be done by swapping in the reverse order using the same key.

Transpositional cipher is also not a very secure approach. The attacker can find the plaintext by trial and error utilizing the idea of the frequency of occurrence of characters.

Block Ciphers

Block ciphers use a block of bits as the unit of encryption and decryption. To encrypt a 64-bit block, one has to take each of the 264 input values and map it to one of the 264 output values. The mapping should be one-to-one. Encryption and decryption operations of a block cipher are shown in figure. Some operations, such as permutation and substitution, are performed on the block of bits based on a key (a secret number) to produce another block of bits. The permutation and substitution operations are shown in Figures, respectively. In the decryption process, operations are performed in the reverse order based on the same key to get back the original block of bits.

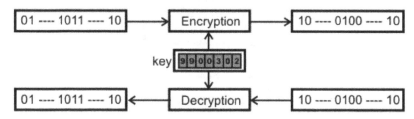

Transformations in Block Ciphers

Permutation: As shown in figure, the permutation is performed by a permutation box at the bit-level, which keeps the number of 0s and 1s same at the input and output. Although it can be implemented either by a hardware or a software, the hardware implementation is faster.

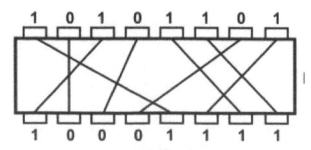

Permutation operation used In Block Ciphers

Substitution: As shown in figure, the substitution is implemented with the help of three building blocks – a decoder, one p-box and an encoder. For an n-bit input, the decoder produces an 2^n bit output having only one 1, which is applied to the P-box. The P-box permutes the output of the decoder and it is applied to the encoder. The encoder, in turn, produces an n-bit output. For example, if the input to the decoder is 011, the output of the decoder is 00001000. Let the permuted output is 01000000, the output of the encoder is 011.

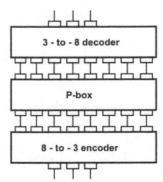

Substitution operation used in Block Ciphers

A block Cipher: A block cipher realized by using substitution and permutation operations is shown in figure. It performs the following steps:

Step-1: Divide input into 8-bit pieces

Step-2: Substitute each 8-bit based on functions derived from the key

Step-3: Permute the bits based on the key

All the above three steps are repeated for an optimal number of rounds.

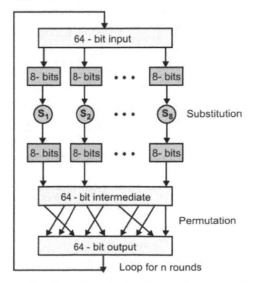

Encryption by using substitution and permutation

Data Encryption Standard (DES)

One example of the block cipher is the Data Encryption Standard (DES). Basic features of the DES algorithm are given below:

- A monoalphabetic substitution cipher using a 64-bit character

- It has 19 distinct stages

- Although the input key for DES is 64 bits long, the actual key used by DES is only 56 bits in length.

- The decryption can be done with the same password; the stages must then be carried out in reverse order.

- DES has 16 rounds, meaning the main algorithm is repeated 16 times to produce the ciphertext.

- As the number of rounds increases, the security of the algorithm increases exponentially.

- Once the key scheduling and plaintext preparation have been completed, the actual encryption or decryption is performed with the help of the main DES algorithm as shown in figure.

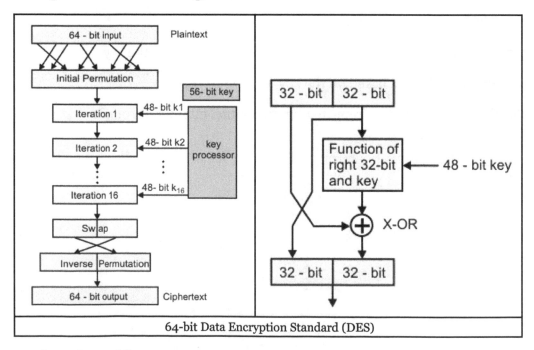

64-bit Data Encryption Standard (DES)

Encrypting a Large Message

DES can encrypt a block of 64 bits. However, to encrypt blocks of larger size, there exist several modes of operation as follows:

- Electronic Code Book (ECB)

- Cipher Block Chaining (CBC)

- Cipher Feedback Mode (CFB)

- Output Feedback Mode (OFB)

Electronic Code Book (ECB)

This is part of the regular DES algorithm. Data is divided into 64-bit blocks and each block is encrypted one at a time separately as shown in figure. Separate encryptions with different blocks are totally independent of each other.

Disadvantages of ECB

- If a message contains two identical blocks of 64-bits, the ciphertext corresponding to these blocks are identical. This may give some information to the eavesdropper

- Someone can modify or rearrange blocks to his own advantage

- Because of these flaws, ECB is rarely used

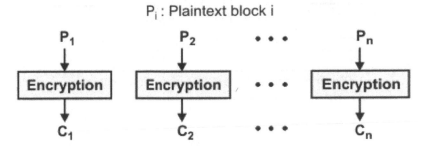

Electronic Code Book (ECB) encryption technique

Cipher Block Chaining (CBC)

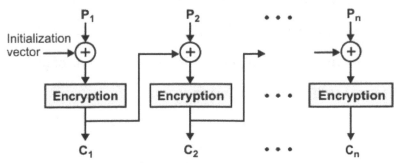

Cipher Block Chaining (CBC) encryption technique

In this mode of operation, encrypted ciphertext of each block of ECB is XORed with the next plaintext block to be encrypted, thus making all the blocks dependent on all the previous blocks. The initialization vector is sent along with data as shown in figure.

Cipher Feedback Mode (CFB)

- In this mode, blocks of plaintext that is less than 64 bits long can be encrypted as shown in figure.

- This is commonly used with interactive terminals

- It can receive and send k bits (say k=8) at a time in a streamed manner

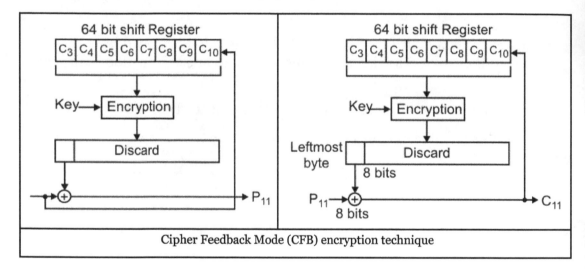

Cipher Feedback Mode (CFB) encryption technique

Output Feesdback Mode (OFB)

The encryption technique of Output Feedback Mode (OFB) is shown in figure. Key features of this mode are mentioned below:

- OFB is also a stream cipher

- Encryption is performed by XORing the message with the one-time pad

- One-time pad can be generated in advance

- If some bits of the ciphertext get garbled, only those bits of plaintext get garbled

- The message can be of any arbitrary size

- Less secure than other modes

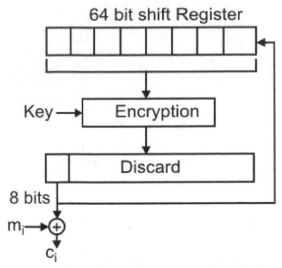

Output Feedback Mode (OFB) encryption technique

Triple DES

Triple DES, popularly known as 3DES, is used to make DES more secure by effectively increasing the key length. Its operation is explained below:

- Each block of plaintext is subjected to encryption by K1, decryption by K2 and again encryption by K1 in a sequence as shown in figure

- CBC is used to turn the block encryption scheme into a stream encryption scheme

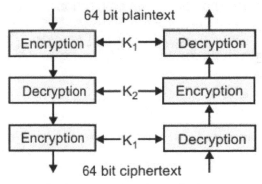

Triple DES encryption technique

Public key Cryptography

In public key cryptography, there are two keys: a private key and a public key. The public key is announced to the public, where as the private key is kept by the receiver. The sender uses the public key of the receiver for encryption and the receiver uses his private key for decryption as shown in figure.

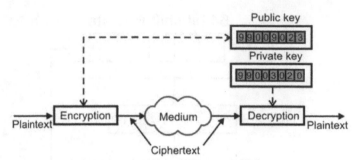

Public key encryption technique

- Advantages:

  o The pair of keys can be used with any other entity

  o The number of keys required is small

- Disadvantages:

  o It is not efficient for long messages

  o Association between an entity and its public key must be verified

RSA

The most popular public-key algorithm is the RSA (named after their inventors Rivest, Shamir and Adleman) as shown in figure. Key features of the RSA algorithm are given below:

- Public key algorithm that performs encryption as well as decryption based on number theory

- Variable key length; long for enhanced security and short for efficiency (typical 512 bytes)

- Variable block size, smaller than the key length

- The private key is a pair of numbers (d, n) and the public key is also a pair of numbers (e, n)

- Choose two large primes p and q (typically around 256 bits)

- Compute n = p x q and z = (p-1)x(q-1)

- Choose a number d relatively prime to z

- Find e such that e x d mod (p-1)x(q-1) = 1

- For encryption. C – Pe (mod n) For decryption: P = Cd (mod n)

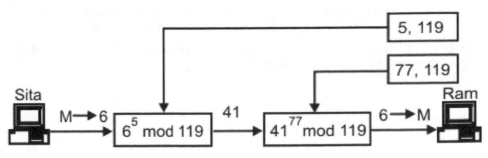

The RSA public key encryption technique

References

- "Cryptology (definition)". Merriam-Webster's Collegiate Dictionary (11th ed.). Merriam-Webster. Retrieved 26 March 2015

- Goldwasser, S.; Micali, S.; Rackoff, C. (1989). "The Knowledge Complexity of Interactive Proof Systems". SIAM Journal on Computing. 18 (1): 186–208. doi:10.1137/0218012

- Menezes, A. J.; van Oorschot, P. C.; Vanstone, S. A. Handbook of Applied Cryptography. ISBN 0-8493-8523-7. Archived from the original on 7 March 2005

- Blaze, Matt; Diffie, Whitefield; Rivest, Ronald L.; Schneier, Bruce; Shimomura, Tsutomu; Thompson, Eric; Wiener, Michael (January 1996). "Minimal key lengths for symmetric ciphers to provide adequate commercial security". Fortify. Retrieved 26 March 2015

- Oded Goldreich, Foundations of Cryptography, Volume 1: Basic Tools, Cambridge University Press, 2001, ISBN 0-521-79172-3

- Biham, E.; Shamir, A. (1991). "Differential cryptanalysis of DES-like cryptosystems" (PDF). Journal of Cryptology. Springer-Verlag. 4 (1): 3–72. doi:10.1007/bf00630563. Retrieved 26 March 2015

- "Case Closed on Zimmermann PGP Investigation". IEEE Computer Society's Technical Committee on Security and Privacy. 14 February 1996. Retrieved 26 March 2015

- Hakim, Joy (1995). A History of US: War, Peace and all that Jazz. New York: Oxford University Press. ISBN 0-19-509514-6

- Coppersmith, D. (May 1994). "The Data Encryption Standard (DES) and its strength against attacks" (PDF). IBM Journal of Research and Development. 38 (3): 243–250. doi:10.1147/rd.383.0243. Retrieved 26 March 2015

- "FIPS PUB 197: The official Advanced Encryption Standard" (PDF). Computer Security Resource Center. National Institute of Standards and Technology. Retrieved 26 March 2015

- Gannon, James (2001). Stealing Secrets, Telling Lies: How Spies and Codebreakers Helped Shape the Twentieth Century. Washington, D.C.: Brassey's. ISBN 1-57488-367-4

- "NIST Selects Winner of Secure Hash Algorithm (SHA-3) Competition". Tech Beat. National Institute of Standards and Technology. October 2, 2012. Retrieved 26 March 2015

- Shannon, Claude; Weaver, Warren (1963). The Mathematical Theory of Communication. University of Illinois Press. ISBN 0-252-72548-4

- "Bernstein v USDOJ". Electronic Privacy Information Center. United States Court of Appeals for the Ninth Circuit. 6 May 1999. Retrieved 26 March 2015

- Levy, Steven (2001). Crypto: How the Code Rebels Beat the Government—Saving Privacy in the Digital Age. Penguin Books. p. 56. ISBN 0-14-024432-8. OCLC 244148644

- Schneier, Bruce (2001-08-06). "Arrest of Computer Researcher Is Arrest of First Amendment Rights". InternetWeek. Retrieved 2017-03-07

Permissions

Index

Printed in the USA
CPSIA information can be obtained
at www.ICGtesting.com
JSHW051409221024
72173JS00006B/1329